Raising Smart Kids

FOR DUMMIES®

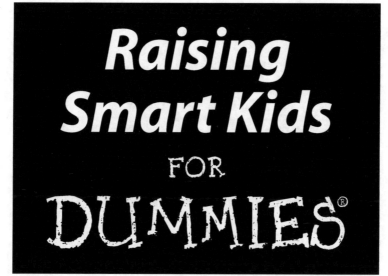

Raising Smart Kids

FOR DUMMIES®

by Marlene Targ Brill

WILEY

Wiley Publishing, Inc.

Raising Smart Kids For Dummies®

Published by
Wiley Publishing, Inc.
909 Third Avenue
New York, NY 10022
www.wiley.com

For general information on our other products and services or to obtain technical support, please contact our Customer Care Department within the U.S. at 800-762-2974, outside the U.S. at 317-572-3993, or fax 317-572-4002.

Wiley also publishes its books in a variety of electronic formats. Some content that appears in print may not be available in electronic books.

Library of Congress Control Number: 2003101877

ISBN: 0-7645-1765-1

10 9 8 7 6 5 4 3 2 1

1B/RZ/QV/QT/IN

WILEY   is a trademark of Wiley Publishing, Inc.

About the Author

Marlene Targ Brill is an author, early childhood specialist, and special educator. More important, she is the mother of a great kid. Her background of multiple degrees in education, 13 years on the front lines of teaching and training other teachers, and practical experience on the home front contribute to the parenting focus and practical suggestions you find in this book.

Marlene has written 50 books and countless articles for readers of all ages. Her *Keys to Parenting a Child with Autism* has received a Parent's Choice Award — so she knows how to make raising smart kids a readable topic and how important a job parenting can be.

Dedication

This book is dedicated to all parents who journey down the awesome parenting road, and to their smart children, who will grow up just fine. I also want to thank my hubby, Richard, and daughter, Alison, for giving me the wonderful and wacky family experiences that helped me write this book.

Author's Acknowledgments

Every book has a story, and this one involves lots of helpful people. I never would have embarked on this book without the professional guidance of my agent, Grace Freedson; prodding of my hubby, Richard; and support from my experienced writer's group: Charlotte Herman, Carolyn Crimi, Mary Jane Miller, Fay Robinson, and Mary Monsell.

Once into the book, countless folks from various areas lent their expertise: Iris Gimbel, speech and language; Lucy Klocksin, reading; Janet Emmerman, science; Robin Campbell, physical fitness; and Arlene Erlbach, special education. Special thanks go to my teen consultants: Alison Brill (yep, my kid!), Rebecca Targ, and Scott Klocksin. Thanks to Tere Drenth, the editor who fine-tuned the manuscript. I am indebted to you all and to the parents, including my own, who gave me inspiration for this book.

Publisher's Acknowledgments

We're proud of this book; please send us your comments through our Dummies online registration form located at www.dummies.com/register/.

Some of the people who helped bring this book to market include the following:

Acquisitions, Editorial, and Media Development

Project Editors: Tere Drenth, Marcia Johnson

Acquisitions Editor: Pam Mourouzis, Norm Crampton

Acquisitions Coordinator: Holly Grimes

Technical Editor: Sue Drenth

Editorial Manager: Michelle Hacker

Editorial Assistant: Elizabeth Rea

Cover Photos: © Philip James Corwin/CORBIS

Cartoons: Rich Tennant, www.the5thwave.com

Production

Project Coordinator: Dale White

Layout and Graphics: Seth Conley, Michael Kruzil, Tiffany Muth

Proofreaders: Dave Faust, John Greenough, Brian Walls, TECHBOOKS Production Services

Indexer: TECHBOOKS Production Services

Publishing and Editorial for Consumer Dummies

Diane Graves Steele, Vice President and Publisher, Consumer Dummies

Joyce Pepple, Acquisitions Director, Consumer Dummies

Kristin A. Cocks, Product Development Director, Consumer Dummies

Michael Spring, Vice President and Publisher, Travel

Brice Gosnell, Publishing Director, Travel

Suzanne Jannetta, Editorial Director, Travel

Publishing for Technology Dummies

Andy Cummings, Vice President and Publisher, Dummies Technology/General User

Composition Services

Gerry Fahey, Vice President of Production Services

Debbie Stailey, Director of Composition Services

Contents at a Glance

Table of Contents

Introduction

Congratulations! You're taking a giant leap into the world of *Raising Smart Kids For Dummies.* You're smart enough to know that being a parent means more than cleaning bottoms and wiping tears: You want high-achieving kids.

Parenting can be incredibly fun. But sharpening minds also brings more challenges than climbing Mt. Everest. Sometimes, the responsibility of increasing your kid's brain cells can be overwhelming. That's where *Raising Smart Kids For Dummies* comes in.

This book helps you encourage your kids to set their sights high and achieve success, whether at school, with friends, or in the community. In these pages, you find suggestions for easing your parenting anxiety and putting out fires, while raising smart, fulfilled kids in the process.

This book also helps put your parenting gig into perspective. Raising smart kids requires long-term sacrifice and diligence — not to mention the patience of a saint — but don't obsess about being the perfect parent, or you won't be able to enjoy the journey with your kids. Having fun is as essential to your child's success as all the other ideas in this book combined. I want you to have so much fun raising little Einsteins (well-rounded Einsteins, anyway) that you forget you're molding minds.

About This Book

In this book, you get plenty of practical advice. I go for easy, low-cost alternatives that matter most in getting your child mentally, physically, and emotionally prepared to succeed. I don't, however, suggest anything that hasn't been tested in my home or classrooms.

- ✔ This book gives you the scoop on what works and what doesn't in growing smarter kids. You find everything from arranging baby rooms to promote language skills to identifying optimum conditions for studying calculus.

- ✔ This book helps you explore the range of skills involved in being truly successful, so you can decide for yourself what "smart" means in the grand scheme of your lives. Remember that being smart means more than getting all As.

✔ This book helps you match activities to your child's level of maturity. You can't expect your advanced 9-month-old wonder who speaks in four-word sentences to pass a spelling test. Therefore, I give you tons of suggestions for making the most of each stage and knowing when to push on to the next.

✔ This book helps you discover the motivating activities and interactions that you share with your kids naturally. By helping you discover what comes naturally, you gain the confidence to orchestrate effortless repeat performances. Then you can enjoy your bundles of joy, while also having the certainty that you're bringing out their best.

✔ This book offers great tips for turning off the tube and getting your couch potatoes excited about being top performers. I prepare you for inevitable parenting trouble spots by offering preventive measures that thwart the most sluggish lazybones.

✔ This book dispels myths and helps you sort through corporate messages that pressure you to pay big bucks for educational products based on dubious theories.

In this book, I offer realistic guidelines and suggestions to bolster your innate parenting know-how. I try to eliminate educational jargon and psychological mumbo-jumbo (although I may slip in just a little — with easy-to-understand definitions, of course — to keep you abreast of the latest terminology).

Conventions Used in This Book

Throughout this book, I use the pronouns *he* or *she.* To give equal time to each gender, I alternate pronoun usage: Female pronouns show up in even-numbered chapters, and male pronouns go in odd-numbered chapters — no pun intended!

Foolish Assumptions

The major assumption made in this book is that you want to raise kids who are smart, but also well-rounded. You want your kids to shoot to the top of their classes and stay there. You want them to appreciate art and the outdoors, be leaders and mentors to other kids, and be kind and caring people.

Another assumption is that you spend significant amounts of time with one or more youngsters. You're probably a parent, but you may also be a grandparent, wild-and-crazy aunt or uncle, coach, or teacher.

My final assumption is that you're willing to go the extra mile for your kids. You are ready, willing, and able to put your kids first — within reason, of course!

How This Book Is Organized

This book includes five major parts that are divided into 22 chapters. The following sections give you an overview of what you can expect.

Part 1: Getting Off to a Good Start

Being smart encompasses more than acing tests, although I admit acing tests doesn't hurt any kid. The first part of this book defines what being smart means and discusses the role parents play in the success of their offspring. This part sets the framework for smart parent-child interactions and gives you tools to evaluate how healthy bodies and minds affect the smarts of every child.

Part II: The Early Years: Birth to Kindergarten

Babies are more than miniature adults. They need different kinds of attention and available activities — not to mention loads of hugs — than adults need. This part shares the latest feedback about activating brain cells in the womb, awakening infant senses, and preparing smart toddlers for the world outside home. You find hints about how to set boundaries and how to play in unique ways that stimulate your baby's little mind and senses.

Part III: The Eager-to-Learn Years: Elementary School

Because you've probably reached for this book with an eye toward making your child an academic genius, I divide this part and Part IV by levels of schooling. In this part, I discuss the nuts and bolts of preparing your kids for elementary school and ensuring they take the school by storm. Stickier subjects, such as homework, parent involvement in school, changing schools, and identifying giftedness, are also front and center.

Part IV: The Know-It-All Years: Middle School and High School

Teenagers are a different breed. Although most of what works for younger kids still applies to teens, much changes, too. This section introduces you to the world of teens, which includes friends, time at school (with emphasis on the extra-curricular activities), and home life — in that order — and gives you tips for ensuring the correct balance. The chapters in this part move you toward the ultimate smart-parenting experience: launching your child to function independently at college or on the job.

Part V: The Part of Tens

This part gives you several bonus chapters that are short and sweet. You find ten family traits that nurture smart kids, ten favorite reading options for various age groups, and ten top-notch resources to help you raise capable people.

Icons Used in This Book

Icons in the margins of this book flag special information. These symbols give you clues about the material coming up on the page. You then get to decide whether the material is a "must-read" or something you consider interesting but choose to skip.

This icon alerts you to creative new ideas for raising smart kids. It also points out some ideas that have worked for generations — possibly even on you, when you were a kid!

This icon marks paragraphs in which I define educational or psychological terms in everyday language.

Sometimes, the best way to highlight a point is by giving you a real-life example from a parent who's on the front lines. This icon highlights those stories and techniques.

If you remember nothing else, tuck away these gems for future use.

This symbol signals you to stop and think about what you're doing, because your actions may backfire.

Where to Go from Here

You have a choice now and can do any of the following:

✔ Read this book from cover to cover, which would thrill me immensely. If that's not practical for you, however, you may at least skim the entire book, especially if you're a first-time parent. A quick scan gives you some inkling as to what your future holds, which may or may not be comforting, depending upon your current baby-induced-sleep-deprived state and how many sibling battles you broke up today.

✔ Read about topics that are relevant to your current situation. The *For Dummies* format makes targeting specific issues easy, because each part, chapter, and section is self-contained. Don't worry about needing to read earlier material to grasp later sections. I suggest where to go, if I think another section helps or enhances your understanding of the current one.

Part I covers smart parenting suggestions for any age, so I encourage you to look over that material. Beyond that, however, parts cover different levels of maturation with age-specific information and tips.

✔ Decide to include sidebars in your reading pleasure. The shaded areas, called *sidebars* in publishing-speak, consist of material that may be of interest to you. Or, if they don't interest you, feel free to skip them: Sidebar information is a bonus, but not integral to understanding the chapter.

Where do you go from here? Simple. Curl up in a comfy chair and enjoy your journey into the world of raising smart kids.

Part I
Getting Off to a Good Start

In this part . . .

Gardeners know how to grow top-notch crops. They determine which plants thrive best under available conditions, plan their optimum placement, and nourish the seeds with plant food and water. Plants that receive the most attention thrive, blossoming into colorful fruits and flowers.

Kids work the same way. With kids, you lay the groundwork for the fruits of your labor by understanding what's important for their success. Then you nurture your seedlings with positive messages and the right environment to grow up smarter and happier. Chapter 1 helps you define the concept of smart, while Chapters 2 and 3 help you prepare the soil that allows your kids to do their best. Chapter 4 adds information about kid fertilizer — the ways to keep your child healthy and ready to learn.

Chapter 1

Defining Smarts

You may as well acknowledge this fact now: The challenge of parenting has never been greater. Your kids experience endless choices, new technology, and outside forces — such as media — that bombard them from babyhood on and compete with you for their attention.

In such a fast-paced, highly competitive world, you have to get your parenting priorities straight early-on. If you want to raise smart kids, you must define what being smart means to *you*. Then you need to understand which resources give kids the ability to succeed. Only after careful consideration can you identify how these concepts translate into a smarter style of parenting.

This chapter explores those basic, albeit intertwined, characteristics that make getting higher grades and pursuing unusual talents possible.

Recognizing Characteristics of Smart Kids

Do you have wild and crazy dreams for your darlings, ones that may have started in the cradle? Perhaps you envision any or all of the following:

- Babies who spring from the womb talking and walking
- Preschoolers who read encyclopedias and compute algebra problems
- Kids who make the honor roll every semester and receive so many first-place blue ribbons in the science fair that NASA calls

> ✔ High schoolers who lead the school play, are first chair in the orchestra, and score so well on college boards that every Ivy League college sends four-year scholarship offerings

WARNING!

These goals, in addition to being a bit unrealistic, demonstrate only one aspect of being smart. Truly smart kids need more than lofty goals and pipe dreams to make it in today's cutthroat world.

I know the idea of raising well-rounded, smarter kids can be daunting. And sadly, no easy formula exists. Kids are as complex, varied, and exciting individuals as you are. The good news is that your child has a natural desire to do well. Your job as parent is to bring out this quality and cherish it until the day your kids leave home, and then some. Doing well involves your nurturing the traits discussed in the following sections.

Nothing beats drive

Being smart involves the drive to succeed, no matter which or how many obstacles cross your child's path. Drive gets you started, and then keeps you going. It challenges you to succeed. Even if your child proves exceptionally book smart, without drive to use the information in a practical way, the facts lead to nowhere.

The best part about drive is that it fuels itself. Interest in throwing a ball leads to pitching little league, which leads to playing on a school team. Some unidentifiable inner resource creates the quest for knowledge. Call it a love of learning or an adventurous spirit. The pleasure is as much — or more — in the doing as in reaching the goal.

Encouraging kids

Children drive themselves almost from birth. They reach for the next step along the path to independence. Your healthy baby:

> ✔ Cries to communicate to you when he needs attention
>
> ✔ Roots until he finds food to suck
>
> ✔ Pushes and pulls until he rolls over, sits, and stands
>
> ✔ Moves about until he crawls, walks, and climbs stairs

Keep encouraging your child, and the drive to succeed kicks in. Potty training, picking out numbers and letters, drawing pictures, tying shoelaces, reading a book independently, playing an instrument — all are important milestones. With each achievement, your child gains the strength and confidence to try new adventures (although some, like drawing on walls, you may not appreciate). Encouraging these endeavors builds motivation to succeed that lasts a lifetime.

Not squelching drive

Every child possesses drive — unless it's stifled. Repeated putdowns, disinterest on your part, or minimizing what your child finds important goes a long way toward smothering drive.

A big time for parents who stifle drive occurs when kids spontaneously offer creepy, gooey treasures, such as the day my daughter found a large caterpillar cocoon. My first reaction, being truly bug-phobic and illiterate on the subject, was, "Yuck! No bugs in this house. End of story." Then I thought of a Plan B. We tucked away the bug house in a safe haven to watch it hatch. We went to the library to find books about the care and feeding of future butterflies. My daughter invited friends to see her treasure. And when a colorful moth emerged months later, we set it free. Today, my daughter encourages young insect lovers as a camp counselor when other group leaders say, "Gross! Get that thing away from me."

Think about the following ways to encourage drive in your kids:

- ✔ **Cherish mud pies, lightening bugs, and dandelion fuzz.** Consider your responses to gross stuff kids bring home and whether these reactions establish, or squelch, the drive to learn more and the interest to get smarter.

- ✔ **Let the laundry wait another day, if you see the first sun in six days.** Take time to explore your kids' discoveries *when* they happen.

- ✔ **Talk with helium you inhale from a balloon or concoct a baking soda volcano.** Figure out what's happening in these and other situations. Help your kids find magic in everyday scientific endeavors.

- ✔ **Encourage effort and always giving a best effort over final results.** When your child shows you a picture or story, ask questions to decipher and extend the learning involved in creating the work. Ask what else could be added. Praise the hard work to make whatever treasure you are witnessing.

- ✔ **Reinforce how earning money helps to buy CDs, books, and other valuables your child wants.** Plant seeds of desire that can be satisfied through hard work and increased knowledge.

- ✔ **Expose your child to volunteer work, such as at a food bank.** Talk about helping those who are less fortunate, but also discuss how to stay out of similar situations.

- ✔ **Allow a healthy dose of competitiveness and challenge to creep into your family activities once in a while.** Find out more about dealing with competition in Chapter 15.

Even when you give textbook responses to all your kid's curiosities (and no parent does that), your job instilling the drive to do the best isn't easy. Many forces work against you. The most obvious are TV, the stress of two-wage-earner and single-parent families, and less family time together for any number of reasons.

Consider, too, the rich and famous who boast how they managed to succeed without doing well in school. President George W. Bush tells Yale graduates that being a C student gets you elected president. Actor George Clooney boasts to television viewers that he ducked out of college early. Although you may believe these folks epitomize drive because they achieved success without being the sharpest tool in the shed, they don't send the right message to kids that the drive for knowledge equals success.

Willingness to work works magic

The sooner your kids appreciate the value of work, the more successful they will be. Work is part of life. You work to earn money, put food on the table, and keep your homes orderly and clean. For your kids, work involves schoolwork, homework, and teamwork at home and in the community. Becoming a responsible, committed worker is one of life's lessons.

Clear links exist between a positive work ethic and success. Studies show that your hard-working 10-year-old has a greater chance for success later in life than the slacker kid next door. In fact, the willingness to work overrides IQ or family economic levels. Establishing a work ethic at an early age brings less unemployment and more fulfilling relationships all around later.

When your kids are able to cheerfully labor at a task until it's complete, they beat their chests and say, "I did it!" Developing a positive work ethic provides other benefits, too:

- Sense of achievement
- Self-confidence
- Awareness of strengths and weaknesses
- Respect for rules and authority
- Skills to cooperate with others to get a job done
- Ability to conscientiously continue until a mental or physical task is complete, in other words, self-discipline

I think work is so important for kids that I explore the value of work and types of jobs kids of all ages can do in Chapters 8, 11, and 16.

Optimism keeps kids going

If your kids display a positive attitude, their chances increase for a healthier and longer life. Your kids can also count on performing better at work and school. The reason is that optimists see all of life a certain way — the I-can-do-it-or-fail-trying way — instead of focusing on individual events that may or may not go well at any given moment.

If your kids truly count on acing a test, getting a lead in the play, or climbing a mountain, they can achieve their dream or come pretty close. If they don't make the grade, so be it. They'll try again.

Bolstering courage through attitude

Thinking positively helps your kids take on life's challenges. Positive attitudes help kids find courage to:

- Refuse harmful temptations, such as dope, alcohol, and unwanted sex

- Avoid other risky or dangerous situations that don't feel right

- Answer questions in class when others think being smart is uncool

- Stick with upbeat friends who may not be in the most popular crowd

- Enter a new classroom or school, especially the lunchroom, without knowing anyone

Optimism versus rose-colored glasses

Being an optimist doesn't mean your child is unrealistic. True optimists never deny reality. Nor are they Pollyannas, who view silver linings everywhere. Instead, your positive-thinking kid uses faith and enthusiasm to change existing reality, whenever reasonably possible, into something constructive. They say, "Maybe if I can run a little faster, study a little harder, I'll make the grade."

Kids who react in this way learn from their experiences. They build on them. And they view their best performances as part of a continuum. With these kids, the bar keeps rising rather than hitting a ceiling.

Creating an optimist

The jury's out about whether optimists are born or made. One thing's for sure. If you're always negative and expect the worst, expect your kids to be downers, too. But if you're an optimist, you give off a can-do attitude that sends positive vibes to your kids. (More about this in Chapter 3.) Kids come to believe that they can make a difference in the world. And they usually do.

Creativity opens doors

Smart kids are creative kids, and they think differently. They grab the brass ring, turn it upside down, and roll it around, inventing a host of uses other than holding onto the carousel. They use a variety of mental skills to make their worlds interesting.

The marvels of creative thinking

Creativity is all about using talents to generate something unique. You can discover clues to your child's creative spirit as you watch him do the following:

- **Think abstractly.** An empty box is more than a box. It's a fort, toy box, or doll house.

- **Reason.** If this block fits on the side but makes the tower wobble, maybe placing a block on the other side will keep the tower from toppling.

- **Solve problems.** This math problem may help understand how to balance a checkbook.

- **Plan.** For example, "Today, I dress, take the dog for a walk to the park, dig for worms with Jamie, and finish the necklace I'm stringing."

- **Grasp complex ideas.** Your child may take the radio apart and see how it works. Then he puts it back together again.

- **Interpret the world through the senses.** Producing music, visual art, or stories is a creativity clue.

Looking beyond the everyday

Unlocking your child's creative streak takes time and patience. To encourage the natural sense of wonder and adventure that leads to creativity:

- Let your kids know you appreciate free thinking and adventuresome spirits.

- Promote thinking in new and different ways by asking questions, such as "What would happen if . . . ?" or "How did you come up with . . . ?" that extend your child's creativity.

- Accept that today's daydreamer may be tomorrow's Mozart. The settling of ideas, mulling them over, and anticipating "what ifs" are all part of the creative process, as long as your daydreamer doesn't let the entire world go by.

- Meet each wild and crazy idea with respect and enthusiasm. Putdowns for impractical or silly suggestions pop creative bubbles. Be supportive and more ideas will surely come.

Encourage your child to keep an imagination journal. Any kind of paper, folder, scrapbook, or blank book can help record fanciful thoughts and images. Audio journals on cassette work, too. Let your child's imagination soar in writing, drawings, narrations, or song. If the creative muse is asleep, offer prompts to send your kids into make-believe land. Very young kids respond to "Pretend you are . . . landing on the moon, playing in a garden of candy plants." Older kids may take a little brainstorming to get them started. You can suggest idea sparkers, such as Robots on the Loose, Wacky Wildlife, or The Day I. . . . You get the idea. Creative musing doubles as great time fillers on long trips.

Friends fuel success

Friendly kids get farther. Even in this impersonal, high-tech world, your child eventually interacts with others: in class, on the job, on teams, and — heaven forbid — on dates. Friendly kids get asked to parties and run for class office because they know how to connect with people. As adults, they get jobs done because they know how to support others and gain support in return. Moreover, studies show that mental and physical health depends on having the social skills to make friends.

The ability to make and keep friends is a quality of life issue that successful kids have. Through interactions with others, smart kids refine and adapt these skills as they mature. To ensure your child's ability to build healthy relationships:

- **Explain the emotions of others.** Say: "Pat cries because he feels sad." "Maria giggles when she's nervous." Besides giving language for feelings and actions, talking about what makes others sad or happy builds empathy.

- **Read stories that show kids expressing their feelings,** so that your child doesn't fear emotions in others.

- **Talk about qualities, such as being supportive, fun, and responsible, that make good friends.** Build your child's confidence in making good decisions early. Reinforce that sound decisions include choosing friends who meet family standards.

- **Help your child accept differences in friends, teammates, and coworkers.** Explain that no one person has all the qualities someone needs in a relationship. That's why most people choose a variety of friends to satisfy different aspects of their personality. Read more about the importance of relationships in Chapters 10 and 15.

Lightening up: The parenting reality check

I know that nothing is more serious than raising kids. And aiming to help them be as smart as possible ups the ante a few notches. But don't get so caught up with your emphasis on smarts that you lose sight of how much fun growing a family can be. Enjoy your kids. Laugh with them. Cry with them. Act goofy with them. By all means, give them lots of hugs and kisses. This give and take will do as much, or more, toward creating smart, happy kids than all the suggestions in any parenting book.

Expect, too, that your kids will try your patience, anger you, sometimes drive you to distraction. That's what they're supposed to do. At times, they'll buck your best efforts to enrich their little lives. Even that's part of their learning process! If they acted like model kids all the time, you'd never want them to leave home. But that's not what parenting is about. Smart parenting instills qualities in smart kids that allow them to fly the coop, be successful, and live independently.

Remembering real-world smarts

All these qualities mean nothing without good common sense, which is another kind of smarts altogether. Common sense involves the street smarts that your child often can't learn in books. It includes sound decision-making abilities that your child learns from life:

- ✔ Thinking on his feet
- ✔ Making safe and healthful choices
- ✔ Trusting his gut feelings, especially the uncomfortable ones
- ✔ Knowing when to act, speak out, or run away
- ✔ Understanding when following instructions is wrong
- ✔ Standing firm about saying "no"

Street smarts don't just happen. You must prepare your kids for life. I talk about planning for situations that your child may encounter at different maturation levels, such as crossing the street and stranger danger, in Chapters 8, 10, and 18. But certain lessons cover all ages. Prime your child for the real world by:

- ✔ Planning ahead for situations your child may bump into at different stages of life, such as telephone predators when your child is old enough to stay home alone.
- ✔ Teaching specific skills that match these situations, such as dialing 911 in emergencies.

✔ Brainstorming alternatives to these and other situations by playing a "what if" game. "What would you do if someone who claimed to be a plumber came to the door and wanted to come into the house?" "What if a stranger called and asked whether your parent was home?"

✔ Preparing safety checklists, keeping them visible, and reviewing them regularly.

✔ Keeping lines of communication open and staying up to date on your child's life at every age.

✔ Role playing responses to situations until they become comfortable and second nature. Pretend you're a stranger who rings the bell and says he needs to use the telephone for an emergency, or act out driving your car next to your child and offering to take him to see new puppies. Practice what to say and do in each situation.

Keeping Kids Smart As They Grow

Throughout this book, you find a smorgasbord of practices to raise smarter kids. Again and again, I drive home the main ways that smart parents help their kids shine.

✔ **You realize the important role you play in raising smart kids and take that role seriously.** This doesn't mean spending every waking hour stimulating your little darlings. It means keeping a healthy perspective and being the best parent you can be.

✔ **You send your kids the right messages that being smart counts.** No, I don't recommend telling your kids over and over again that they must be smart. Instead, I suggest subtly sneaking the idea into their brains by what you do and say, as I mention in Chapter 2.

✔ **You take care of your kids and yourself,** understanding that healthy, fit kids grow into smarter kids. More about this in Chapter 4.

✔ **You find out about normal child development.** You learn how little brains work (Chapter 6) and what makes them grow. Then you expand your kids' minds with activities that match their levels of development.

✔ **You give your kids room to be the best they can be.** You keep an eye on their social and emotional development, as well as on academics. But you let them flounder, succeed, and grow at their own pace until they become independent beings and leave home, which comes quicker than you may think.

Chapter 2

Realizing That You Can Raise a Brain

Come clean. Does your stomach flip-flop at the awesome task of raising brainy kids? Has this anxiety sent you running for the latest parenting books, videos, and Web sites? Do you probe, dissect, and analyze every parenting step you take because you worry about ruining their potential?

Take heart and save your hard-earned money. What your kids need comes from home. Look no farther than the resources you already have — within yourself and your family. This chapter helps you do a little soul-searching to identify the strengths you already possess for your smart-parenting gig. If you've done some personal accounting for your other children, you may want to scan this chapter for what's new to you and quickly jump to another chapter.

Assessing What You Already Know

Even if you're a first-time parent, you're not a novice at parenting. You were a kid once, and that's one notch in your knowledge belt. And you probably spent time with at least one parent or parenting figure. That's another notch.

If you've worked with children (as a day-care provider, a teacher, a physician, an aunt or uncle, and so on), you've already experienced childhood interactions that offer dress rehearsals for raising your own family.

Don't be surprised if, from time to time, you respond exactly like your parents did. To your amazement — and horror — you may find reflections of your youth lying dormant inside you. Your parents' words, actions, and replies may reappear to haunt you when you least expect them with your own children, like when they try your patience with whining or by playing ear-splitting music — just like you did to your parents.

Take a minute to think seriously about your relationships with the folks who raised you. Ask your significant other, if you have one, to do the same thing. You may want to list pros and cons like the sample in Table 2-1. Think about how your parents responded to you.

- ✔ What did they do that worked for you and your siblings?
- ✔ What didn't work?
- ✔ Which of these responses do you want your kids to experience?
- ✔ What family traditions are worth continuing?
- ✔ Which desperately need to be scrapped?

Analysis of these reflections provides a framework for how you choose to respond as a parent.

Table 2-1	Sample Family Pro and Con List
Pros	**Cons**
Kissed me goodnight routinely	Told me to be brave when sick or that scrapes didn't really hurt, negating my feelings
Hosted regular birthday parties	Told me to stop crying or I'd get something to cry about
Treated me and my siblings equally	Followed different rules for boys and girls
Spent weekends together as a family	Left me out of choosing family activities
Told me I could do anything	Suggested I take courses in teaching, in case "anything" didn't work out

Don't panic. You're *not* your parents. But you received their gene pool at birth, and you lived in the same household for years. Chances are, you've combined their positives and negatives — and some qualities in between — to form your own distinct personality.

Treasure the good stuff from your folks and work on losing whatever you think contributes to your quirks. Remember, too, what you bring to the parenting table. Look to your own values, dreams, strengths, and ways of handling life experiences.

Talk with your significant other to find commonalities that make parenting work better. Kids catch on quickly when parents disagree about how to handle child rearing and use this information to their advantage. They either play one parent against the other or ask permission for doing something they know full well the other parent will veto. Then they go to the vetoing parent and say, "Dad (Mom) said I could keep the snake under the bed" or "Mom (or Dad) said I could sleep over with my boyfriend." Resolve your differences ahead of time so that you present a common front to your child.

Another two notches in your parenting belt involve your good common sense and love of your child. Never underestimate how important love and intuition can be to raising smarter kids. If something feels right to you, go with the feeling, no matter what the child-guidance books say. Trust your judgment, hug your kids regularly, and reap the rewards of raising smarter kids.

Taking a Look at Other Parents' Tricks of the Trade

You love being a parent. But don't feel bad if talking to an infant for hours on end when you're used to trading on the floor of the stock exchange leaves you pretty lonely sometimes. Adult stimulation is good for smart parents. Parenting is too important a job to carry out in a vacuum. So get out of the house and look to the resources around you.

Communicating with family elders

Parents who didn't have a clue when you were growing up may be filled with wise gems about raising grandchildren. Raising one child eases the way for second and third children. Ask your parents how they raised such a smart brood. If you can't talk with your folks, call Grandma, Aunt Sadie, or Uncle Phil.

Practicing ten ways to nurture smarter kids

Sadly, no magic potion exists to raise smarter kids (or I'd bottle and sell it instead of writing books). But parents in the know mix a brew of these general guidelines to wind up with success stories. If you want smarter kids, do the following:

✔ **Set family standards high and keep everyone focused on what's really important.** Expect the best. If grades fall one time, explore why the dip occurred and express confidence for better grades the next time. Studies show that parents of smart kids dream loftier dreams for their kids than other parents do, and their kids live up to them.

✔ **Encourage your child's intellectual curiosity.** Extend curiosities with activities and family outings. Talk about your child's dreams — and even fears — as starting points. Explore together. Point out constellations, watch sunsets, and analyze how crickets chirp.

✔ **Create balance in your child's life.** Establish routines, but make time to enjoy the wonders of the world around you together. "Taking time to smell the roses" applies to kids, too.

✔ **Stay connected and involved in your child's life.** Show interest in your children and their daily activities. Don't assume that because your child goes off to school, your job is done. It's only beginning, as you find out in Chapter 10.

✔ **Provide a supportive atmosphere for learning and growing.** Keep lines of communication open, and be a good listener. Ask about and rejoice in what's going well with your child. Create an appropriate atmosphere for schoolwork to take place, as discussed in depth in Chapter 13. Most of all, offer hugs for when life goes awry.

✔ **Help your children organize for success.** Your kids need safe, stimulating environments at any age. They also need someone who sets realistic boundaries and helps them arrange their days of studying, homework, and activities without micromanaging.

✔ **Proclaim your house a reading house.** In a reading house, you read to your kids regularly, encourage reading of anything and everything from cereal boxes to billboards to magazines, and you model reading newspapers and books yourself.

✔ **Reinforce that education ranks number one in your home.** Maintain a keen intellectual level at home. Schedule schoolwork as the primary activity, as expanded in Chapters 13 and 14.

Think of "education" more than "schooling." Your kids can experience many wonderful interactions, such as taking vacations, meeting different types of people, and visiting museums, that expand their horizons as much as school.

✔ **Give your kids responsibilities as early as they can handle them.** Shared chores build an interconnectedness, a family feeling. Fulfilling responsibilities leads to the abilities of organizing and working well with others outside the home.

✔ **Foster creativity.** Reward the joy of discovery. Bite your tongue when the gooey experiment to create the perfect dessert boils over on the oven. If Thomas Edison's parents could forgive his burning down the barn to see how flames react, you can stand a little mess in the kitchen. Welcome new ideas.

Checking out how other parents handle behaviors

Other parents provide a wealth of answers to everyday problem situations. Meet folks while walking your baby or watching your kids at the playground. Big cities often have community centers where families go to hang out or join in activities.

Post a note on bulletin boards at the community center or at the local grocery store to find others with children of similar ages to yours. Contact other parents to form discussion groups. Sharing with someone in the same boat helps you sort through all the parenting hype from media. Read Chapters 9 and 22 to find other types of help and support.

Ask for help when your kids stump you and drive you crazy (which, by the way, they live to do). Take advantage of wise words from the wounded warriors who've come before you.

Dispelling Parenting Myths

Do you have ideas about what you think smart parenting involves? Maybe these ideas come from how your folks raised you. Or maybe ideas come from your research or from TV sitcoms.

The following are parenting myths you may have encountered but should wipe from your mind:

- **Unless you stimulate your kids all day every day, they become lazy.** Wrong. Kids need downtime to absorb, synthesize, and play with information. They need to do some of that absorbing without you around and without a tight schedule of play dates and activities.

- **The best way to grow smarter kids is to put their lives first all the time.** Reality check. You're no good to anyone, much less your intelligent offspring, unless you take care of yourself. If you're unhappy, your kids will be, too. You owe it to yourself and your family to lead the same well-balanced lives that other smart people lead.

- **The best way to raise high-achieving kids is to micromanage everything they do.** Leave your extreme managerial skills at the office. Hide your latest version of those cute little computerized schedulers and planners. Using some form of a calendar is great to show your kids how to organize, and providing a little family structure is fine. But hang a little looser with your kids. After you've guided them with your organizational wisdom, let them schedule for themselves.

✔ **Raising a smart kid ensures raising a nerd.** Erase that old-fashioned notion from your parenting crib notes. In fact, smarter kids love learning, and that includes anything that suits their fancy. So it's possible that the smarter, more high achieving your child, the more areas she'll delve into — sports, the arts, academic subjects — creating balance in her young life.

On a more personal note, because your smart child experiences frequent successes, she probably feels better about herself. So she's emotionally healthier, which gives her a better shot at practicing social skills and making friends. Now does that sound nerdy to you?

✔ **You can speed up your darling's development by pushing developmental timetables.** No way. Kids learn better when they are developmentally ready.

Remember the family secret about why Uncle Harry is neurotic? Grandma potty trained Uncle Henry at 9 months, well before he could walk. Potty training is just the beginning of pushing. Grandmas like this one probably expect their kids to eat with a spoon at 10 months, read by age 3, and make a perfect bed by age 5. Some things are just not going to happen when you want them to, no matter how hard you push, until your child naturally develops the skills.

✔ **Smart parents never get upset or annoyed.** I have never known a parent who has never gotten bent out of shape over something their child did. If I ever meet one, I'll consider him or her delusional and maladjusted.

You're a person, like any other. Parenting doesn't change that. And as a normal person, you experience ups and downs. Some days are easier to handle your child's difficult behavior than others.

Just like you, kids need to separate feelings from actions. It's okay to get angry; it's not okay to kick the baby or berate your teen because you're in a twit over something else.

You need to be honest about your feelings. How you handle life's experiences sends a powerful message to your child about expressing feelings and emotions. Explore more about reacting to your child's behavior in Chapter 3.

Getting a Handle on Growth and Development

This book gives you tons of ideas about what smart parents do. But you may be wondering, "How do I know when to apply these suggestions?"

Children go through definite stages of development. Your baby rolls over, sits, and crawls before walking. Your school-age youngster learns counting to 100 and addition before being expected to multiply and handle percentages. Milestones occur generally around the same time for most kids, although all kids vary, which is totally normal. This said, throughout this book, I tuck developmental info into chapters where I discuss specific age groups. That way, you have a frame of reference when your cousin boasts that her 3-year-old recites "Ode to a Grecian Urn."

Recognizing that children go through stages of development makes parenting easier because the information creates more realistic expectations. You think twice before expecting a 2-year-old to sit still in a fancy restaurant for a seven-course meal. You understand that your preteen can't have a party at home without adult supervision. Realizing everyone goes through stages helps you guide your smart kid wisely because you have an idea what childhood is about.

Try not to be the kind of parent who views developmental transitions as traumatic and tries to avoid them. Instead of potty training and enjoying that new phase with your child, you rack up extra diaper bills for years, waiting for some sign from your little darling that the toilet is where she chooses to place her jewels.

Burn into your brain that moving from one developmental stage to another isn't life-altering. A little frustration at one step or another doesn't scar your child for life or produce a mentally unbalanced adult. Most stages are part of the natural evolution of growth and maturation. You've passed through numerous phases in your life and probably will go through still more. Your kids will move along just fine, too.

Understand, too, that not every child goes through every stage. Some kids skip crawling and leap right to standing and walking. Moreover, your child may go through the same stage later or earlier than her best buddy. Does this mean your child has a problem? Probably not. This merely means your child is following her own time frame for developing, and that's okay.

Evaluating Whether You're Pushing Too Hard

You naturally want the best for your child. But what if your desire for success causes more trouble than it helps? You pressure your child into activities that she is neither ready for nor capable of doing. Or you throw too much at her in an effort to help her zoom ahead.

Animal trainers know better. They would never expect a turtle to jump through a hoop the way a dolphin can. Why? They're practical. They understand that turtles are genetically or developmentally incapable of hoop-jumping.

You probably understand what your child is capable of doing, too. But you want her performing to the max, or you feel you're not being a good parent. So you buy more educational toys, read more parenting books, and schedule more music lessons, gymnastics, art classes, and other activities. You try to transform your turtle into a dolphin.

Readiness and genetic predisposition play critical roles in raising smart kids. Kids who aren't ready to learn the next step because they haven't learned the one they are on struggle. Then they battle you for forcing them through hoops.

You aren't the only factor in pushing your child. My daughter's school district, as is becoming more common, keeps pushing curriculum into lower grades. What has been traditionally a fifth-grade skill is now taught in fourth, and so on down the line. She agonized over fractions and decimals in third grade. Even in fourth and fifth grade, she struggled with the same problems. By sixth grade, the light bulb went off in her head. Her math development caught up with her teacher's expectations. She finally understood fractions and decimals.

Realize that your child can get too much of a good thing. Your child needs time to veg-out, regroup, and play independently. So I give you permission to spend less time, money, and energy on your child. I urge you to put raising smart kids into a more balanced perspective that includes more fun, more family time, and a broader definition of smart (see Chapter 1).

Opening Doors to Success

You know you want smarter kids. You want kids who focus on achieving what they set out to accomplish, whether writing a haiku poem or getting into medical school. But have you figured out your role in the success-building process?

You can stand on your head and talk until your eyes bulge. But if your kids don't welcome success, they won't stay in the race to cross the finish line. The messages you send your kids encourage them more than gold ribbons, stars, and trophies ever will.

Your job begins by creating a mindset to raise success stories. This section gives you some general guidelines for acquiring the mental attitude for raising smarter kids of any age.

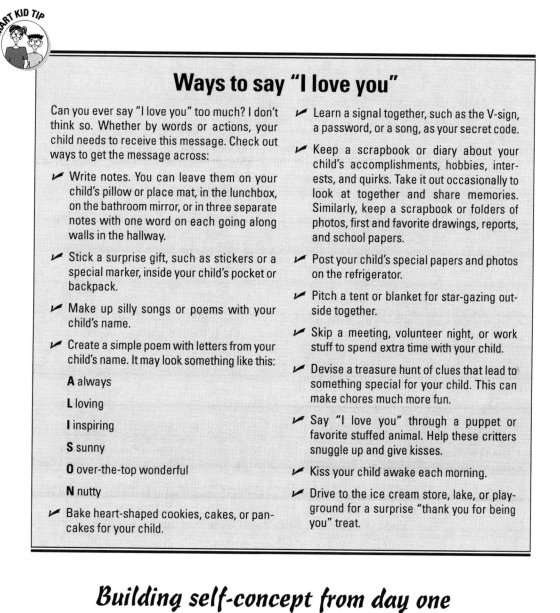

Ways to say "I love you"

Can you ever say "I love you" too much? I don't think so. Whether by words or actions, your child needs to receive this message. Check out ways to get the message across:

✔ Write notes. You can leave them on your child's pillow or place mat, in the lunchbox, on the bathroom mirror, or in three separate notes with one word on each going along walls in the hallway.

✔ Stick a surprise gift, such as stickers or a special marker, inside your child's pocket or backpack.

✔ Make up silly songs or poems with your child's name.

✔ Create a simple poem with letters from your child's name. It may look something like this:

A always

L loving

I inspiring

S sunny

O over-the-top wonderful

N nutty

✔ Bake heart-shaped cookies, cakes, or pancakes for your child.

✔ Learn a signal together, such as the V-sign, a password, or a song, as your secret code.

✔ Keep a scrapbook or diary about your child's accomplishments, hobbies, interests, and quirks. Take it out occasionally to look at together and share memories. Similarly, keep a scrapbook or folders of photos, first and favorite drawings, reports, and school papers.

✔ Post your child's special papers and photos on the refrigerator.

✔ Pitch a tent or blanket for star-gazing outside together.

✔ Skip a meeting, volunteer night, or work stuff to spend extra time with your child.

✔ Devise a treasure hunt of clues that lead to something special for your child. This can make chores much more fun.

✔ Say "I love you" through a puppet or favorite stuffed animal. Help these critters snuggle up and give kisses.

✔ Kiss your child awake each morning.

✔ Drive to the ice cream store, lake, or playground for a surprise "thank you for being you" treat.

Building self-concept from day one

The late Mr. Rogers, the rock-star of preschoolers, used to say that success is a four-letter word: L-O-V-E. The loving relationship between you and your child lays the groundwork for all relationships that follow. Loving parent-child interactions help your child learn who she is and how much she can accomplish. She feels worthwhile because somebody loves her unconditionally.

When your child knows she is loved, she believes she can conquer the world. See the "Ways to say 'I love you'" sidebar for tips on how to communicate the love you feel for your child.

Connecting with family

Nothing is more important to a loving relationship and raising high-achieving kids than the feeling of belonging. The glue that holds your child's self-concept together is family. Through family interactions, your child begins to trust herself and others. She becomes optimistic about life.

When your child feels secure as an individual, she explores the world knowing the safe family haven will welcome her back with open arms. These early interactions help your child gain the strength to weather any storm. Just as important, loving relationships feed the love of learning.

Making time for your kids

How do you create that family feeling? By spending meaningful time together. Time is the greatest gift you can give your kids to help them grow happy and successful.

Parents and kids agree that time together is the best. Yet, a recent survey by Boys & Girls Clubs of America reports that one in five kids believe they have "too little" or "hardly any" quality time with their folks.

Time together probably sounds like an admirable goal that's easier to say than do. But staying connected with your kids isn't impossible, no matter how chaotic your schedule. Try to arrange some of these options:

✔ **Meal times:** Long-range studies show that kids who eat with their families achieve greater academic success. And one national study reports that 75 percent of adults agree that meaningful conversation with their kids is important. So eating together is a simple way to get a little chit-chat in while boosting brain cells.

  Try to eat at least one meal together each day. Food calms the spirits and opens minds to discussions. Talk about your child's day, the news (if it's not too depressing), or a specific topic of relevance to the family. And you don't have to be a gourmet to make family meals work. I'm talking quick and nutritious meals here.

✔ **Family outings:** Family excursions build bonds and provide time to practice skills learned at home, such as good manners, taking turns, and respect for others. Think about trips to museums, stores, libraries, forest preserves, and beaches. Pick apples and pumpkins, watch leaves turn color, and make snow angels. Walk, run, ride bicycles, or drive in cars, planes, or trains. Vote on where to go, depending upon your kid's age, interests, and the family budget. The choices are endless but mind expanding.

✔ **Chores and vegging out together:** Quality time together doesn't have to be fancy or planned. Kids discover bundles from sorting laundry (colors and shapes), fixing lunches (cooking, nutritional value of foods), cleaning the house (health and safety, camaraderie and motor-skill practice), and planting gardens (environment, insects, plant growth).

Your kids don't always have to be learning for time to be valuable. Watch TV together, read books in the same room, or have tickle fights — whatever you need to relax. Being close and accomplishing something together goes a long way toward building family togetherness.

✔ **Times when you're apart:** If you can't be with your kids, stay connected by telephone, e-mail, even fax.

Creating family traditions

Traditions comfort children — and adults. They provide security in an ever-changing world. They add joy to already fond memory banks. They give reassurance that you and your kids can count on and hold dear certain events and experiences. Who knows? Maybe family traditions are why you and your significant other clash over whose family to visit on Thanksgiving or which ornaments hang front and center on the holiday tree.

Start smart and memorable traditions in your home. You find ideas for traditions sprinkled throughout this book, but here are a few to get you started:

✔ Each night, share something good that happened during the day.

✔ Read a story each night before bedtime.

✔ Hold a mini tea party with crackers and milk before beginning bedtime routines.

✔ Make birthdays special. But you don't have to buy the most expensive present to arrange a successful birthday. Let the birthday person choose a favorite meal, decide where to go on the next family excursion, or wear a special crown (which works well with young kids).

✔ Schedule a family night the same night each week or month. Plan on spending the time together in some fun activity, such as playing games, taking walks, baking cookies, or going to movies. Institute backward night, where you wear clothes backward and talk backward, or silly suppers, in which you eat outrageous combinations of food. Do whatever tickles your funny bones.

✔ Celebrate a holiday with similar foods or activities each year. You may be surprised what sticks with kids.

I know someone who, on Thanksgiving, must eat sweet potatoes with miniature marshmallows just like her mom used to add, even though she prefers healthier food today.

✔ Visit special relatives regularly. Listen to stories about long ago with grandma every Sunday afternoon. Eat dinner with Aunt Maria's family every other Friday night to ring in the weekend.

✔ Volunteer together. Check out food banks, senior's homes, homeless shelters, local political offices, or worthwhile organizations that can use help.

✔ Have reading time each night. Someone can read a story aloud, family members can take turns reading aloud, or you can each read want you want.

Family rituals are a funny thing. Sometimes, you don't know you've created one until your kid says, "I want the same . . . as you did it before," or "I sure did like when we. . . ."

Holding family meetings

Another way to ensure much-needed family-communication time is to hold family meetings. These are sacred times when the entire family — dog and cat included — connects during regularly scheduled get-togethers. Meetings can be problem-solving sessions, gripe sessions, or happy sharing times. The purpose is to reconnect with each other and the fact that you're a family.

Setting a positive tone

Smart kids thrive in positive environments. In fact, studies prove that gifted kids live in families with greater acceptance and less conflict. I don't mean unnatural Pollyanna homes where voices never rise in anger. I'm talking about homes where you and your kids strive to be as even-tempered and positive as you can, given your day. And you treat each other with respect any age person deserves, no matter what your mood or how many times the dog pooped in the house.

Being positive and respectful is contagious. When you're happy, so are your partner and kids. One kind word usually leads to another. Try it some time. Listen how "Thanks for helping" or "You did a great job on your homework" ripples from person to person in kind words, like waves in the ocean.

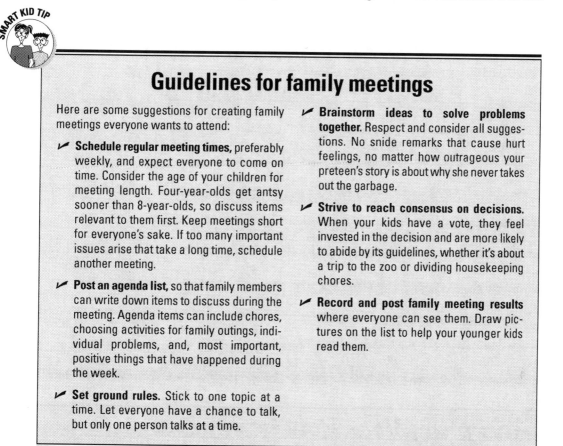

Guidelines for family meetings

Here are some suggestions for creating family meetings everyone wants to attend:

✔ **Schedule regular meeting times,** preferably weekly, and expect everyone to come on time. Consider the age of your children for meeting length. Four-year-olds get antsy sooner than 8-year-olds, so discuss items relevant to them first. Keep meetings short for everyone's sake. If too many important issues arise that take a long time, schedule another meeting.

✔ **Post an agenda list,** so that family members can write down items to discuss during the meeting. Agenda items can include chores, choosing activities for family outings, individual problems, and, most important, positive things that have happened during the week.

✔ **Set ground rules.** Stick to one topic at a time. Let everyone have a chance to talk, but only one person talks at a time.

✔ **Brainstorm ideas to solve problems together.** Respect and consider all suggestions. No snide remarks that cause hurt feelings, no matter how outrageous your preteen's story is about why she never takes out the garbage.

✔ **Strive to reach consensus on decisions.** When your kids have a vote, they feel invested in the decision and are more likely to abide by its guidelines, whether it's about a trip to the zoo or dividing housekeeping chores.

✔ **Record and post family meeting results** where everyone can see them. Draw pictures on the list to help your younger kids read them.

Watch how the opposite occurs. Your spouse grumbles at dinner because of a bad day at work. You react with less patience when your kids protest eating their broccoli. If they harbor ill feelings from eating the foul-smelling greenery, they shove the dog, who chases the cat, who lunges at the fish bowl. Pretty soon everyone is griping about something.

You can't check your moods at the door, but you can control how you express them. Your kids find out from you how to handle their feelings. If you feel out of sorts, explain why without the gory details. Your youngest child, in particular, may think she causes your anxiety, so reassure your kids that the problem is with you, not them. Let your kids know what helps you regain your composure: time alone, exercise, or talking with a friend. Being honest and modeling different ways to handle problems does a lot to lift the household mood.

A positive environment is a welcoming environment, one that supports learning, growing, and healthy well-being.

Confidence builders

Remember the old adage, "Actions speak louder than words"? Show your kids you respect and value them as people by doing the following:

✔ Recognizing efforts, no matter how small.

✔ Giving them time to respond without your answering or prompting them for answers.

✔ Listening carefully by establishing eye contact when they talk. This means turning away from the computer and putting down the potato peeler.

✔ Knocking on the door before entering bedrooms. This should be an absolute rule with teens in the house, but it applies to all kids.

✔ Saying "please" and "thank you." That's the least you expect from your kids.

✔ Taking discussions about infractions somewhere private. Nothing deflates like being bawled out in public or in front of friends or a favorite relative.

✔ Introducing your kids to friends and acquaintances you bump into.

✔ Including them in conversations, whenever appropriate, rather than talking past them like they were objects or not there.

✔ Notice something positive about each of your kids every day. Appreciate the little things, the way they put underwear in the laundry bag, how they always remember to feed the dog, when they say thank you to Aunt Martha.

Accepting Your Role as Teacher

I don't mean to scare you, but you're your child's most important teacher. Facts memorized for tests come and go, but lessons experienced at home linger for a lifetime. Your interests and attitudes (especially about education), your expectations, the rules you set, and how you maintain balance in your life all make a difference. These factors all rank high in studies that evaluate what makes kids smarter.

Practicing what you preach

Your kids love to imitate. From toddler house cleaning to teen shaving. So use imitation as your secret teaching weapon.

Act as a living model for the personality and work habits you want your kids to acquire. Be the best role model you can be — without exuding obnoxious perfection. Instill the love of learning in your children. Mold their relationships by letting them see how you treat people. These traits seep into your kids' brain unconsciously through imitation. Show your kids by example how smart learning comes from life.

Fall down a few times, though, so your kids see how you rise up again. Making mistakes offers important learning lessons, too.

Whatever you do, don't say one thing and do something else. Inconsistencies generate disastrous results. Older kids especially love to catch their parents not practicing what they preach. Talk respectfully to your spouse, if you want respect from your kids. Bite your tongue when you feel the urge to yell, "Damn!" or worse. Otherwise, expect to hear these words, and then some, later. In other words, your kids are watching you while you watch them.

Managing parent ego: Yes, yours!

Stay alert to what's important about raising your child: nurturing a confident, independent person who likes herself. Parenting a smart kid is *not* about:

✔ **Growing an extension of yourself:** Check your ego at the door if you prefer a child who dances, but your child loves racing cars instead. This is her life.

✔ **Creating a status symbol:** Your child has not been put on this earth to glorify you. If you have a high achiever, remember the little person inside. She doesn't exist so you can brag about grades, test scores, or the number of batters she strikes out.

✔ **Smothering your child in the name of love:** Your child should not be the total focus of your existence. Yes, your child takes considerable time and energy, not to mention loving. But she needs some space to ever be able to separate from you.

That said, do remember that smart parenting involves being proud of your child. Give liberal amounts of love and respect and reread the "Confidence builders" sidebar often.

Chapter 3

Disciplining in a Positive Way

*T*ime to read (or reread) *The Little Engine that Could.* If you aren't familiar with this wise children's book, its main theme revolves around a woebegone train engine that bolsters his seeming lack of strength by saying, "I think I can. I think I can." Because of his inner strength and positive self-image, this bedraggled train believes he can deliver an overload of toys uphill and save a town's Christmas. And he does. What a great message for your smart kid.

In the spirit of that little train engine, this chapter focuses on boosting your child's confidence to achieve impossible goals. The sections in this chapter concentrate on stressing the positive and structuring your child's world for success — while acknowledging that a few behavior lapses are bound to happen. If you have your bases covered on disciplining for success, jump to another chapter.

Accentuating the Positive

Nothing encourages learning better than your love and attention. Saying "Great job for . . . (you fill in the blank)!" provides a dynamic way for you to shape your child's behavior. Meaningful praise helps you structure an environment that says, "You're headed for greatness, kid."

Disciplining for fun and family peace

Smart kids need discipline, and so does your child. You may be thinking, "Discipline isn't for my little sweetie." Think again. Unlike punishment, which comes *after* some dastardly deed has been done, discipline provides a frame-work to train your child to act appropriately. Without discipline, your brainy kid faces a lifetime of trouble.

- ✔ Other kids don't want a friend who can't play by the rules.
- ✔ Teachers balk at teaching a child who constantly pushes the limits.
- ✔ You certainly don't want a bratty kid.

Your child needs discipline to feel secure and confident in this crazy world, just as you set certain parameters to run your home or job. Discipline is the smart way to grow a happier, more productive human being.

Provide well-defined rules and guidelines about what will happen when they are broken, and then follow through.

Think about the following key factors that encourage your child to thrive:

- ✔ **Be consistent.** For your own good, avoid flip-flopping at all costs. Here's an example: You say yes to midweek trips to the mall one time, but try to keep your preteen home the next school night, because it happens to be the night before a test. In your child's mind, flip-flopping is a show of weakness. He gets the message that the unacceptable will eventually be allowed if he continues to badger you long enough. His brain grabs onto the inconsistency and keeps trying to break you, because it has happened before.

- ✔ **Devise rules that are fair.** Your 12-year-old shouldn't have the same bedtime as your toddler. Set guidelines that make sense for every member of the family.

- ✔ **Make sure rules are realistic.** Rules need to match your child's level of development and maturity. They must be simple and understanding to follow, and they should always fit the situation they pertain to. Expecting a 10-year-old to keep his water glass off the marble table because it leaves a ring is fair and realistic. Expecting your son home from the prom for his usual eleven o' clock curfew is not.

- ✔ **Give reasons for rules when possible.** You don't always have the luxury of time to explain, and you don't want to go into long monologues. But providing a brief rationale for why a rule is important gives your child a chance to incorporate the rule into his own system of beliefs. He is empowered.

✔ **Bend rules for the rare but wonderful situations when they make sense.** Let your toddler stay up past 8:00 to finish the story. Allow a pillow fight between siblings once in awhile, as long as light fixtures are glued to ceilings and tabletops. Allowing what's usually out of bounds gives your kids the message that you're not unreasonable. You appear less perfect and more approachable in their eyes when you put down your policing stick once in awhile.

Traveling the behavior-shaping road

Kids are often unsure how to act. Here's where you come in. You help your child determine how to behave by praising or rewarding the behaviors that you want to reoccur. You even praise those behaviors that are on the road to approximating what you want to happen. Gradually, the approximations grow into full-blown actions that hit the mark head-on. This string of interactions is how you shape (or mold) behavior.

The reason praise works is that your positive response helps your darling feel good about himself. His feeling cheerier about accomplishments increases the likelihood of that behavior occurring again.

Educators and psychologists call this sort of interaction *positive reinforcement*. Focusing on the positive gives you two bonuses:

✔ You put conscious effort into noticing how well your offspring functions.

✔ You pat yourself on the back at his successes, gaining more confidence as a parent who's raising a smart kid.

Make sure you expend more time and emotion on appropriate behavior. I've seen kids who continue to be fussy eaters because picking at foods sends Mom or Dad into a tizzy, and the kids love the attention. But if Mom or Dad spent more time and effort noticing how great it is that little sister tries new foods, perhaps big brother would get the idea to join in.

To be effective, you must offer praise that's not only honest but specific. Never bluff praise. Kids have radar that detects when you don't mean what you say. As for the specific part, decide which you would rather hear: "That's nice," or "I like the way you wrote the opening paragraph. It's a grabber." The more specific you can be, the better your child knows what you like and want repeated.

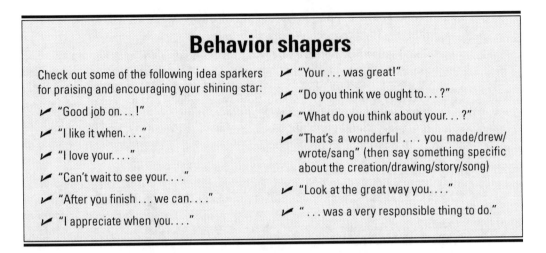

Behavior shapers

Check out some of the following idea sparkers for praising and encouraging your shining star:

✔ "Good job on. . . !"

✔ "I like it when. . . ."

✔ "I love your. . . ."

✔ "Can't wait to see your. . . ."

✔ "After you finish . . . we can. . . ."

✔ "I appreciate when you. . . ."

✔ "Your . . . was great!"

✔ "Do you think we ought to. . . ?"

✔ "What do you think about your. . . ?"

✔ "That's a wonderful . . . you made/drew/wrote/sang" (then say something specific about the creation/drawing/story/song)

✔ "Look at the great way you. . . ."

✔ " . . . was a very responsible thing to do."

Letting natural consequences do their job

Sometimes, you want to let nature take its course where your child's behavior is concerned. By this I mean that you let your child suffer consequences for misdeeds, and maybe, just maybe, he won't do it again.

Everything you do has consequences. If you work, you get paid. When you don't work, you don't get paid. Seems logical enough. Yet too many parents forget how they learned that lesson — on their own.

How many times have you covered for your child, thinking you're doing him a favor? In actuality, you're depriving him of powerful learning experiences.

Sean finds getting to school on time difficult. For months, his mother sets the alarm, which he ignores, and prepares his breakfast. And when he misses the bus, she dutifully drives him to school. She feels sorry for him. Two miles is such a long walk to school when he misses the bus. Then Mom gets smart. She decides to let him suffer the consequences of being late on his own. After a few days in detention for missing the late bell, Sean now views his morning differently. He sets his own alarm. He picks out his clothes and stacks his books by the door the night before to save precious sleep time in the morning. If he has to wake up earlier than usual for a special event, he's been known to sleep in his clothes. Being wrinkly the next day beats detention. He also makes his own breakfast. And best of all, he catches the bus that gets him to school on time — all without his mother's help. What a learning experience!

Troubleshooting When Kids Misbehave (And You're Tearing Your Hair Out)

Every so often, your little darling will try your patience. In fact, you can plan on it. But don't despair. As with most aspects of raising smarter kids, you have choices. The following sections can help.

Arranging for kids to do the right thing

Before you work on your child's behavior, consider structuring surroundings so your child doesn't get into trouble in the first place. You may be surprised at how many parents create picture-perfect homes and yards and expect even the youngest kids to adapt to the surroundings instead of the reverse. So kids live up to the challenge. They invariably break lamps, soil furniture, or take apart items that are either a temptation or simply in the way. That's not a smart way to raise brainy kids. In fact, it's downright restrictive.

Arranging where your kids spend time

Take a hard look at where your child spends most of the time: in the bedroom, playroom, living room, or backyard. Then consider your child's age, your child's interests, and what the next stage may bring. Put these tidbits of information together and decide to:

✔ **Put a few treasures away for when your child leaves for college,** so your rambunctious primary grader can build forts, while your middle schooler can hold talent shows and parties without breaking anything.

✔ **Designate a special place for science experiments, if science is your kid's thing.** Think about an area as secure as Los Alamos. Strip the area down. Remove carpets that can stain or even catch fire — just in case.

✔ **Rearrange furniture, so that your supertot doesn't fall on the corner of the glass table after a flight to save the world.** Open spaces without decorative pieces to get in the way promote play and reduce accident headaches for everyone.

✔ **Carve out enough space in the backyard so that your child isn't always struggling to avoid ornate flower beds and veggie gardens.** Leave room for running, throwing, or whatever creative play your child gets into.

You can't prevent every catastrophe. But you can create places where your child behaves better, and you yell less.

Arranging what kids have handy to play with

Besides enough space to spread out safely, think about whether your child has age-appropriate toys and enough toys and equipment to play with. I'm not talking about anything fancy here, nor am I sending you to the store. I'm merely suggesting that you provide a small assortment of items to imagine or create with: old clothes, blocks, books, and toys. An interesting mix of play things keeps kids out of mischief. More about choosing and using books and toys for varying ages in Chapters 6, 7, and 21.

A bored child finds something to do, and not always the "something" you intend. So head off problems before they happen by arranging an interesting, stimulating, and safe environment for your child's play.

Arranging for outings

For trips, outings, and long travel times, plan ahead. Bring snacks for your child to eat at restaurants, while you're waiting for the meal. Tote a bag of tricks, coloring supplies, miniature games and puzzles, and books to eliminate whining and fighting that can make everyone miserable. And make sure you talk about where you're going and how you expect your child to behave. Then you can lavishly praise his compliance as it occurs, and your child learns how to behave in a specific environment.

Turning misbehavior around with a planned approach

Letting consequences happen and creating an ideal play environment may not ward off misbehavior. Your child is only human, not some scripted robot.

The most effective strategy for turning around your little devil is to create a *plan* based on reinforcing good behavior and, thus, eliminating wrongdoing. Professionals have a variety of formal names for what's discussed in this section: *behavior modification, behavior management, applied behavior analysis,* and *behavioral intervention.* But each plan follows the same basic principles:

- Every behavior has an established consequence.
- Consequences are rewards (as discussed in this section) or punishments.

Your hair may stand on end at the mention of managing behavior with rewards. You may believe that all this reinforcing stuff is really another way of saying "bribery." I urge you to think again. You work for rewards. You earn grades in school. You receive pay for putting in your eight or more hours a day at a job. And you prefer to hang out with people who think well of you and say so. I'll even bet that a huge squeeze from your child or significant other perks up your day. These sound like rewards to me.

Reinforcement is part of life. Try to think of modifying behavior as another tool for leading your child down the smart road to doing what you think is right. By creating a behavior management plan to counter problems, you offer a nonthreatening, nonemotional, and organized way to deal with your little monster at a time when all you want to do is scream obscenities.

To develop a behavior modification plan, consider these general guidelines:

- **Clearly identify what drives you up a wall about your lovely child.** Is it the way he acts as if he's Hansel and Gretel, leaving crumb trails from his homework desk to the kitchen? Does your preschooler tap dance on table tops?

  Define only one or two trouble spots to work on at a time. That way, you increase the likelihood you'll remain committed and consistent. And your child has a greater chance to succeed without feeling confused or overwhelmed by too many messages to sort through at one time.

- **Jot down when and how often the dastardly deed occurs.** You conscientiously write it down because your memory can play tricks on you, especially if the deed really irks you. The intensity of your response may color your judgment, so you think your darling is purposefully repeating the crime more often than actually happens just to punish you.

  This brings out the real reason you write things down: You may discover a pattern that gives you great wisdom into why your kids acts so off the wall.

One mom I know saves her climbing toddler from falling off the dining room table, the table from scratches, and herself from headaches. How does she do it? She collects information about when he climbs and finds that her high-wire acrobat only hikes his little body onto the table when a chair is nearby. With some minor furniture rearranging and reminders that "We climb at the park," she saves the shiny surface and her son's head. Now he's on to other great feats that she hopes will be within her tolerance level.

- **Decide on a reward (*positive reinforcer*) that tickles your child's fancy.** You're in luck if your child does a behavior turnaround for hugs,

smiles, or a happy voice. But you may need to find something more tangible, at least at first. Your young child may like stickers or non-sugared cereal. Your older child may like coins or stickers or may go for tokens to collect or exchange at the end of the week for prizes, like baseball cards or release from unappealing chores. Be as creative as you want.

Ask your child for suggestions. The new crop of dollar-type stores makes concrete reward selection less expensive.

Always keep in the back of your mind that your ultimate goal is to phase out material goods in favor or more sociable rewards, such as your words of approval. With time and patience, your child behaves the way you want because it feels good.

✔ **Decide the timing for presenting rewards.** After you decide what your child needs to work on and how you plan to praise these glorious deeds, think about how often to present rewards. You can present your little rascal with a reward immediately after completing the task correctly, or every hour, or at bedtime. Timing depends upon your child's ability to connect the reward with doing the right thing.

The less your child understands, the more frequently you give rewards. In the beginning, reward each time your child performs the desired task. Gradually, lengthen the time between rewards as your child proves he can follow directions.

Offer liberal but targeted praise at the same time. For example, say "I like the way you cleaned up the crumbs after your snack" (or whatever your child is doing well). This tells your child which behavior deserves the reward, so he knows what to repeat again. You want to indicate what behavior is acceptable, so that your child doesn't replace one problematic deed with another. You also eventually want your kind words to be enough to motivate your child to the higher road of behavior.

✔ **Chart the number of times you catch your child doing the right thing.** A chart helps your child see how much he improves. Each day, he can follow his progress by counting his marks or stars.

With a chart, you have a visual evaluation of whether the plan is working. A chart is a simple table or calendar with boxes that show with words or pictures what your child is expected to do (see Table 3-1).

Don't be surprised if the number of unwanted behaviors increases at first. This is your child's way of learning and testing the rules to keep you on your toes. But stick with your plan and be consistent. After a couple of weeks, you start to see more checks, stickers, or whatever you choose to mark the calendar, each day.

As your child shows his competency, gradually reduce the number of times you give rewards. For example, instead of after every good deed, record good deeds at noon, dinner time, and bedtime. But keep the verbal praise up after every occurrence.

Table 3-1	Happy Homework Habits				
My Jobs	**Monday**	**Tuesday**	**Wednesday**	**Thursday**	**Friday**
Bring all books home					
Clean up after snack					
Begin homework without reminders					
Finish homework					
Read for 20 minutes					

You may ask at this point, "What do I do if the plan doesn't work after a couple weeks and my child continues to drive me crazy?" You have three choices:

✔ Change the reward to something more desirable to boost his motivation.

✔ Change to smaller time intervals between rewards, so that you can catch your child doing what you want.

✔ Reexamine whether you identified the correct behavior to work on.

Thinking like a behavioral therapist won't end all your parenting woes. But this sort of framework helps you find smart answers to your kid's creative challenges.

Behavior management does work. My young neighbor learned to use the potty, focus on homework better, and study for tests with the help of a couple positive and rewarding parents who followed a few charts.

Choosing your battles

One benefit of managing behavior is that it forces you to focus on what you really think is important. You take a hard look at what you really need to change in order to have a more peaceful home life and a smarter, well-balanced kid. All the inconsequential rubbish fades away when you choose your battles.

Show your displeasure about a specific behavior that upsets you or that you find unsafe. That's your right as a parent. But never attack your total kid. You can criticize the behavior, but not in a personal way that berates your child.

You hear a big difference between, "I don't like when you pull the cat's tail," and "You're so stupid for pulling the cat's tail." Your child hears the difference, too. Keep talking like the second example, and he starts to feel bad about himself. He feels you already don't like him, so why should he bother to please you. Eventually, he stops trying.

Another mode of operating that stops your kid dead is constant picking about everything he does. Think about how you would feel being judged at every turn. I'll bet you wouldn't show your best side. Same with your child. If nothing seems right to you, your child stops trying to do anything. Therefore, pick your battles.

Overlooking the negative

Ignoring is another technique for eliminating objectionable behavior. With ignoring, you take away the reward, which is your attention. It's much like your reaction to a friend who never returns your telephone calls or e-mails. You're willing to continue just so long before you stop trying to make contact.

Here's how *planned ignoring* works with problem behavior. You decide which behavior needs to go. Perhaps you want to end tantrums, interrupting conversations, or teasing. After you pick your battle, you consciously refrain from any eye contact, touching, or talking whenever your child engages in the behavior. Your child thinks, "Hey, I don't get any attention for this, so I better try a different approach."

Similar to behavior management programs, expect an escalation in the behavior to test your resolve. If you're consistent, though, eventually the behavior will stop.

Sometimes, you may find certain behavior very difficult to ignore. As long as your child is safe, find something to busy yourself. If that doesn't work, leave the room.

Timing a time-out

Some disruptive behaviors are impossible to ignore. If your child wigs out, you may need to hold him to calm him or keep him safe. Otherwise, you can try a timeout.

A *timeout,* a term you've probably heard about by now, is when you calmly remove your child from the setting and deposit him in safe place, such as in another room, his bedroom, or a chair in the corner, possibly called the *timeout chair* for lack of anything more creative. The good part about a time-out is that it gives your child a chance to calm down and gives you respite from whatever behavior is so bothersome to you.

Sometimes, kids refuse to stay where they're put. Mine did. So I chose to pick my battles and not worry about her lurking in the halls instead of where I put her in the bedroom. I merely ignored her for the allotted time or until I felt she could reenter the situation in an appropriate fashion.

You may have to hold a thrashing child for safety until he settles down. Be careful, though, that the holding doesn't become a reward. For an older kid who won't budge, leave him in timeout where he is. But take the offending material or anything your child likes with you.

You can set a timer to signal the end of a timeout. Or you can tell your child he can resume regular activity after he calms down. Never make a timeout like a jail sentence or incarcerate your child for undetermined amounts of time, no matter how tempting this may seem. Some experts suggest a minute in timeout for each year of life. But judge the seriousness of the situation and your child's remorse. The idea is for you and your child to regain composure enough to talk about what's happened and act appropriately.

Remember to tell your child why a timeout is necessary. Keep your message positive. Always recommend a behavior replacement, so that your child knows what you expect of him:

- ✔ "You can come back to play after you calm down and learn to keep saliva in your mouth."

- ✔ "You can come back when you're ready to finish the puzzle without throwing the pieces."

- ✔ "You can play with the hamster when you remember to hold her gently and not spin her by the tail."

For your child, being banished to the bedroom, den, or wherever may be the perfect reward. In fact, he may act up repeatedly just to get removed to this palace. Where else could he find a computer, VCR, television, or telephone, as some kids have? So evaluate ahead of time where to put your little cherub in case of trouble. Decide whether this place is somewhere he can think about what's happened and repent, or somewhere that can be misconstrued as a payoff for acting terrible?

Be assured that your child wants to behave. Realize, too, that you have a right to expect acceptable behavior. Help your child manage behavior, and you're really offering a fairer, more loving way to live.

Taking Advantage of Teachable Moments

Timing is everything — in comedy, baking cookies, and raising smart kids. Never try to impart wisdom when your offspring is tired, sick, racing out the door, or despondent over the latest breakup with a significant other. Nothing sinks in. It's like trying to hold a conversation in a noisy restaurant. No meaningful communication gets transmitted.

At times, though, the planets line up and the world is blissful. Your child is alert and awaiting your every word — or is plain bored and wants your attention. That's the time to strike with food for thought. The following sections share some tactics for making your parent-as-teacher sessions more productive.

Organize learning step by step

Your kids are more open to learning something new when, besides having fun and spending time with you, the activity is something they can understand. This is especially true for young children who want to perform a task that has many steps.

Running through steps to tie a bow and saying "Voilà! Now you know how to tie your shoes," only brings bewilderment. But if you divide bow-tying into simple and manageable steps, present each step in order, and work on one step at a time, you offer a plan your child can grasp.

Here's how this works:

1. **Pretend you're having show-and-tell, only you're the one in front of the class, and the class is made up only of your child.**

   Perform the first step for bow tying, for example holding up two laces already in a shoe.

2. **Tell your child to do what you do.**

   Use the same familiar wording to cue each step. This reduces confusion.

   Guide your child's hands, if he has difficulty responding. This hands-on direction is called a *prompt* in psychology talk.

3. **Before moving onto the next step, practice the first one until it comes naturally.**

4. **Present the next step in the bow-tying process, such as crossing the two laces.**

5. **Repeat Steps 1 through 4.**

6. **Put two bow-tying steps together, beginning with Step 1.**

7. **Continue with the next step until your child performs all steps to tie a bow.**

In much the same way, breaking schoolwork into bite-size, manageable pieces works for your older overwhelmed kid, too.

Another way to learn steps for something new is to use a backward approach, where success comes after the first step and is the final result. Here's an example:

1. **Place your child's pants almost on.**

2. **Tell him to pull the pants completely in place.** Your child gets the feeling of pulling up pants until they reach the right place.

3. **Proceed with positive reinforcement.**

   This reinforcement may include — but doesn't have to be limited to — verbally praising him for following directions and pulling up his pants.

4. **Pull your child's pants down a tad farther and repeat Steps 1 through 3.**

   Keep pulling the pants somewhat lower on your child's body and jumping up and down when your child pulls the pants to their rightful position. With patience and persistence, your child eventually takes pants that are completely off and puts them on independently.

Capitalizing on basic principles of learning

People in the know — including parents with brainy kids — have discovered assumptions about most learning situations, including those parents with brainy kids. Tuck these notions in the back of your mind. Put them to good use when you want to structure opportunities to enhance your child's learning.

✔ **Kids repeat what they find pleasurable and lose interest in what becomes unpleasant.** No surprises here. So if you want repeat performances, up the fun quotient and follow up with praise, hugs, toys, or other rewards.

   Kids naturally like to explore and experiment because it's fun and satisfying.

✔ **Kids learn more readily if information you present makes sense and goes together.** For example, your kids remember meaningful words more easily than scrambled syllables. They recall words in sentences better than jumbled words. And they remember table manners better at mealtime than during odd times of the day set aside just for practice.

✔ **Kids' brains link what you present in the same place and at the same time.** In other words, they master the information together. For example, your child understands the concept of bow-tying better if you not only say but also model each step to tie the bow.

✔ **Kids discover best through hands-on experiences.** Solving real problems by seeing, touching, testing, and smelling is much more rewarding than being on the receiving end of a lecture.

✔ **Kids learn what they practice.** Repetition increases the likelihood that an activity will reoccur. So practice with your child before oral reports, tests, and events at which you may worry about questionable behavior. *Role play* (act out in a pretend play) what to do until your child feels comfortable with the information and can follow through.

Chapter 4

Growing Smarter Minds from Healthier Bodies

You plan a perfect outing. And what happens? It turns into a disaster because your child is tired, hungry, or worse, sick. Any of these occurrences can bring out the monster in your child and keep all of you from having a good time.

Now think of the same child in school. How can you expect your child to get tiptop grades with a body that isn't working properly? This chapter reinforces the importance of a healthy body for a smarter mind and gives you suggestions about how to raise kids that come to school prepared to learn.

Keeping Your Kids Physically Healthy

Kids always pick up germs. If they're playing and investigating the way kids do, they can't help it! But repeated illness keeps kids from wanting to explore and learn, makes them lose school days, and causes inattention. You can do your part to prevent serious illnesses and learning problems before they occur and before they interfere with learning.

Scheduling regular checkups

and immunizations

Regular checkups keep kids healthy — and smart. Your child's doctor monitors general growth (height, weight, head size, and so on), evaluates emotional and physical health, and administers immunizations.

Usually, parents schedule the most visits in a child's lifetime during the child's early years. In fact, you may feel like you're living at the doctor's office, especially if you're a new parent. But take heart. The number of visits drop greatly as your child ages. See Table 4-1 for well-kid checkups that the American Academy of Pediatrics recommends.

Immunizations, inoculations, or shots are a fact of life for smart kids, and mostly a healthy one at that. Shots protect your youngster from diseases that interfere with learning big-time. Particles in the shot serums activate the body's normal network of antibodies to fight off any other intrusion of that particular bug. Today, many diseases, such as polio and measles, are rare thanks to immunization.

Prepare for your child to receive about 20 shots recommended by the American Academy of Pediatrics before entering kindergarten (see Table 4-1). Most occur within the first two years of life, which is good. Chances are slim to none that your chicklet will remember as an adult the torture you put her through.

Knowing whether your child is sick

Young kids often can't tell you why they lack enthusiasm for exploration. If they can talk at all, they can tell you only that they hurt or feel "yucky." Older kids don't want to miss out on what's going on at school or some after-school activity. Or they fane illness as a way to get out of something, such as a test they never studied for. So you have to play detective and look for these signs of physical distress:

- Ornery or weepy
- Prolonged sleeping during the day

- Change in skin color (pale green, gray, yellow, and pasty white are signs something isn't right)
- Rubbing a part of the body, such as stomach, head, or ears
- Favoring one side of the body over another, such as with feet or hands
- Bloodshot eyes, dilated pupils, runny eyes
- Fever above 101°F

To immunize or not: The great debate

Not everyone buys into the amount of immunizations a child should have. Of course, government and doctors, not to mention pharmaceutical companies, believe in them. That's why they legislate a slew of shots that your child must get before entering different levels of school.

But many scientists and parents question the wisdom of the more-is-better route. Some identify links between certain shots and conditions, such as autism, although the U.S. government claims no connection as yet.

Some kids react to certain serums. Combined serums, as with the DPT (diphtheria, pertussis, tetanus) shot, may cause a problem with one ingredient. You have a right and responsibility to question inoculations if your child has an adverse reaction from a shot.

If you find shots are detrimental to your child's health:

✔ Contact your doctor immediately about any reaction.

✔ Request that an offending serum be removed from a combined one. Doctors usually know which serum in the mix contributes to specific problems.

✔ Check with your local school district about whether you have an out with shots. Some districts have parents sign waivers before their child is admitted to school.

✔ Contact the National Vaccine Information Center at www.909shot.com or call 800-909-SHOT for the latest information about immunizations and alternatives.

Table 4-1	Checkup and Immunization Schedule	
Ages for Checkup	*Immunizations*	*Checkup*
Newborn		General evaluation on ten-point scale
2–4 weeks	Hepatitis B	General evaluation
2 months	Hepatitis B (1 to 4 months)	General evaluation
	DtaP (diphtheria, tetanus, lockjaw, pertussis)	
	Polio, pneumonia/meningitis	
	Hib (Influenza type b)	
4 months	DtaP	General evaluation
	Hib	
	Polio	
	Pneumonia	

(continued)

Table 4-1 *(continued)*

Ages for Checkup	Immunizations	Checkup
6 months	Hepatitis B (6 to 18 months)	General evaluation
	DtaP	
	Hib	
	Polio (6 to 18 months)	
	Pneumonia	
9 months		General evaluation
12 months	Hib (booster 12 to 15 months)	General evaluation
	Pneumonia (12 to 15 months)	
	MMR (measles, mumps, rubella; 12 to 15 months)	
	Varicella (chicken pox; 12 to 18 months)	
15 months	DtaP (15 to 18 months)	General evaluation
18 months		General evaluation
2 years	Hepatitis A (if recommended)	General evaluation
3 years		General evaluation
4 years	DtaP (4 to 6 years)	General evaluation
	Polio (4 to 6 years)	General evaluation
	MMR (4 to 6 years)	
5 years		General evaluation
6, 8, 10 years		General evaluation
11 to 21, yearly	Td (Tetanus and diphtheria only: 11 to 16 years; boosters every ten years thereafter)	General evaluation

You may question the amount of times your child acts as a pin cushion. But she won't be able to go to school to show her smarts without most inoculations. Most shots are safe or, at the very least, their benefits outweigh the small reactions some kids experience. See the "To immunize or not: The great debate" sidebar for further discussion.

Testing vision

A large portion of learning during your child's first 12 years comes through vision. That's why specialists believe visual preparation for school begins at birth.

Take your child for regular eye checkups to make sure she sees well. Kids often can't express why they can't see the blackboard or why they hold objects up to their noses to investigate them.

Your regular physician checks for muscle problems and infections. And your child's school should offer preschool evaluations upon registering. But whisk your child off to the eye doctor at any time if you notice the following:

- ✔ One eye turning in
- ✔ Crusted eyelids
- ✔ Your child holding playthings and books close to the face
- ✔ Unusually red eyes or eyelids
- ✔ Sores or sties on eyelids
- ✔ Excessively watery eyes
- ✔ Droopy eyelid
- ✔ Excessive blinking

Testing speech and hearing

Babies can't learn language and social cues without the ability to hear clearly. At minimum, hearing loss affects the ability to learn how to talk. Hearing screening for newborns should be standard at your maternity center. If not, have your infant screened for hearing loss by three months of age. Yes, it can really be done accurately.

If you find that your child is at risk for hearing loss, don't panic. Even if your child shows some hearing loss early on, she can shine with her peers by the time school starts, if the loss is picked up and corrected early.

After an initial hearing screening, check your baby's hearing every six months until age 3. After that, screen at the following times:

- ✔ When entering school
- ✔ Every year from kindergarten through third grade

Risk factors for hearing loss

You want to screen your child for hearing loss more frequently than recommended in this chapter if the following factors are involved:

- Speech/language delays

- Family history of childhood hearing loss

- Prenatal infections

- Postnatal infections, such as meningitis, that may affect hearing

- Degenerative conditions that affect the nervous system

- Head trauma

- Continuous ear infections or fluid in the ear

- In seventh grade

- In eleventh grade

- Any time your child shows learning problems that may indicate the need for special education classes or grade retention

Examining teeth and gums

Tooth decay, bloody gums, or discolored gums: These can be signs your child isn't getting enough of the right nutrients to boost brain power. Taking care of teeth seems obvious. But did you know that the American Dental Association recommends introducing your child to a dentist within six months after the first tooth appears?

The thinking is that your child gets used to the dentist and starts on the right track for cleaning and flossing. That way, she never has to face the drill or pain of tooth decay later on, which sounds great, doesn't it?

Feeding Brain Cells

Food furnishes the fuel that keeps kids healthy — and smart. By providing a variety of good foods, your child receives enough essential vitamins and minerals to be able to think, remember, reason, and have enough energy to stay awake in class.

Well-nourished kids come to class ready to learn. That's been the reasoning behind the school breakfast and lunch programs. Because hard-earned tax dollars go into feeding school kids, plenty of studies have followed their progress. Not surprisingly, research supports that kids who eat breakfast exhibit:

- ✔ Increased standardized test scores

- ✔ Reduced tardiness

- ✔ More class participation

- ✔ Improved attendance

The same goes for lunch. Even the slightest ongoing undernourishment is enough to affect development and school performance. The quality of your child's diet can make the difference in academic, behavioral, and emotional performance.

Choosing brain foods

You'd think choosing healthy brain food for your child is a no-brainer. But considering how often the U.S. government changes nutritional guidelines — not to mention regular news reports and supposedly ground-breaking studies touting wonder foods — finding healthier brain food can be confusing at best. So what's a caring parent to do?

Prepare a variety of foods for your family, so that all the healthy stuff is available. Be sure to give your child a balanced diet that includes grains, fruits and vegetables, dairy products, and some form of meat or meat substitute. Check out the food pyramid in Figure 4-1 as a starting point for getting your smart kid on the right diet track.

The following are some other recommendations that provide the right diet to keep brain cells firing:

- ✔ **Ask your doctor about DHA, or docosahexaenoic acid, for your baby.** This omega-3 fatty acid has been linked to early brain development and later academic performance. Because DHA is found in breast milk and not infant formula, consider breastfeeding. Even then, make sure you eat DHA-rich foods, such as salmon, herring, and tuna, so your milk has more punch per drop.

- ✔ **Offer a nutritious breakfast.** Even if your child hates to have breakfast, start her day off energized instead of droopy with at least small amounts of protein and grains.

- ✔ **Supply healthy lunches with nutritious desserts and snacks.** Check out the nutritional guidelines article at www.parentsplace.com for healthy lunchbox ideas.

- ✔ **Remember to include iron-rich foods.** Studies show that kids with iron deficiencies score lower than their iron-rich classmates on math tests and are more irritable, tired, and unable to concentrate. Good sources of iron are red meat, poultry, beans, and whole grains.

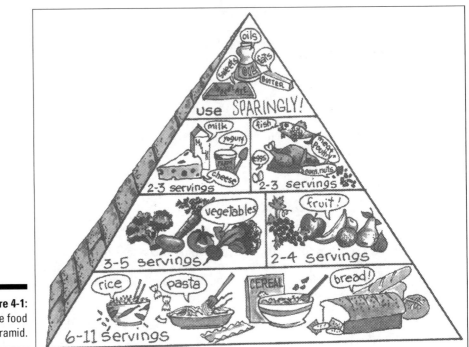

Figure 4-1:
The food
pyramid.

✔ **Include plenty of water in everyone's diet.** Usual recommendations of six to eight 8-ounce glasses a day keep the body, and especially the brain, well-lubricated.

✔ **Never buy pop.** Soda is mainly sugar water with a bunch of chemicals that rot your teeth and provide loads of empty calories. And then there's the inevitable crashing of your kid's brain after the sugar rush. This happens when sugar levels in the blood that feeds the brain become elevated from the surge of sugar and then drop suddenly, leaving the brain with fewer nutrients to function. If soda isn't around the house, your child won't get used to drinking it.

✔ **Limit sweets.** Sugary and junk foods, like fatty chips, provide empty calories that cause brain rushes and crashes and add too many calories that contribute to weight gain. Sweets once in a while aren't the worst thing in the world. But having large amounts of sweets and junk food around regularly is more temptation than anyone needs.

✔ **Limit trips to fast-food restaurants.** I know time is precious. But fast-food restaurants process the few vitamins and minerals the food originally has out of them. And they douse your food with too many unhealthy fats, salt, and sugars.

✔ **Read labels to omit unhealthy types of fats from the family diet.**
Certain kinds of fat cause health problems, such as high cholesterol and
arterial disease. If you have a choice, choose nonanimal-based monoun-
saturates and polyunsaturates over animal-based saturated fats. Also
avoid the trans-fats that are in hydrogenated vegetables oils. The way
the oil is processed changes its character, turning it into a cholesterol-
builder. One way to tell what's saturated fat and trans-fat is to discover
whether it hardens at room temperature, like butter (saturated fat) and
many types of peanut butter (hydrogenated oils). Also, read labels, which
list many types of fats and show hydrogenated oils in the ingredients list.

✔ **Turn off the tube.** Television projects disproportionate amounts of time
per show of hard-sell commercials for fast food and sugar-laden foods. If
your child watches TV, take some time to go over what commercials aim
to do and why, so she becomes a savvy consumer early on.

Heavy-duty commercialism invades most kid's magazines, too, so stay
vigilant. I mention pulling the TV plug and crash commercialism influ-
encing your kids in unwise ways many times throughout the book, but
see Chapter 12 for more about monitoring media.

Your job is to raise a child who knows how to make wise food choices that
keep her body in tip-top shape. These healthy eating habits your child masters at a young age contribute to a lifetime of success.

Handling fussy eaters

Mealtime is for pleasant conversation, not battles over which food expands
brain matter most. If you find yourself locking horns over food regularly, step
back and question whether something else is going on:

✔ Does your child not eat in order to gain your attention?

✔ Do you reward your child with food, which increases its value, not to
mention the chance of weight gain?

✔ Do you cater to your child's whining and prepare special foods on
demand, thereby relinquishing mealtime control and responsibility?

✔ Do you bribe your child with cookies for eating cauliflower, which
inflates the importance of dessert and possibly devalues more
nutritious foods?

If any of these apply to you, time to change behavior — yours. When your
child squawks about what's on her plate, matter-of-factly ignore the protests
and stay as positive as you can. Keep preparing the same meals as you do for
the rest of the family.

Tips to end food battles

Try some of the following ideas to help reduce fights about food:

✔ **Give your child a say in meals.** Let her help plan and prepare them. Go to the grocery store together, and let her choose the fruits and vegetables she likes. Play color and naming games to select the prettiest new foods to try. The more involved she is in creating the meal, the greater likelihood she'll happily eat it. Besides, feeding the family is a pretty important job, so joining the process should boost her ego.

✔ **Encourage a taste, or "no thank you," helping of new foods.** But don't worry if you get turned down. Kids normally broaden their food choices as they age.

✔ **Discover creative alternatives to foods that cause problems.** For example:

• Allow more fruits, if your child refuses vegetables. Many fruits have similar vitamins and minerals to vegetables, and your child may prefer their sweetness.

• Grind vegetables into baked goods, such as carrot or zucchini bread or casseroles.

• Mix new foods with old, such as substituting ground turkey breast or a soy substitute for beef in spaghetti. Introduce new foods that are similar to familiar ones, such as tangerines instead of oranges or parsnips and sweet potatoes instead of white potatoes.

• Offer separate foods to younger kids, rather than mixes. For some reason, kids through the primary grades prefer distinct tastes, which knocks out most casseroles. Mixing peas and corn into mashed potatoes comes later, when kids become more experimental with foods.

• Never, ever tell ingredients to your family before they eat something new. Even if they love your burgers, after they hear you mix ground soy or liver into them, they (including your spouse) may never trust your burgers again.

✔ **Cut foods into fun shapes or decorate them with colorful foods.** Hardware stores and kitchen shops sell thick versions of cookie cutters in different shapes. With these thicker cutters, you can pour pancake batter or mold whipped potatoes into them and decorate the results with raisins, herbs, chopped olives, or whatever suits your creative fancy. This is an old trick, but you may be surprised how well it works.

✔ **Display healthy snacks prominently.** Healthy snacks bolster vitamin and mineral intake for a smarter diet that your child may avoid at mealtime. If the healthy snack is front-and-center on a reachable shelf or toward the front in the refrigerator, I guarantee that's what your snacker will grab first.

✔ **Fill a bowl with washed fruit or cut veggies in bite-sized pieces.** That way, whenever your child gets the munchies and opens the refrigerator, she spots colorful bowls of enticing fruits and vegetables first.

✔ **Stock a healthy freezer.** Prepare homemade Dreamsicles with yogurt, vanilla, and orange juice and make juice Popsicles in ice-cube trays. They taste better than store-bought and take less time than schlepping to the store.

✔ **Leave out bags of nuts and raisins, seeds, and popcorn.** Let the first snack your child sees be a healthier choice. If they're lying around, your child probably won't investigate further.

> **✔ Offer an assortment of foods at mealtime.** This way, your child gets used to choosing from what's available.
>
> Consider what your child eats over the long haul, rather than concentrating on one meal or day. If she gobbles a bag of carrots after school but won't eat vegetables at dinner, consider the day a dietary success.

Try not to call attention to your child's lack of enthusiasm for the intellectually stimulating cuisine on her plate, which places undue importance on food.

If she won't eat, let her miss a meal or two. She won't starve. A hungry child is more likely to eat what you serve at the next meal. I don't mean to sound hard-hearted about this. I understand that kids, and adults, have food preferences. But over-the-top, generalized fussiness is another story. Check out the "Tips to end food battles" sidebar for more tips to end food wars.

Walk, Run, Hop: Making Fitness Part of Your Kids' Lives

Kids who exercise bring home better grades. Fitness promotes healthy physical and mental health and physical activity improves self-confidence and self-discipline (both of which are tools for getting ahead). In addition, without regular activity, your child may face a lifetime of weight problems, illness, and slower motor development.

Knowing why fitness builds brighter kids

Research supports the connection between physical activity and mental capabilities. Some long-range studies have been the basis of Title IX, the law that requires schools to give girls the same opportunities and budgets for programs as boys to participate in sports.

Research supports the following facts and figures:

✔ Aerobic activities, the kind that are vigorous enough to boost your heart rate, increase the amount of oxygen sent to the brain. No, your active child isn't an airhead after exercise, but she does have more neurons firing from the extra oxygen, which helps with thinking and memory.

Backpack tips

You may have thought a backpack is your child's friend. Nowadays, though, your child may be hauling up to 50 pounds in oversized textbooks and school supplies. The resulting poor posture and backaches can reduce your student's energy and performance. To alleviate muscle strain, find a backpack with wheels. If that's impossible, help your student do the following:

✔ Buy a backpack with wide, padded straps and a hip strap.

✔ Fasten straps so that the backpack sits two inches above the waist with the most weight closest to your child's body.

✔ Tie all the straps to keep the backpack tight against the child's center of gravity.

✔ Wear the backpack with both shoulder straps to distribute the weight more evenly.

✔ Pack books and supplies evenly in the backpack, also to distribute weight evenly.

✔ Try not to carry more than 10 to 15 percent of body weight. This may be the difficult to do, especially at test time. Nineteen pounds of books require someone who weighs 130 pounds to carry them without strain and a 200-pounder to carry a 30-pound backpack easily.

✔ Make more trips to the locker. That's one way to carry less. Another way is to buy another set of books (or use a set at the library) to provide a second set away from school, thus eliminating the need to carry books back and forth.

✔ Kids who receive 240 minutes per week in physical activity earn higher math scores.

✔ According to the Institute for Athletics and Education and the President's Council on Physical Fitness, active girls earn better grades than their less-active sisters.

In fact, physically active girls are three times more likely to graduate from high school than their couch-potato counterparts. These figures relate to boys, too.

✔ Eighty percent of women leaders in the top 500 U.S. companies have participated in sports, according to the Big Ten Conference.

Sports make kids feel better about themselves. Now there's an easy, low-cost investment in your child's future.

Getting physical education at school

Rush out to your child's school now and find out what kind of physical fitness your child receives, if any. Your school's program should expose kids to a fun mix of sports, dance, and exercise activities. Numbers differ about the optimum length of time per week, but figure at least 30 minute-periods, preferably daily, to allow enough time for kids to drag themselves into the gym and dawdle back to class.

Don't be surprised if physical activity is minimal at best, with school budgets being what they are. If that's the case, you need to decide whether you have the stamina and persistence to try and move school bureaucratic mountains to get programs reinstated. Should you remain undaunted by the task, try some of the following options:

✔ Talk with the principal about adding physical activities. Propose extending in-class physical time or sharing a physical education teacher with another school, if budgets don't allow hiring a full-time PE teacher.

✔ Work through your local parent-teacher organization to institute change. See whether pressure from a vocal and interested group makes a difference. Check whether your PTO raises funds that could go toward physical education.

✔ Contact the district superintendent. Make a case for the benefits of physical activity for kids. Even though school budgets are tight, perhaps a creative superintendent can come up with alternatives that benefit your child.

✔ Keep up with legislation. Some national politicians keep trying to roll back Title IX, which could give local schools ammunition for cutting girl's teams. Lobby your state congressperson to introduce and pass a bill requiring regular physical education in schools.

✔ Push for recess every day, so kids can at least run around and play: Games, playing tag, and chasing each other around a playground count as physical activity, too.

✔ Suggest after-school athletic programs, which work best with older students. Sometimes, money for extracurricular programs becomes available through other sources than an education budget.

Creating a fit, healthy environment at home

As the prime family role model and rule maker, show your child that you believe in physical activity and its contribution to living smart by doing the following:

✔ **Plan a family physical activity at least once a week.** Try walking through a forest, bicycling, skating, picking strawberries, or challenging another family to a baseball game.

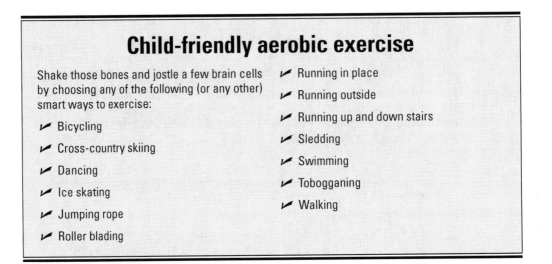

Child-friendly aerobic exercise

Shake those bones and jostle a few brain cells by choosing any of the following (or any other) smart ways to exercise:

- Bicycling
- Cross-country skiing
- Dancing
- Ice skating
- Jumping rope
- Roller blading
- Running in place
- Running outside
- Running up and down stairs
- Sledding
- Swimming
- Tobogganing
- Walking

- **Encourage your child to try different individual or team activities.** Help her find something she enjoys enough to stick with it.

- **Participate in regular activity yourself.** Show your kids how exercise can be a lifelong activity. Start your own physical fitness program. If you don't like exercise, try parking a little farther from the store so you have to walk, dancing around the house to your favorite song, or parking your shopping cart in one aisle while you run up and down the aisles to get individual foods. Every little bit helps.

- **Offer physical activity as a reward.** Set up a trip to the playground or a bicycle ride together as more positive than getting a cookie for a job well done.

- **Assign chores that involve physical activity,** such as raking leaves, mowing the lawn, gardening, and vacuuming the house.

- **Unplug the television, video games, and computer.** If your child must be a viewer, alternate these inactive forms of play with physical activity.

Ensuring That Kids Get Enough Zzzs

Want an easy way to boost grades? Make sure your child gets enough sleep. And I don't mean shut-eye slumped over a desk in school.

Research supports the strong connection between enough sleep and academic achievement. Improvements with more sleep have been so noticeable that Minneapolis Public Schools now juggle starting times to accommodate recommended sleep schedules: By opening school later in middle and high schools, the district reports increases in attendance, alertness, and overall academic achievement. All this without threats of whips, detention, or expensive tutors!

Being well rested translates into better grades.

Judging when enough is enough

Kids need different amounts of sleep to feel alert, depending on their ages. Mercifully, your newborn requires about 16.5 hours of sleep but unfortunately, it comes in spurts around the clock, so you always feel exhausted.

As babies mature, they gradually reduce the hours of sleep they need. By a year, their bodies require just under 14 hours with two shorter nap times. By two years, you wrestle your active toddler down for about 13 hours, which includes only one nap. (Sorry.)

Kids need slightly less sleep each year. During elementary grades, expect your sleepyhead to zone out for about 10 hours, compared with your grownup needs of 8¼ hours.

Teenagers should have at least 9¼ hours of sleep, but their bodies turn weird at puberty. Their body clock shifts, which creates havoc on them and the family schedule. Suddenly, their hormones tell them to stay up later and sleep later. Even when they turn out the lights at 10:00 to get their normal nine hours of sleep, they may lie staring at the ceiling. Adolescents aren't all lazy. Many are just sleep deprived.

Push for later starting times for junior high and high school students. Contact your school's PTO/PTA or the principal to get the idea rolling. If the school isn't interested, write letters to your local newspapers and other media outlets. At the very least, all the teens in the neighborhood will be your friend, but keep in mind that research does support your stance.

Looking for signs of sleep deprivation

You know your child — whether a preschooler or high-schooler — needs more sleep when she:

- Finds concentrating and remembering difficult
- Looks tired (puffy or red eyes, sallow skin color, disheveled) — at least more than normal

✔ Acts irritable (more than usual)

✔ Tends to make mistakes or seems clumsier

✔ Seems slower acting and less creative

✔ Loses interest in activities or social life

✔ Catches more colds or other bugs

✔ Falls asleep in class

If your child exhibits any of these signs, see the "Sleepytime tips for bedtime resistors" sidebar for assistance.

Sleepytime tips for bedtime resistors

Falling asleep isn't always easy to do. But helping your child get a good night's sleep is imperative to functioning well in school. As the one in charge, you provide the structure for your child's good sleep habits. If you absolutely find bedtime horrible, curl up with the book, *Solve Your Child's Sleep Problems* by Richard Ferber (Fireside, 1985). Otherwise, help your child feel rested by:

✔ Setting regular times to wake up and go to bed.

✔ Establishing a relaxing bedtime routine that allows for winding down. That means no TV, video games, computer games, or otherwise mentally stimulating activities right before bed.

✔ Turning out lights at bedtime. Lights prompt alertness. If your child fears the dark, stick a cute nightlight in a wall socket. If ghosts are the problem, do a complete room and closet search, including under the bed and blanket, and proclaim the room ghost-free before lights out.

✔ Avoiding big meals, caffeine (as in chocolate and tea), sugar, and exercise shortly before bedtime.

Part II
The Early Years: Birth to Kindergarten

The 5th Wave   By Rich Tennant

"Nurse! It's another baby with the Mozart Effect."

In this part . . .

*B*abies are like gifts: You never know what surprises come inside. Usually, your bundle of joy catapults onto the scene with a pretty complex bag of tricks. So don't expect a smooth ride raising smart little ones.

Yet, even though you have your work cut out for you, rewards lie ahead. Smart babies lead to smart kids who lead to capable, independent adults. Therefore, you're never too early starting to work toward that goal.

In this part, you find pregnancy tips for expanding brain cells. You also get plenty of techniques for enhancing those lively infant and toddler years. Finally, you find one chapter each on behavior/discipline and resources for you to contact (when you need a time out for yourself).

Chapter 5

Before Your Baby Is Born

In This Chapter

▶ Enriching the prebirth environment

▶ Making smart choices that influence your fetus

▶ Playing music for what's inside your tummy

▶ Reading to your fetus

*P*regnancy can be a wonderful time in your life, and this chapter helps you have the healthiest, safest pregnancy possible, so that you do what's best for your smart baby.

During those nine months, you're likely to come across people who want to cash in on your new role as a parent to sell you something, especially some new gizmo that makes your baby "smarter" while in the womb. These shysters develop high tech, expensive products that commercialize what should be a fun and enjoyable experience.

Don't get me wrong. The added information is welcome. What I find overwhelming are the numbers of products designed to help you give birth to a super baby before the newborn sees the light of day. This chapter sorts through the hype of enriching unborn baby brain cells.

Enjoying a Positive Pregnancy

No matter how many products companies try to sell you during pregnancy, your child won't be as healthy as possible unless you take care of yourself. Your health and well-being play a tremendous role in growing a healthy, successful infant.

Conversely, not taking care of yourself, such as by taking drugs, drinking alcoholic beverages, smoking, and not eating right, contributes to producing a not-so-smart kid, resulting in a baby that

✔ Has a smaller head and, therefore, less brain power

✔ Is addicted, which messes up about every system in his little body

✔ Has neurological problems, which result in sensory disturbances that interfere with learning

✔ Exhibits learning disabilities down the road

I don't mean for you to obsess about every morsel you eat or every stressful situation you encounter. But try to follow these and your doctor's general guidelines as best you can. It's critically important right now.

Choosing wisely for your baby

Much of the following pregnancy information is probably no surprise. But this section's words of caution are so important to a successful pregnancy, and ultimately a smarter baby, that I include them anyway. Feel free to skip to the next section if I'm preaching to the converted and otherwise knowledgeable.

Tossing the alcoholic beverages

Whatever you do, don't drink alcohol if you want a smart kid. Alcohol consumption is known to retard brain development.

Chemicals in alcohol destroy the developing nervous system, which causes a host of other learning and maturational problems. So many problems come from Mom's drinking too much alcohol that docs gave the bundle of symptoms a name, *fetal alcohol syndrome.*

Recent studies point to as little as two or more alcoholic drinks at one time as a measurable problem. This amount is shown to decrease the amount of oxygen in your blood, which in turn reduces the amount of oxygen flow to the placenta, the sack that holds and nourishes your baby. In fact, because you and your unborn share the same container for nine months, when you're drunk, so is your fetus. This isn't a smart way to go through a pregnancy.

If you're used to consuming mass quantities of alcoholic beverages for whatever reason, especially without food to absorb them, throw the bottles away right now to reduce temptation. If you have withdrawal problems or can't

stop, get to a doctor or rehab clinic immediately. Your baby's smarts depend on it.

Quitting smoking

U.S. government requires makers of alcoholic beverages and cigarettes to print warning labels for pregnant women on their products for a good reason. They both harm fetal brain cells.

Several chemicals in cigarettes influence how the unborn baby develops. Nicotine shrinks blood vessels and decreases blood supply to the fetus, which does terrible things to developing baby cells, especially the nervous system. Smoking also increases the risk of low birth weight, which may mean a reduced head and brain size, along with other birth problems. Cigarettes may be a tad less damaging than alcohol, but they act on other organs, such as the lungs and heart, that contribute to illness after birth. So why take a chance with your child's health when you can prevent possible retardation and illnesses altogether?

The greatest risk for damage from smoking comes during the third trimester. Quitting smoking for even a couple months lessens the harm done. Of course, the best is to quit altogether. But nicotine is highly addictive. You may need help to stop smoking, so don't be afraid to ask your doctor for recommendations.

Don't forget about dads, too. Before conception, smoking dads may be damaging their sperm. Even second-hand smoke is known to negatively affect intelligence. Make sure everyone in your household stops smoking when you plan to get pregnant and after you become pregnant and have your baby. This is the smart thing to do for your baby's smarts.

Passing on drugs

All drugs, and that includes over-the-counter and herbal remedies, alter the environment in the womb. Some cross into the placenta, wreaking havoc on fetuses. Much is still unknown about exactly what specific drugs and herbs do to the unborn. Most studies focus on illegal stuff, such as cocaine, heroin, and marijuana, which you know is a no-no for myriad reasons, mainly for causing premature birth and tons of problems with learning and growing. As for any other meds, your best bet is not to take any, if you can help it.

Does this mean you can't expect relief if you get really ill? Not really. It means you need to have a heart-to-heart talk with your physician about the costs and benefits of each substance you put into your body just before and during your pregnancy. Check out Table 5-1 for a more complete list of stumbling blocks to watch out for during pregnancy.

Table 5-1	Top Ten Biggies to Avoid for a Smart Pregnancy	
Problem Substance	*Known Problems*	*Limit Exposure by . . .*
Alcohol	Retards brain development; can cause deformities	Abstaining from drinking alcoholic beverages
Smoking	Causes slow learning; retards birth weighting	Stopping smoking; avoid second-hand smoke
Drugs	Varies with drug	Avoiding illegal drugs (consult a healthcare provider first)
Solvents, hydrocarbons, oil-based paints	Increased risk of miscarriage; malformations	Ventilating rooms; avoiding exposure
PCBs (polychlorinated biphenyls)	Growth and mental retardation	Limiting freshwater fish intake
Pesticides	Varies with substance	Avoiding exposure; never applying
Caffeine	Lowers fertility at high doses; increases miscarriage	Ingesting no more than 300 mg/day
Excessive heat	Neural tube defects	Avoiding saunas and hot tubs; contacting physician if you have a fever
Severe stress	Causes birth problems; physical/mental problems	Exercising regularly; meditating; building social supports
Housework	Taxes the mind/body	Having your partner take on more!

Reducing stress

Reducing stress is one of the more ridiculous recommendations, I know. But focus on avoiding extreme stress. Not your usual demanding-but-rewarding job or raising your other kids. I mean the stress of an abusive situation, an overbooked schedule, loud noise of rock concerts, the over-the-top stuff.

Stress reduces blood flow to the placenta, which in turn reduces brain cells and the ability for those pre-baby brain neurons to fire. So now is the perfect time to reconnect with light exercise, meditation, or other activities that have reduced your stress in the past.

Don't forget to schedule regular prenatal checkups throughout your pregnancy. That way, you get started on much-needed vitamins, and you receive one of those neat ultrasound photos where your fetus looks like a feathery blob. Nothing like seeing your fetus's heart beating to jolt you into working on your kid's smarts before birth and taking better care of yourself.

Eating for two

Be forewarned: Unhealthy mothers have babies who are less intelligent. And one of the ways to stay healthy is to eat healthy foods. Why? Because pre-birth babies get their nourishment from you, the almost mom.

Don't get me wrong. I'm not advocating eating the house to cover all your nutrition bases. I'm talking about eating enough healthy foods to get your vitamin, mineral, and energy requirements. If you don't, chances are, your infant will come out malnourished, which may mean a less-developed brain. This is definitely *not* a smart way to go through a pregnancy.

Don't take pregnancy as a time to diet. You'll lose plenty of weight chasing your toddler around later. For now, concentrate on feeding your placenta a well-balanced diet that includes a range of foods and enough essential vitamins and minerals to keep you both in tip-top shape.

Eating well

Your child's brain experiences its greatest growth during the second half of pregnancy and through the first two years after birth. Although every stage is important, these are the most crucial times for good nervous system nutrition. So those early months when you may have morning sickness are the least important for brain growth.

After morning sickness disappears, however, you eat for two. Doctors recommend that you add an additional 300 calories beyond your nonpregnant diet to nourish you and your developing fetus. You may need extra calories later in the pregnancy.

Choose foods from the food pyramid (see Chapter 4). Drink at least eight glasses of fluids per day; drink more as your body fluids increase with the pregnancy. Get most of your fluids from water and limit caffeine from coffee, tea, cocoa, or colas.

As with any diet, make healthier choices for a smarter fetus by:

✔ Eating complex carbohydrates, such as whole grains, fruits, and vegetables. They are loaded with vitamins and minerals to stimulate healthy fetal growth, and the fiber in these foods keeps your system working better as your abdomen gets a bit cramped.

- ✔ Limiting fats and sweets, such as asking for baked and broiled foods instead of fried.

- ✔ Choosing four servings a day of lower-fat proteins, such as lean meats, low-fat dairy products, beans, and other legumes.

Getting enough vitamins and minerals

Fetus brain food requires enough iodine, iron, folic acid, and vitamin B12. Without these nutrients, brain development and thought processes can be compromised. So beyond a well-balanced diet, your ballooning body needs plenty of these vitamins and minerals:

- ✔ **Calcium:** Taking 1200 mg of calcium (400 mg more than for nonpreggies) builds strong muscles and bones. Choose at least four calcium-rich servings a day from milk, cheese, yogurt, orange juice, nuts, green leafy vegetables, or tofu soybean curd.

- ✔ **Iron:** Plenty of iron (60 to 120 mg) helps expand your blood supply and the blood going to your fetus. You can find iron in red meats, dried fruits, dark green and yellow vegetables, egg yolks, iron-fortified cereals and grains, and wheat germ.

- ✔ **Vitamin C:** Vitamin C increases iron absorption, so drink at least two servings of orange juice with your iron intake. Other vitamin C–rich foods are grapefruit, mangos, papaya, cantaloupes, spinach, broccoli, tomatoes, berries, and kale.

- ✔ **Folic acid:** Folic acid (400 mg) prevents neural tube defects, which can cause brain damage among other problems. Since 1998, the U.S. government has required companies to add folic acid to enriched grains, but you need at least 0.4 milligrams every day, which is more than you get in processed foods.

  Start taking multiple vitamins with folic acid before you expect to get pregnant to ensure your folic acid intake. In addition, good folic acid food sources are avocados, navel oranges, asparagus, and black beans, but they alone aren't enough to fulfill your pregnancy requirements for a neurologically healthy child.

- ✔ **Vitamin E:** Vitamin E acts as an antioxidant, protecting your developing fetus against tissue damage, which includes the brain and nervous system. Vitamin E-rich foods are wheat germ, green leafy vegetables, soybean oils, egg yolks, nuts, and whole grains.

- ✔ **Choline, which is a B-complex vitamin:** Choline is important for growing neuron connections in the brain. Add foods rich in choline when you're about 18 weeks pregnant. Natural sources are egg yolks, liver and other organ meats, yeast, soybeans, peanuts, beans, peas, wheat germ, and seaweed.

Eleven steps to a smarter pregnancy

This sidebar isn't rocket science. But these pearls of wisdom sum up solid tips for enriching your child's brain power during pregnancy, in the absence of morning sickness, swollen feet, and an outie belly button, of course.

✔ Eat well.

✔ Schedule regular checkups.

✔ Get enough rest.

✔ Take your vitamins.

✔ Reduce stress by keeping active and paying attention to your emotional health.

✔ Exercise regularly but moderately.

✔ Avoid alcohol.

✔ Stop smoking.

✔ Stay away from chemicals, both ingested and smelled.

✔ Look in the mirror every day and say, "I am beautiful," even with a daily-expanding abdomen.

✔ Enjoy the pregnancy journey.

Revving Up Baby in the Womb

Until the 1980s, everyone figured that baby's life in the womb consisted of wallowing in a confusing watery bubble machine and that brain cells didn't begin firing until months after birth. Then studies of newborns rolled in, telling how smart infants really are. They see objects after all, albeit a bit like a drunken sailor. They even recognize Mom's voice after birth.

New questions emerge from these findings. What do infants really know at birth? When and where do they acquire these sensations? If they learn before birth, can outsiders teach them in the sack? Is teaching early on really better?

Kicking to the beat

Ever since news that babies learn in the womb catapulted onto the scene, get-rich-quick artists have capitalized on the idea of tuning up baby's hearing skills in the womb. For a couple hundred dollars, you can strap a belt with two speakers and a bunch of tapes around your belly so that your fetus can listen to special beat patterns that trigger movements. You can buy other expensive tapes with music based on a tempo of 60 beats per minute, which some scientists consider a resting baby's heart rate. One package claims that these heartbeat rhythms produce babies who talk at 6 months and read by age 2.

Prebirth sense development

Fetal senses are usually limited at best. But they do start developing inside the womb. Here is the order they mature:

☑ Touch   About 5 to 8 weeks

☑ Taste   8 weeks first taste buds form

☑ Hearing   6 to 9 months

☑ Sight   6 to 7 months sight begins to develop

No one asks the fetus whether this or any other expensive gizmo is a pleasant experience. Some even speculate that your baby kicks to the beat to get away from the sound. Others worry that continuous exposure to sound waves alters the baby's natural sleep and awake patterns, which could be harmful, long-term.

Although I question much of this theory, your fetus does begin hearing at about the end of the second trimester or the beginning of the third. Some babies have indicated in their babylike way that they recognize Mozart and Debussy, postbirth. Baroque music has the same 60 beat per minute pattern that gets all the hype. Hence the term, *Mozart Effect* and the rather new emphasis on playing classical music to unborns.

Studies with school kids and adults, however, indicate that listening to classical music does the following:

☑ Calms kids, lowering blood pressure and reducing muscle tension just as well as 10 mg of Valium, the sedative, does. Baroque music has also been known to decrease breathing and heart rates.

☑ Speeds learning and improves concentration, unless you're like me and can't work with music in the background.

☑ Improves coordination and productivity. Ever take an exercise class that doesn't play music? Silence can sound too much like work.

☑ Increases high-level pathways in the brain, such as those used for math and chess.

☑ Boosts the amount of *endomorphs*, the chemical in the brain that lifts your spirits, lessens pain, and promotes a natural high.

☑ Improves concentration and memory.

But the jury is still out about whether tampering with nature produces life-long music lovers or toddler readers. Some studies show that although baby may recognize music right after birth, within a month, he forgets. So all your work may be for naught — except for strengthening your bond with this wonderful little creature growing inside you.

Chances are if you're that interested in enriching unborn fetal cells, you're motivated to be a nurturing parent anyway. And your baby is exercising muscles and hearing sounds with or without your spending lots of dollars on formal programs. Singing, playing beautiful music, and talking to your unborn baby never hurts. These activities give you and your family a head start in the bonding process. So focus on loving your child, unborn and born, rather than always trying to teach something. Save your hard-earned money, relax, and enjoy whatever kind of music you like. If you want a music lover, or any other kind of lover, expose your child to these experiences when he is ready to appreciate them.

Reading to your belly button

If you want to read to your fetus, fine. No harm is done, and you may get another leg-up on the parent-baby bonding relationship. But don't expect your toddler to read or your older child to love books solely because you read to your belly button.

Fetuses gain an awareness of voices and certain stories, if they hear them repeatedly. One study involves one of my favorite children's books, *The Cat in the Hat.* Moms read this story to their unborn child twice a day for about six weeks. After birth, researchers test the newborns by allowing them to suck on nipples attached to recorders that play either *The Cat in the Hat* or *The King, the Mice, and the Cheese.* All of the read-to babies prefer sucking on a machine that lets them hear *The Cat in the Hat.*

Now you may consider *The Cat in the Hat* a superior story, which accounts for the newborn choices. But researchers take these findings to mean that what fetuses hear in the womb influences their preferences after birth. Some believe learning takes place in the womb. Yet the problem is the same as with music (see the "Kicking to the beat" section) — learning, in this case remembering the stories, doesn't stick for long unless you keep up the experiences after birth.

Some fetal-stimulation gurus suggest not reading scary or sad stories to pre-borns. The thinking is they get enough spooky stuff after they're born.

Babies are natural learners. They exercise their muscles inside the womb and use their senses within the limited confines of the placenta. After the fetus is outside the womb, you can expect that inborn desire to learn to continue without all the repetition, scheduling, and concentrated effort of early embryo stimulation. So spend your time, energy, and money on the best insurance for a successful child — letting the unborn and later-born know how loved and capable he is.

Chapter 6

Energizing Your Baby through the Senses

* *

In This Chapter

▶ Stimulating newborn senses as a beginning down the smart road

▶ Awakening your baby's love of learning

▶ Choosing smart baby toys and books

* *

*B*abytime is a great time. You get to act goofy and blame it on your desire to stimulate and entertain your child. You sing, dance around, and talk in tongues — all in the name of smart parenthood. And the best part is that your infant doesn't cover her ears or complain about your act, unless you count occasional wailing, spitting up, and pooping as forms of protest.

At some point, though, your baby needs more than a vaudeville act to enrich her little life. Babies require stimulation for their brains to develop and for them to become well-rounded kids. In other words, your child's surroundings — along with a good set of genes provided by you and your partner — influence how intelligent and well-adjusted your child grows to be. This chapter shares some experience-enhancing ideas to launch your baby in a smart direction.

Becoming a Brain Architect

The way you bring up your infant actually frames how the brain grows. One-hundred billion brain cells called *neurons* lurk inside your newborn's noodle. These miniscule cells like to move and connect with each other. The bridges they form create wiring that enables your darling to process information and experience the world through the senses. More connections mean a smarter kid.

So what causes neurons to get together? Baby stimulation. The sounds, colors, smells, and touches you provide trigger new and improved circuitry inside your baby's brain. But you don't have to drop the rest of your life and devote yourself to consciously stimulating your newborn. Instead, you do this stimulation naturally.

Every time you wiggle her fingers, rock her to sleep with a lullaby, sprinkle water on her tummy during bath time, and act silly, you stimulate more brain cells to form vibrant new pathways. And when you decorate her surroundings and supply different ways to play, you cause actions and reactions that prompt additional brain bridges. Therefore, with everything you do, you're a natural-born baby brain architect.

Before you launch into improving your baby's chances at Harvard, a word of caution. Kids demonstrate different learning styles, even as infants. One baby may perk up or stare or flail all body parts at anything in her path. Another holds back, looks quickly, and then turns away.

As the two individuals mature, hyper Harry explores the world with unsuppressed exuberance. Meanwhile, careful Carolyn cautiously approaches each new situation. And their playmates mix the two strategies in a thousand different ways to interact with their surroundings. None of these styles exudes superiority over the other: Just concentrate on how your child responds best.

Your baby has an individual approach to life that needs respecting from day one. If you can truly understand her unique personality, you're better able to give your child the support and freedom to be her own person. Cherish your baby's uniqueness, and she won't disappoint you.

Most kids follow the same basic developmental path. But some take their time, while others whiz through each stage or speed along and plateau at different rest stops. And then many kids exhibit uneven mental and physical progress. The schedule your child is on provides another sign of your infant's uniqueness.

Table 6-1 gives you some general milestones you can expect from your infant, the child from 0 to 12 months old. These are just guidelines, not hard-and-fast rules of developmental conduct.

Table 6-1	A Baby's First Year		
	Newborn	*3–6 months*	*9–12 months*
Language	Follows sounds, cries when uncomfortable, startles at loud sounds	Differentiates cries, imitates sounds and syllables, laughs aloud, babbles, shakes head "no"	Understands words, says first words, waves "bye-bye"

	Newborn	*3–6 months*	*9–12 months*
Senses and motor	Tracks moving objects, hears well, lifts head, flails all body parts, sees best at 10 inches, sucks, yawns	Grasps and holds, sits independently, rolls from stomach to back, explores with mouth, holds rattle	Uses spoon, feeds with fingers, crawls, takes first steps, bangs objects, makes objects disappear
Social and mental	Smiles, quiets down with comforting, recognizes sight and smell of parents	Says "no" without understanding, reaches toward caregiver, shows interest in surroundings, recognizes toys or bottle	Begins to understand routines, connects with parents, cries when parents leave, sometimes stops at "no"

Including Random Acts of Play (An Infant's Daily Work Routine)

Whether your child reaches her potential depends on how much intellectual and sensory stimulation she receives during the first five years of life. So let your baby play, play, play from day one — at least when she's awake.

Sensing life

Because young babies can't move anywhere, you have to bring the world to them. Your role during the first few months is to provide items to play with (besides yourself, of course). These objects titillate the senses of touch, sight, hearing, and smell.

Choosing toys that foster learning

This quest for perfect toys, more specifically learning toys, is way overblown. Don't believe hype about "jumpstarting" your child's learning at two weeks or advertisements that scream, "Genius in the making." Sure, expensive, pretty toys brighten your baby's room, but you don't have to buy those sorts of toys. Your baby doesn't care how much you spend, at least not now. She's just as happy with a ball of aluminum foil on a string as she is with a fancy, expensive mobile, and her enthusiasm for simple fun stuff lasts for years. The quest for name-brand, I-want-what-my-friend-has stuff comes soon enough. (I believe in low-key, low-cost child accouterments so much that I expand the topic further in Chapter 7.)

Playing baby brain games

You want some inexpensive, and worthwhile, games to play with your infant? Can't get much simpler than the following:

- ✔ **Play music, any kind that suits you, and make sounds for your baby to track.** Clap your hands, snap your fingers, and utter unusual sound effects in different positions around your infant's head, while she lays on her back or stomach.

- ✔ **Hold a bright-colored ball or toy in front of your baby to track the object as you move it.** By about eight to ten weeks, encourage your bundle of joy to reach for the object.

- ✔ **Hang a safety mirror over the crib so she can see herself.** As she gets older, make sure a tall mirror is fastened to a door to give her a good look at how she plays.

- ✔ **Draw line art of a face on cardboard and tuck it into your baby's infant seat or the side of the crib.** Babies respond to simple patterns. They get most excited by faces. As my daughter got older she kept herself busy babbling and cooing to this no-talent-needed happy face on a piece of rectangular cardboard tucked in her car seat.

- ✔ **Offer familiar but safe household objects to babies 3 to 6 months and up who love to explore with their hands.** Nothing fancy here. Think about plastic and metal bowls and bottles, measuring cups and spoons, which are favorites, along with keys, clothes pins (relics of the past), and swatches of bright nonfuzzy cloth that won't come off in her mouth. Consider, too, frozen teething rings to gnaw on while in the throws of painful teething, wooden spoons to bang, empty cardboard boxes for your crawler, and paper bags to shake objects in and out. And keep in mind that for the first year or two, gift wrap is much more exciting as a toy than the gifts inside.

- ✔ **Cut the toes off brightly-colored baby socks and put one on each hand.** Your baby will have hours of fun wiggling her fingers and focusing on her colored hand.

Positioning infants

You can't see much lying on your back, and your baby isn't ready to sit up, even with support, until between 4 and 6 months. So you need to provide different points of view, as follows:

✔ **Lean your infant in your lap while you sit.**

✔ **Swing her in an automated swing.** Besides providing a different height perspective, a swing calms babies long enough for you to finish dinner or an important conversation. Some swings come with battery-operated music boxes, a definite improvement over the crank type that needs rewinding every few minutes and jolts your snoozing babe awake.

If your infant is too floppy, prop her sides with rolled towels or diapers.

✔ **Lay your baby on her stomach a couple times a day.** This encourages her to lift her head and get the idea of crawling some day.

✔ **Carry your baby in a sack close to your body.** Besides your being able to talk to your child easily without snoops listening in, infants thrive on physical contact and being close to the heartbeat that sustained them for nine months in utero. For a different perspective, turn baby around, so that she can watch the world as you move along.

You can buy two different types of front pouches, as pictured in Figure 6-1. Both allow your hands to be free to do other things. A sling works best for newborns who sleep a lot. Front packs provide more support, so your baby can look around.

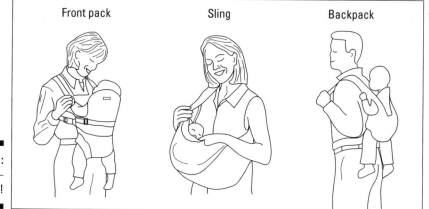

| Front pack | Sling | Backpack |

Figure 6-1:
Look ma —
no hands!

Babies get heavy after a few months in either front carrier, so you won't use yours for long. Try to borrow a baby pouch or buy one at a resale store to use until your baby grows too heavy for you to carry kangaroo style. Because most front carriers are washable, using someone else's shouldn't be a germ problem.

✔ **Plop your baby in a backpack after her head stops bobbing.**
Backpacks elevate baby, giving her the same birds-eye view that you see, and they distribute weight better, which lessens your chances of back-aches and reduces your trips to the chiropractor. Some are limp, as in

Figure 6-1, while others have a metal frame to support heavier babes. With either version, you may want to tie lose tendrils back. Babies grab and pull anything in their reach — it's part of the learning process.

Unless you want your hair conditioned with soggy slobber or sticky crumbs, refrain from giving your baby nibbles while being carried in a backpack. These snacks can also cause choking, so steer clear.

✔ **Strap your baby into an infant seat.** New versions adjust for sitting and reclining or they bounce, which you can activate with your foot while busying yourself with other occupations.

You can take the seat from room to room with you as you go about your daily activities. Infant car seats double as infant carriers, but they are sometimes heavier. Here, too, prop floppy babies with rolled diapers or towels.

My daughter, who wailed when out of my sight, enjoyed life in a car seat from the bathroom floor while I showered. I could talk with her and pop my head out occasionally, and eventually, my voice was enough to sooth her savage beasts. We also cooked together with her car seat in the kitchen, and she helped me write while I was at the dining-room table.

Exercising your baby

Sometimes, even with the best intentions, knowing what to do all day with a newborn is difficult. But you don't need to sign up for baby classes to have fun with your kid. Use your organizational skills to come up with a schedule that incorporates everything you believe stimulates your baby's body and mind. In other words, exercise your baby!

Exercise activities make your baby's body more flexible. And the time together builds on the bond you already have.

Lots of books give precise instructions for manipulating your baby's body parts. But you don't need to get fancy. Just lay your baby on her back, look into her eyes, and try these ideas:

✔ **Massage:** Rub a vitamin E oil, baby oil, or other cold-pressed oil over one body part at a time. Gentle massage awakens nerve endings and the senses. Use different textured materials, such as terrycloth or velour, to evoke different sensations.

Talk about what you're doing with your infant. Try some music — it doesn't have to be Mozart to get a smooth rhythm going — so your baby begins to connect the pleasurable sounds and touch.

Massage now can pay off later. Down the road, during times of stress, you'll be pleasantly surprised that you can calm your baby by gently rubbing a hand, a leg, her back, or her stomach. The calming memory lingers throughout the body.

✔ **Movement:** On days when enthusiasm and energy lag, you'll benefit from having an exercise routine with your baby to fill small blocks of time. You don't need to be a rocket scientist to think of your own routine.

- Take one body part (such as the right arm) at a time and gently stretch it, move it up, move it down, cross it over to the other side of the body, and place it back down. Go to the left arm, and do the same thing. Then move on to other body parts.

- Turn your baby over and gently try similar exercises. Play music and keep time by moving your baby to the beat.

- Place your baby face down over a large ball. Rock her up and back. As she matures, her arms will go out to protect her head. This game gives your baby a sense of her body in space.

- Push your baby in a swing, after she can sit without flopping.

- Hold and carry your baby around town. Nothing stimulates better during the first three months of life than snuggling with a parent as the world flies by.

Decorating Your Baby's Room

Ideally, a baby's space is more than a pretty place to sleep. The room is a total environment where your child can play, grow, and learn. It's also a place to go when the outside world closes in, when parents become unreasonable, or when your little someone needs a calming or stimulating place. (Of course, that's more for teenagers, so I'm getting ahead of myself.)

I personally view a baby's room — or nook, if you don't have space — as a way to keep your baby happy when you can't be there. The room can allow for visual and tactile exploration as your baby begins to move about. Everything for your baby is handy and organized for use on demand.

Some educators recommend keeping the room exactly the same for at least the first year. This gives your child the opportunity to feel safe while discovering new wonders at each new developmental stage. These same folks suggest that you crawl around the room to get an idea what your baby sees, hears, and feels.

More than anything, your baby's room should be a safe haven without sharp objects that can cut or tiny toy parts that can be swallowed. Check www.cpsc.gov/cpscpub/pubs/grand/12steps/12steps.html or call the U.S. Consumer Product Safety Commission at 1-800-638-2772 for a free pamphlet called *Childproofing Your Home*. You can also check out www.theparent club.com for safety tips.

Your choice of decorations, from furniture to toys to wall hangings, says a lot about what you expect for your child. Here are some suggestions to help you and nature walk your baby along the developmental road.

Touchy-feely baby rhymes

Nursery rhymes go great with body movements. They help teach language and rhythm and enhance your baby's ability to acquire and use language. And they keep you on track with the movements. Besides, they're silly and fun. You were probably raised on these rhymes, so they're likely familiar to you. Just add tummy strokes, arm raises, and tickles to start touching and exercising your baby.

Rhyme for toes and up:

> This little pig went to market,
> This little pig stayed at home,
> This little pig had roast beef,
> This little pig had none,
> And this little pig cried wee-wee-wee-wee-wee,
> All the way home.

Head-moving rhyme:

> Here's Sulky Sue,
> What shall we do?
> Turn her face to the wall
> Till she comes to.

Rhyme for arms:

> Pat-a-cake, pat-a-cake, baker's man,
> Bake me a cake as fast as you can;
> Pat it and prick it, and mark it with B,
> Put it in the oven for baby and me.

Rhyme for moving baby around:

> Up to the ceiling, down to the ground,
> Backward and forward, round and round;
> Dance, little baby, and mother shall sing,
> With the merry gay choral, ding, ding-a-ding, ding.

Rhyme for a belly rub and/or finger walk up to the armpit:

> Round and round the park
> Went the teddy bear,
> One step, two step, tickly under there!

Rhyme for touching your baby's face:

> Brow bender,
> Eye peeper,
> Nose dreeper,
> Mouth eater,
> Chin chopper,
> Knock at the door,
> Ring the bell,
> Lift up the latch,
> Walk in . . .
> Take a chair
> Sit by there,
> How'd you do this morning?

Spending time in the crib

Babies don't always sleep. And you aren't always carrying around or interacting with your infant. So think about the following ways to enliven your baby's world and improve her brain circuitry with stimulating crib decorations.

- **Hang brightly colored pieces of cloth or paper on the sides of the crib or overhead.** Babies respond to bright colors visually and with body movements. With time, they elicit wonderful baby sounds, the beginnings of speech and language. Colorful bibs tie easily to crib slats. Inexpensive place mats, especially of animals, double as touchable, washable crib artwork.

- **Make or buy a baby mobile to string in the crib.** Remember that your baby keeps her head turned toward the side for the first six weeks. So hang the mobile to one side or the other initially. After about six weeks, your infant can focus straight up toward the ceiling and appreciate stimulation from overhead. This trains her eyes and contributes to her understanding of where objects are in relation to body parts.

- **Consider musical mobiles.** They may be more expensive than non-musical ones, but the sounds help baby miss you less, which translates into more time for you to do other things. Modern battery-operated music boxes also keep the auditory stimulation coming for unlimited amounts of time, soothing your baby and helping her focus her hearing and differentiate sounds.

Some educators advocate a floor bed or mattress on the floor, turning the entire room into a giant playpen. This setup allows free exploration of the entire room after your baby begins to crawl.

To keep your baby — and the rest of the house — safe with this setup, put a baby gate in the doorway. And make sure the room is baby-proofed for tiny objects that can be swallowed and heavy objects that can topple on little heads. Remember to check the child safety Web sites mentioned in the preceding section of this chapter for extensive baby-proofing guidelines.

Changing the changing table

To you, a changing table serves two main functions: to change your baby's diapers and clean and redress her. But to baby, the changing table provides other wondrous options for learning:

- **Place a mirror on the wall next to the changing table.** Your baby can watch both of your movements as she's changed and dressed. You aren't creating a narcissistic individual, just a self-aware one who is visually stimulated with her own reflection and body parts.

I used a mirror with a plastic frame, just in case my darling flailed toward her reflective self. You can reinforce the back with extra strips of tape to keep parts from shattering. Or look for a mirror that reflects from metal rather than glass.

✔ **Attach a shoe bag with six or eight pockets to the table to hold diaper essentials, as well as toys or rattles** to distract your little darling, who definitely doesn't appreciate the fine points of diaper-changing. The varied objects offer sights and sounds that stimulate her senses.

Other holders of diaper-changing and kid-distracting necessities include a hanging plant holder for large, light items and ice cube trays for the small objects, such as cotton balls for tickling toes and tummies.

Going from crib to floor

Make or sew a textured mat with squares of different materials affixed to a rubber pad that you can place under your baby, either in the crib or on the floor. Each movement gives your infant another tactile experience. One square can be fuzzy, another rougher, another velvety. You get the idea.

If you have a choice for floors in your baby's room, consider indoor/outdoor rugs. They're warm, washable, and slip-proof, which is what you want as your baby starts pulling herself up to explore.

Gettin' comfy with your own chair

If you have room, an adult chair is great for interacting with your baby. The more comfy you are, the more you'll be inclined to spend time with your baby, reading, singing, and discovering life together.

I thought a rocking chair would be perfect for me and my daughter, but it often made me sleepier than I already was. Still, my daughter and I loved the relaxing motion, which helps baby learn about her body in space.

Naming objects

Label anything with a flat surface that doesn't move much. Use your best lowercase primary printing to write *bed, door,* and *table.* I included my daughter's name on items whenever it seemed reasonable, such as *Rebecca's toys* for her toy box. As she grew older, she attached the idea of names, including her own, with the written words and started to develop a sight vocabulary before her formal reading began.

I'm not suggesting that infants start reading. The reason I suggest that you label objects now is because you probably won't have the time or the inclination for such details after your baby is off and running.

Sprucing up the walls

Hang pictures, posters, photos, or whatever you want your baby to observe. She does notice what's on the walls as you carry her around, and she begins to point at them and make sounds. These simple experiences around the house build language.

Babies particularly like pictures with lots of little objects in them to point out and name — pictures of animals and family members (not that these two categories go together). Expect your baby to first notice brightly colored images or primary colors that have plenty of *contrast,* like black or red against a white background.

Recognizing color theory

Babies love color and contrast. The brighter the better. That's why so many new toys and baby products come in black, white, and red, the colors your baby sees best until six months of age. High-contrast, bold colors hold your infant's attention longer, visually stimulating her to kick, wave the air, and wiggle around, usually all at once.

But softer colors are useful, too, because they're soothing. Think about what effect you want for your child's room. Whatever your choice, consider the following:

✓ Use washable — that means really scrubbable — paint or wallpaper only. You'll thank me later for reminding you about this.

✓ Make nonsexist color choices. Choose a pastel because you want a soothing environment, not because your baby is a girl. All babies prefer primary colors, so don't program your girl for passivity and boy for boldness from birth because of the color of your baby's room.

Containing yourself

Plan ahead to organize your baby's room in an orderly fashion, because the room won't stay that way long after she starts moving around. But even though the room will get messy, by organizing it, you're helping your child understand how to categorize and sort objects, which enhances language development and early math skills. A bonus for you is easier cleanup.

Use boxes, plastic containers, stacking crates, and laundry baskets for different sizes of toys. As your baby matures, she can sort with you and later toss objects into their rightful places on her own. (More about organizing rooms for older kids in Chapter 8.)

Talking to Your Baby — Even Though She Can't Talk Back!

The easiest and proven most effective way to create a child who loves learning is to talk to her. Describe to your baby what she's seeing, feeling, and experiencing. Because the ability to hear and speak language comes before understanding, your voice inflections tell your baby a lot about what you're saying. Talk to your baby to develop language, stimulate auditory senses, and, of course, interact with her.

- **Talk to your baby about her day from wakeup to final shut-eye.** Go about your regular activities and talk about them. At the store, point out fruits and vegetables. In the car, watch other cars and trucks and houses. At home, review names of different furniture, toys, and cleaning supplies.

  I don't mean baby talk. Use understandable, simple words in short, simple sentences. You want to model the type of language your child should speak as she gets older.

- **Point out links between real objects and pictures of objects.** Name what you call objects to provide language for the visual cues.

- **Create a photo scrapbook that shows important people in your child's life.** This is particularly a good idea for keeping the memory of out-of-town friends and relatives alive. But don't forget everyone in your household, too, so that you provide a framework for linking people with pictures and names.

  To keep family peace, balance folks from both sides of the family. And include the family dog, cat, or whomever ruled the roost before baby came.

- **Prepare another scrapbook of pictures of common objects in your child's life.** Photos are best because they look more like the real thing, but pictures from newspapers, magazines, catalogs, and junk-mail work, too. Kids love spending inordinate amounts of time picking out and later naming objects in their lives.

✔ **Gather more photos, this time of actions, like eating and sleeping, that your child experiences.** This type of scrapbook provides a way of developing verbs, those action words that are critical for making a complete sentence when you talk and write.

My daughter's dog-eared scrapbook contains pictures of her bed, changing table, toy shopping cart (a favorite), balls, collapsible tunnel, and cherished stuffed "baby."

If these last few ideas seem too time-consuming for you, assign them to a relative, friend, or the older kid next door who loves babies. Or enlist your older child, who usually thinks helping with the baby means bopping the infant on the head or carrying her precariously through the house under the guise of playing with her.

Reading to Your Baby

If you've read to your bellybutton (see Chapter 5), you already value reading to expand your baby's brain cells and act as a springboard to a nurturing relationship with your child. If you skipped reading to the stuffed hole in your bloated belly, you may wonder about the sanity of telling stories to someone who can't understand the words, let alone focus on the page. But the value is immeasurable. Reading at every stage is critical for raising smart kids.

Recognizing the value of reading aloud

Call it snuggle time, quiet time, something-to-do together time, or whatever else works for you. Nuzzling up with your baby and a book feels good. It provides special time for baby to absorb language and pay attention without the fuss of your other must-do, scheduled activities. Regular reading lets your baby know that you care, want to spend time together, and find reading so important you schedule it every day or evening.

This togetherness sets the stage for reading with any age child. You're not expecting your child to read *Moby Dick* by age 1. You're merely committing to what parents of smart kids do: Provide a loving situation that shows a strong interest in their child's activities.

Reading to infants offers the bonus of presenting rhythmic patterns that the developing brain craves. Unlike everyday speech, formal writing for books often organizes *syntax* (the grammar and structure of words) so that your baby receives orderly incoming auditory information. Even though your infant can't understand the meaning of what you read, she gains helpful hints about how to acquire linguistic competency. Similar types of patterns and repetitions come from listening to classical music, as mentioned in Chapter 5.

Reading aloud and acting silly for beginners

Time to let your hair down. Awaken your drama skills. Tickle your funny bone. Let your voice soar. It's reading time.

When reading aloud to your child, be sure to:

- **Cuddle.** Try to read together in a comfy, quiet place away from the family hustle. Designate a reading chair, spread a blanket on the floor for a book bed, or pile pillows into a reading corner. Reading should be relaxing, casual fun.

- **Be silly.** This is a must. Use different voices and body language to express the action, sound effects, and voices of characters. Acting out all aspects of the character's actions while reading aloud makes the story come alive. Your baby can see how imagination works and how wild and crazy you can be.

- **Take many trips to the library.** Unless you have unlimited funds for books, use the library liberally. (And remember, as soon as your child can write her name, which comes years from now, bring her to sign up for a card. Think how grown-up that feels!)

- **Choose books with interesting designs, colors, and textures.** Your baby wants to touch and explore books as you read.

- **Encourage baby participation.** At first you'll be lucky if your infant focuses on the page. As your baby gains more motor and visual control and starts putting words together with objects and pictures, you can ask for help, such as, "Point to the car," "Point to the baby," "What sound does a dog make?" or whatever is in the book.

- **Act out parts of the story together as you read.** This works best with books that have sound effects or a refrain, such as the classic story of *The Pokey Little Puppy*. Whenever you come to a point in the story where you say the refrain, signal your baby to chime in. After your baby acquires more language, you can assume the role of one character in the book and assign your baby another.

- **Suggest that your baby help you turn the pages.** After more language develops, add questions about the story, which is discussed more in Chapter 7.

Encouraging a reluctant reader

While it's never too early to begin reading to your child, don't expect literary miracles in babyland. (See what young babies can do in Table 6-2.) Your infant can still get into college and

✔ **Gnaw on books like a dog on a bone.** In fact, count on a lack of respect for the printed word. Babies haven't yet distinguished books from other playthings.

✔ **Become otherwise engaged while you read.** Generally, the younger the child, the shorter the attention span. If you see your child's eyes and body wandering, skip to a favorite page, point out something your child especially likes, or switch activities completely until later.

✔ **Refuse to read.** This too shall pass, so try again another time. Your baby has plenty of time to hear *Gone with the Wind.*

✔ **Read the same book over and over again until you want to tear your hair out.** This is normal, at least the over and over again part. Kids love repetition. It's comforting, and they learn language this way.

The medical community believes an interest in reading is so fundamental to successful growing up that the American Academy of Pediatrics provides a Reading Checkup Guide for parents and their docs to reinforce regular reading time. Check the Web site www.aap.org/family/readmeastory.htm.

Table 6-2	What Baby Learns from You the First Year
What You Do	*What Baby Discovers*
Respond to cries needs;	People can be counted on to satisfy my beginnings of trust in self and others
Cuddle and carry	I am loved; physical contact is comforting
Provide a loving relationship	I must be pretty special; based on my first encounter with a human, emotional relationships with others feel good
Feed, change diapers, clean	The world is a pleasurable place to live in; basic needs are met, so I am free to seek new challenges
Provide objects and experiences to stimulate senses and intelligence	The world is an exciting place: Bring it on.

Board books that aren't boring

Young babies need books they can sink their teeth into, literally. So publishers have obliged them with books made of plastic, cloth, and heavy-duty cardboard, also known as *chub* or *chubby books*. Most plastic books won't win any awards, but they withstand drooling, bath water, and stuffing into diaper bags. For interesting board books, consider:

- **Any books with photos of babies:** One baby per page is more than enough for the 0-to12-month set. Babies love to look at likenesses of people their own size.

- *Dr. Seuss Book of Wonderful Noises* and *Mr. Brown Can Moo, Can You?* (Random House) are board books that every kid loves: They have bold, primary-color pictures and simple words. Dr. Seuss books rhyme, which trains the ear for language and is plain fun for adults to read.

- *Playtime* series (DK Publishing): The company publishes several books with vivid, realistic, simple pictures and single words, including *First Word* books. These books are great for growing your child's vocabulary. Ask your child to, "Point to the . . . ," and say what it is.

- *Spot* books by Eric Hill (Putnam): These charming books about a black and white dog have been baby favorites for decades. Some are flip-tab, too, which stimulates babies who have more dexterity or are ready for objects to disappear and reappear. Check out other Eric Carle books, such as *The Very Hungry Caterpillar.*

- *Max* books by Rosemary Wells (Dial): Here are baby books you won't get tired of because of Wells's great sense of humor. Max and his sister Ruby have single-word interactions on each brightly-colored page. They share everyday experiences your baby knows about, such as eating and dressing.

- *Pat the Bunny* by Dorothy Kunhardt (Golden Books): This is another classic, but this one boasts different textures and interactive shapes.

- *The Very Busy Spider* or other books by Eric Carle (Philomel): This author/artist uses bold colors with simple text and playful but meaningful messages in his books.

- *Goodnight Moon* by Margaret Wise Brown (HarperFestival): This book is a classic, simple, sleepytime favorite.

- **Nursery-rhyme books:** They're short, sometimes weird, and in rhyme, which babies love to hear.

- **Homemade books:** Gather photos, line drawings, or cut-outs from magazines, catalogs, and junk mail to assemble a creative masterpiece that comes from the heart. Protect the book from drool by sealing pages either by ironing on plastic wrap or by laminating them. Your baby will treasure this book forever, and it costs pennies.

Chapter 7

Pumping Up Your Smart Toddler/Preschooler

In This Chapter

▶ Playing for fun and learning

▶ Talking and listening to your child

▶ Connecting to your child through reading

*T*he honeymoon's over. Get your running shoes on, because your toddler or preschooler is on the move. No more will your child lie in bed or crawl around, looking to you as the main source of stimulation. Now, your baby's ready to explore.

Your toddler has entered what some childhood authorities call the *golden age of exploration*. This chapter helps you get your child off on the right foot while he enters his larger world of experiences.

Learning to Play, Playing to Learn

Toddlers and preschoolers play without your constant stimulation. But that doesn't let you completely off the hook. Nor should you want to be. Your job is to stay involved with your child's play, acting in the following roles:

✔ Participant or observer

✔ Provider of toys

✔ Supporter of whatever feats your child performs (within reason, of course)

Play is your child's work, not a time-filler. This means that you have to continue to present new play options — opportunities that expand your youngster's world and create varied learning situations.

Playing outside: Moving muscles and building confidence

Toddler/preschooler play reinforces the mind-body connection (see Chapter 6). Baby brain cells continue to multiply as your toddler runs, climbs, touches, manipulates, throws, and experiments with objects in different settings. The following are some ways to move your child's muscles and build confidence in the process:

✔ **Make lots of trips to the playground.** Allow your child to climb, run, spin around, and swing.

Try not to be overprotective. Unless your child has particular motor or behavior problems, he usually won't try something he can't handle. But stay close when he climbs higher than usual. Your nearness lends support. You're also nearby, just in case you hear an emergency call for help.

If you find yourself a nervous Nelly, close your eyes when your child entertains daring exploits. If blocking out scary sights doesn't work, let someone else take your child to the playground. A healthy respect for dangerous equipment is wise, but you don't want your child to pick up your fears unnecessarily. Unreasonable fear of situations undermines your child's confidence in his ability to manage his environment. And you don't want that.

One fearful couple I know talked repeatedly in front of their daughter about how clumsy she was. Sure enough, the self-fulfilling prophesy penetrated their daughter's psyche. Although she was physically able, when she ran, she tripped. When she climbed, she clutched and begged for assistance. Thankfully, her inborn talents, including balance and coordination, won out. Today, she is an accomplished and agile dancer.

✔ **Buy or make some equipment that exercises large toddler muscles.** Consider the following toys, especially if you live far from a playground:

• **Sandbox:** A 2- or 3-inch depth of sand enclosed in a wooden frame provides a medium to explore the wonders of texture, science, and fantasy play. Build a sandbox big enough for your toddler's friends, too. And add plastic toys, smooth pieces of wood, and shovels and pans for making sand pies and pouring fine particles.

Don't forget to cover the sandbox when it's not in use. Exposed sand draws outdoor cats looking for a litter box like a magnet.

- **Plastic tunnel:** A tunnel is inexpensive and can go outside or in, even in an apartment. It is colorful plastic over a curled hollow wire frame that looks like a giant covered Slinky. Buy a tunnel as soon as your child starts crawling. It's a great place to play hide-and-seek, and when your baby finishes crawling up and back in the tunnel, the 6-foot snake folds into its flat box.

- **Dome climber:** Domes look like high-top sturdy metal turtle shells. Their rounded top dome shape allows for climbing bravery without the fear of falling, and this builds confidence as well as large muscle capabilities. Best of all, your creative kid can throw a sheet or tarp over the top and pretend the hollow inside of the dome is a fort, tepee, igloo, or secret hideout. In fact, *you* may want to use it for a hideout, too!

- **Water play:** Splashing in a large container or running through hose water are other kid favorites, particularly on warm days. You don't need a fancy water slide or wading pool, but they're fun. A sprinkler works fine for running through.

Indoor water play saves my sanity on many boring days when weather outdoors turns crummy or someone is in a bad mood. If you have space — and funds — you can buy a water table that doubles as a sand table, just not at the same time. But filling the sink with water works fine. Toss in a few plastic containers, measuring spoons, and boats, and your child will play happily for hours.

For younger or messier kids, strip them down and put them in the bathtub. Your child keeps happily busy and gets clean at the same time. Give him a paint brush to water paint sides of the tub, and he turns into a budding Georgia O'Keefe. Just remember to stay in the room for safety and remove him before he looks like a prune.

- **Tricycles, tike bikes, or other wheeled modes of transportation:** Try your child out on these before buying. Bicycle pedaling and steering take coordination of many muscle groups and visual coordination. If your child gets frustrated with what you purchased, put it away until he's ready to take a spin.

Toddlers and preschoolers are busy people. The more they do, the greater their confidence that they can climb any mountain. You want to encourage these positive play experiences. They become the seeds of courage that bolster your child's confidence. Your child will study a little harder, read a more difficult book, or sing on stage when he really wants to hide because he has the spirit to try harder, a spirit you fostered through constructive and varied play when he was too young to notice.

Selecting smart indoor toys

Two- to five-year-olds love their fantasy play. Through fantasy, your child alters the real world. Fantasy play provides a safe way to experience pretend scary situations and work them out. Play offers a chance to change the frightening into joyful. Kids test more worldly waters through fantasy without having to get completely submerged.

To encourage your child's imagination, find the following:

- ✔ Toys that can be used for more than one thing. Check out the "Home-grown toys that trigger imagination" sidebar for ideas.
- ✔ Toys that aren't so delicate that you're constantly hovering over your child, telling him how to use them, or showing your displeasure when they are thrown, dropped, or otherwise abused.

You don't need to buy expensive toys for your child to recreate the world. At this stage, your child is old enough to change everyday items into play props, for example:

- ✔ A washing-machine-box fort in the living room
- ✔ Your reachable clothes worn as dress-up costumes
- ✔ A towel transforming into a Super Cape
- ✔ Boats made from blocks that help imaginary friends sail to magical islands in search of fantastic treasures

These props allow your toddler to

- ✔ **Stay entertained for hours:** He'll play alongside others throughout his second year, not really interested in much sharing at that point. By about age 3, however, your little introvert may blossom into a social butterfly, playing with others the same age and pushing, shoving, and squabbling with the best of them.
- ✔ **Express emotions:** Your child acts out everything from personal feelings to what transpires between members of the household. So watch out! You're in for eye-opening views into how family interactions, jobs, and roles are perceived by your child.

Home-grown toys that trigger imagination

Keep a variety of these toys around for rainy-day and not-so-rainy-day fun. Most can serve many functions for years. Before you load up the house, though, consider how you want to store them: separate shelves, containers, boxes, toy box, or some workable combination. Keep some toys hidden away and switch them with visible ones for variety. You'll find your child doesn't really need so many toys — just a change now and then. Provide your child with a mixture of:

- Bean bags
- Box of mixed items, such as keys, wheels, zippers, large (and later small) blocks, tinker toys, empty tape circles, old clocks, door stops, and snap blocks
- Box of pictures to sort, paste, and cut
- Box of wheels and spools to sort and build
- Chalkboard and large chalk for sidewalks
- Clothespins and sticks for craft projects
- Different sizes of boxes
- Empty boxes and cans for play and storing
- Flashlight
- Housekeeping/grocery supplies
- Large beads for stringing
- Large blocks for climbing and building

- Magnet letters and numbers
- Manipulative toys, such as LEGOs
- Old clothes, hats, curtains, and large material pieces
- Paper bags, plates, and cups
- Paper, pencils, markers, crayons, and blunt scissors
- Parts of flour and salt mixed with water
- Pegboards
- Play dough, which can be made from equal parts of salt, water, and flour
- Puppets
- Rug samples
- Scraps of different fabrics
- Simple puzzles
- Smaller blocks for building and pretend play
- Stack of catalogs to cut pictures and name items
- Stuffed animals and dolls
- Town and farm play sets
- Unused or play telephone and clock
- Varied pasta shapes/foods for stringing and collages
- Wooden and metal cars and trains

Doing nothing and loving it

You may have even gotten the idea in this book (and in others) that the more stimulation a baby receives, the wiser he will be. If this is your interpretation, keeping totally busy is not what I mean.

Yes, stimulation builds brain cells, confidence, and all that good stuff. But I wholeheartedly recommend that you also show respect for your child's downtime, which has merit, too. Give your child — and yourself — a break from a constant diet of structured stimulation.

Match the type and quantity of stimulation to your child's level of maturation and temperament at the time.

Be alert to the messages your child sends you about embarking on yet another enriching activity. If your 2-year-old fusses or runs away before entering yet another class, he may be telling you he's had enough. Your preschooler may steadfastly say, "I hate skating!" And watch out for telltale messages in sudden or specifically timed temper outbursts, crankiness, and clinginess that can occur at any age. These may be strong signals that too much enrichment is creating a stressed-out kid.

Talking, Talking, and More Talking

I talk about the power of speech being a great baby brain cell booster in Chapter 6. For the toddler/preschool age, I recommend that you not only keep chatting with your child but also up the ante with richer language.

- Expand your child's words into phrases, and then phrases into sentences.
- Ask questions to be answered.
- Enhance how you describe situations by using adjectives and adverbs to include concepts your baby needs to understand, such as:
  - **Likenesses and differences:** "Show me which balls are the same." "Show me a different toy."
  - **Shapes and sizes:** "Roll the round ball." "You have the square puzzle piece."
  - **Colors:** "Give me the green sock." "Eat the red apple."
  - **Counting:** "I give you one, two, three carrots." "Let's count the bears we put away."
  - **Qualities of things,** such as cold and hot, fat and thin: "The oven is hot." "Coats are for when it's cold."
  - **Body parts:** "Take your sock off your foot." "Show me your stomach."
- Examine spatial relationships together:

- **Positions of objects:** "Put the peg in the hole." "Walk up the stairs." "I threw the ball away from you."

- **Right and left:** "Shake your right arm." "Point to the cat on the left side of the book shelf." "Your spoon is to the left of your plate."

REMEMBER

Don't expect overnight understanding. These concepts take time (sometimes years) to develop. As with most learning, every child is different. The important thing is to keep conversations light. Learning new things should be fun and exciting times together.

Sometimes, people get the mistaken assumption that after toddlers begin to talk and walk, they're miniature adults who should know all words and respond when spoken to. Table 7-1 gives some general milestones to help you adjust your expectations.

Table 7-1	Toddler Milestones		
	12–15 months	*15–18 months*	*18–24 months*
Language	Says first word	Names several common objects, or at least says close approximations; begins to repeat what you say; points to let you know what he wants	Says up to 300 words; makes two-word sentences; puts emotion into talking
Senses and motor skills	Climbs stairs on all fours	Walks alone; pulls toys	Scribbles with crayon
Social and mental activity	Stands independently; climbs into adult chair	Shows interest in turning book pages; fits two-piece puzzles; tries to throw	Turns book pages; runs without falling; fits five-piece puzzles; masters stairs

Listening to Your Child

Smart kids (and adults) know how to listen. Kids listen to learn. They listen to show respect, empathy, and other qualities of being a good friend and family and community member. Therefore, listening to others is the most important skill your child develops. In fact, the ability to listen now is critical for language development and reading prowess, referred to in Table 7-2, as your child grows.

Table 7-2	Preschooler Milestones		
	3 years	*4 years*	*5 years*
Language	Plays with words; combines four- to five-word sentences; has 900-word vocabulary	Questions everything; gives orders; uses 1,500-vocabulary; loves potty talk and word games; may stutter	Defines things realistically; uses 2,200-word vocabulary
Senses and motor skills	Pedals tricycle; puts on shoes; feeds self without many spills; paints and pastes	Traces; sews cards; helps with chores; cuts with scissors	Jumps rope; uses toilet unassisted; dresses self; skates; colors within lines
Social and mental activity	Shows independence; cooperates; begins making decisions; plays cooperatively; develops imaginary playmate	Becomes more social; fixates on routines; demands and brags; rhymes; loves to tell stories; loves being silly	Moves around neighborhood by self; matches and sorts; knows what's missing; completes activities

According to a survey, listening absorbs an average of 55 percent of your daily communication time, while speaking occupies 23 percent, reading 13 percent, and writing just 9 percent.

The following interactions not only increase listening skills but lay the groundwork for your future parent/child relationship:

- ✔ **Focus your toddler's attention on sounds around the house,** such as the telephone or vacuum. Help him connect sounds, objects, and their names.

- ✔ **Point out sounds outside the home,** such as a barking dog or fire truck siren. Show him what makes the sound, again to connect the sound with the object named.

- ✔ **Give your toddler simple one-step directions to follow,** such as "Bring me the ball." Remember to praise each accomplishment or its approximation. Gradually, increase to two-step commands, then three.

✔ **Tape sounds around the house to listen to.** Ask your toddler to name or find the source of the original sound.

✔ **Allow your child to listen to people, such as grandparents, on the telephone.** At first, your child will say very little. But he's curious about the sounds. With time, he learns to recognize familiar voices and eventually talk back to the odd-looking gizmo that has voices coming out of it.

✔ **Play hide-and-seek.** Call your child to find you from another room. Let your child follow the sound of your voice.

✔ **Sing songs together or play CDs or tapes with kid's songs.** Make sure to include songs that suggest movements, such as the familiar "Here We Go 'Round the Mulberry Bush" or "Ring Around the Rosy."

As your preschooler gets older, play books on tape. Some tapes come with printed books. Your child can turn the pages with each signaled beep, so he feels like he's reading.

✔ **As your child begins to converse, be a good listening role model.** Get in the habit of doing the following:

  • **Establish eye contact when your child speaks.** Your undivided attention sends a powerful message to your child that he's important and worth listening to.

  • **Hear your child out without interrupting.** When you interrupt, you tell your child that what you have to say is more important than what he says. That's a big no-no in the confidence-building arena.

  • **Refrain from finishing his sentences.** You can't be in that much of a rush that you can't hear your little one out. Even if he stutters, which is normal at this stage, let him complete his thought.

  Never call attention to stuttering if your child talks in a halting way. This makes him feel self-conscious, which increases the stuttering. And make sure family and friends bite their tongues, too. Give your child a couple months after stuttering begins before worrying about this speech pattern becoming more permanent and having him tested by a speech pathologist.

  • **Resisting putting words in his mouth:** Even little guys have their own thoughts and opinions. You know a lot about your child, but don't assume you know everything.

Start the activities now, and you'll find you have better communication with your child during the parents-don't-know-anything preteen and teenage years.

Reading to Your Whirlwind

Reading is critical to mastering most other subjects in school. So why not help your youngster develop a love of words, stories, and books from an early age? The number-one way to instill a love of books is to read aloud to your active toddler/preschooler every day.

Beating the drum for early reading

Reading aloud offers tremendous benefits to a toddler:

- **Provides emotional cues your child can pick up:** When you use a happy voice for a happy character or a sad voice for a sad character, your child understands what these emotions are, how to identify them, and how others handle them.

- **Increases attention span:** Your child will gradually be able to sit for long, involved stories or for many favorites at one session. In fact, prepare to tire of reading aloud long before your preschooler tires of hearing you read. This is especially true if you read at bedtime, when your child prefers staying awake to going to sleep.

- **Builds vocabulary:** Kids naturally understand more than they say. Hearing read-aloud stories expands vocabulary and comprehension, which gives your child familiarity with and a leg-up on reading varied words later. Hearing stories enables your child to experience the rhythm and richness of language through description, action words, and the interplay of different letters, sounds, and words. These are the building blocks of reading readiness, which is discussed in Chapter 10.

- **Expands your child's knowledge base:** Reading aloud stories about different subjects, social situations, and activities brings more of the world home, broadening your child's interests and storehouse of information.

- **Engages your child's imagination:** By reading about familiar characters in unique settings, your child discovers alternatives — new ways to handle feelings and situations. He encounters goofy ideas and factual information. He becomes curious about exploring the world beyond home. He begins to love learning.

- **Presents your child with different visual art experiences:** Book illustrations are high-quality examples of where imagination can take your child. They provide the opportunity for your child's first attempts to "read" what the book is saying by explaining what's going on in the pictures.

✔ **Introduces your child to the love of books:** When your child asks to read the story "one more time," he's beginning to love books. When he gets to choose favorites from among a shelf of books, he's discovering how special stories and books truly are.

✔ **Cements the nurturing connection between you and your child:** This key opportunity to bond is so important for your child's development into a happy, self-confident person who wants to learn. Reading together calms and relaxes both you and your child. It's a great cuddle-time activity.

Hunting for good toddler/preschool books

A giggle. Broad smiles. Extended snuggle time. Finding good kids' books takes a little time and effort, but the results are worthwhile. And if your child picks up some facts along the read-aloud way, that's icing on the cake.

But not all books produce the desired results. So I offer these suggestions to help you find books that appeal to you and your child:

✔ **Read through choices before buying or taking them out of the library.** Covers can fool you, so dive inside to find out what the book is about. Also, keep in mind that award winners aren't always the best match for your family. Judges sometimes choose winners from an adult perspective, forgetting who the books are really for. Read snatches of the beginning, middle, and ending and consider the following:

- Will the topic interest you and your child? Even though your child is your prime target, you may be reading this book repeatedly. You need some remote interest in the topic, so that *you* don't come to hate reading time. As the reader, you make the story come alive for your child. You can't give read-alouds your all if you lack enthusiasm for the book.

- Is the text written in a clear, understandable, and interesting style? Nothing hamstrings your reading time like deadly boring or cloyingly cutesy language. You want a book that engages you and your child.

  If the book is nonfiction (sometimes called *informational* in recent teacher/librarian-speak), do you find the information accurate and consistent with your understanding? An approach to a topic may differ from your belief system and what you want your child to hear at a young age.

- Do pictures match the text and age level? Some art in children's books is masterful in design, color, and skill involved. But the art may be too intricate for young readers. If your child can't make out the pictures, what good are they to the story?

✔ **Identify whether the book matches your child's level of development.** The zero-to-five crowd requires picture books with illustrations on every page. In addition, books for younger readers should only have a word or two on each page; a couple of sentences per page for toddler or preschooler readers. Both groups require books or stories that can be read in one sitting.

✔ **Check out the story's pacing.** Does the plot move enough to keep your child interested? Large chunks of description are nice in novels, but they put little ones and their parents to sleep.

You know your child best. Trust yourself to choose fun and enjoyable books that you both can share.

Fun read-aloud books

So many great toddler/preschool books; so little time. To help you narrow the field, consider some of my family's favorites. They include a few classics and a few newer titles worth exploring, depending upon your child's interests. (Be sure to include a mix of fiction and nonfiction in your read-aloud selections.) Additional solid choices are recommended by librarian, educator, and author Betsy Hearne in *Choosing Books for Children: A Commonsense Guide* (University of Illinois Press).

✔ *A Frog Inside My Hat* (poetry) by Fay Robinson (Bridgewater)

✔ *Bein' with You This Way* by W. Nikola-Lisa (Lee & Low)

✔ *Corduroy* by Don Freeman (Viking)

✔ *Don't Need Friends* by Carolyn Crimi (Doubleday)

✔ *Flying Bats* by Fay Robinson (Scholastic)

✔ *Get to Work Trucks* (nonfiction) by Don Carter (Roaring Brook Press)

✔ *Good Night Richard Rabbit* by Robert Kraus (Simon & Schuster)

✔ *Mama Provi and the Pot of Rice* by Sylvia Rosa-Casanova (Atheneum)

✔ *Market Day* (nonfiction) by Lois Ehlert (Harcourt)

✔ *Stranger in the Woods* (nonfiction) by Carl Sams (Carl Sams Photography)

✔ *Strega Nona* by Tomie de Paola (Putnam)

✔ *Tess's Tip-Tapping Toes* by Carolyn Crimi (Orchard)

✔ *The Carrot Seed* by Ruth Krauss (HarperTrophy)

✔ *The Little Puppy* by Judy Dunn (Random House)

- *The Poky Little Puppy* by Janette Lowrey (Golden Press)

- *The Rainbow Fish* by Marcus Pfister (North-South Books)

- *The Runaway Bunny* by Margaret Wise Brown (Harper Trophy)

- *The Snowy Day* by Ezra Keats (Viking)

- *The Tale of Peter Rabbit* by Beatrix Potter (F. Warne)

- *The Wild Baby* adapted by Jack Prelutsky (Greenwillow)

- *Trains* (nonfiction) by Seymour Simon (HarperCollins)

- *Where the Wild Things Are* by Maurice Sendak (HarperTrophy)

Chapter 8

Setting Boundaries That Matter

*J*ust when you get a handle on raising your smart toddler, you get blind-sided by temper tantrums, rampant "no's," rebelliousness, bossy pickiness, and — the worst — limp body drops. You may wonder how your smart kid will ever progress under these circumstances.

Relax. Believe it or not, the way you know your child is progressing is *because* these uproars occur. Your child rebels because she wants more to life. She's curious. She's talkative. She has new interests. She's becoming her own person.

Some experts call this tumultuous toddlerhood *first adolescence.* This is your child's passage — for some, kicking and screaming — from babyhood into childhood. (Don't confuse this time with teenage years, which have been called the *second adolescence* and are discussed in Chapters 17 through 19.) This chapter explores how to keep family equilibrium when one member works hard to break out of bounds.

Drawing Lines in the Sand: Identifying Priorities

Toddlers want what they want *now!* Stamp your foot for emphasis, and you're pretty much behaving like your toddler. In order for her to let you know she's not a baby anymore, she feels compelled to shout the message from rooftops, or the middle of the grocery store floor, whichever is more convenient. In other words, your toddler asserts her growing independence any way she can, but because a toddler's options for expression are limited, you get the screaming, demanding, and contrary foot-stamping.

To handle this probable change of pace, my first suggestion is for you to carve out a rest break from your busy day, breathe deeply a few times, and read Chapter 3, which is about managing behavior. Then, in your quiet moments, consider which rules are really important for your child to learn.

Yes, rules. Even though your tot bucks you every step, she really wants the comfort of your guiding parameters. She needs boundaries, as all children do, to feel secure and safe knowing that someone else is in control and keeping their little lives on a predictable, even course. Your little one needs rules to discover more about herself and about how to be with others.

The trick is to provide rules that are like Goldilocks and the Three Bears: Not so overbearing that you stifle her feelings of self-worth, not so free-form that she can't grasp how to function, but just right. She needs guidelines for acting so that others can stand to be around her, but she can still have some wiggle room to develop her weird-and-wacky or quiet-and-serious personality.

Be sure you follow your just-right rules consistently, or your sweetie won't know which direction to go. By "consistent," I mean providing the exact same response handled in the same way every time your child flops on the grocery store floor and wails, no matter how stressed you are one time versus the next. As emphasized in Chapter 3, your child sees flip-flopping as a real weak spot in your character, and one to be exploited. She understands that the unacceptable will eventually be permitted if she continues to badger you long enough, so be vigilant.

Allowing choices: Yours and yours

Smart older kids know how to make wise choices. Their everyday decisions influence how they learn, behave, and get along with others. In this way, the ability to make choices becomes one of the most important abilities your child can acquire.

But choices bring consequences, both good and bad. Sometimes the choice between two desired options means losing one or the other. Being able to make difficult choices early provides roots for future decision-making and provides your child with the following:

- The confidence to hang up the telephone when she has to study for a test
- The gumption to say "no" to riding in a car driven by a friend who's drunk
- The confidence not to smoke when all her friends do
- The strength to avoid the pressure of sexual intercourse

Guilt-tripping your kid — don't!

The first inkling of conscience develops with understandable language. But even when your child says she won't do something, it takes another three or four years before she really knows how to control herself. Your 2-year-old may be able to say "no-no" or "no climbing." But she won't be able to stop herself from climbing on the table or emptying your drawers for another couple years.

You can say, "Look at the work you've caused me," or "You can do that, but I'll be sad" all you want. Guilt-tripping your kid won't help her learn anything but to feel guilty *after* she's done something you find problematic.

Guilt is a wasted emotion that deflates self-confidence and your child's sense of dignity. So why impose guilt, particularly at the toddler age? If that's how you were raised, this is a great time to change family history.

The following is a quick review of the top three ways to stop the cycle of guilt that you may have experienced in your youth.

✔ **Keep emotion out of rules**. You want your child to internalize socially acceptable behavior because it's right, not because of your reaction. So set rules with realistic consequences, should they be broken. Review them regularly, even for your non-reader, so that everyone understands your expectations.

✔ **Make prevention your goal.** Arrange your home so that kid toys and other treasures are accessible, while adult special objects aren't. By placing your child's necessities at arm's reach, you increase independence. Similarly, hiding your Greek vase or other valuables for a few years ensures their longevity while decreasing the likelihood of your child breaking them. See Chapter 3 for details about how to manipulate your child's world to decrease unwanted behavior.

✔ **Keep talking about your child's emotions in different types of situations.** As your child puts more words together with the actions she's mastering, she'll get more control of the correct way to interact with her environment.

REMEMBER

Choices are part of life. The right choices separate those who succeed and those who find hardship later in life.

But the skill to make choices doesn't come easy. Your child needs years and years of practice from babyhood on. The simple choices you orchestrate for your child now allow her to practice, and maybe falter, while still surrounded by the safety net of home and family.

Your baby chooses between one toy or another all the time. Now it's time for you to expand the options for your toddler/preschooler. Whenever possible, give your toddler a choice. Allow her to choose clothes, foods, and which activity to do first. She'll feel grown up, respected, and important.

The biggest trick at this age is to allow choices that don't offend your adult sensibilities in some way. To do this, make the choice yours or yours: Offer a choice between two options you prefer but that also interest your child.

- **Do you want to take a bath or brush your teeth first?** You know full well your preschooler prefers to stay up until midnight.

- **Do you want juice or milk for breakfast?** You understand that your preschooler really wants the out-of-bounds coffee Daddy is drinking.

- **Should we go to the post office or supermarket first?** You know errands aren't favorites, but they have to be done.

  Be sure to save bonus places, such as the library or toy store, for last, or your agreeable kid won't want to leave these places and definitely won't be agreeable any more, if she does go.

- **Would you rather wear the red shirt with blue pants or green-striped shirt with green pants.** This avoids seeing your toddler in mismatched clothes when going to a dressy wedding or restaurant.

Allowing choices shows respect for your child's opinions without giving up your responsibility as parent. As a smart parent, you relinquish small decisions while keeping control of the big-ticket items that can affect your child's health and safety. Your preschooler assumes control over her life, practicing making simple choices. Unless you allow your child to make decisions now, she may not be able to later, when the stakes are higher.

Making the most of "I can do it myself"

Welcome to the I-can-do-it-myself (or me-do-it) stage. This is the age of the:

- Quick-change artist, or if you're really lucky, outdoor stripper
- Mechanical wizard who unfastens the car seat belt while you're zooming along the expressway
- Self-help queen who pours her own juice, spilling enough to wash the table and create a wading pool on the floor for the dog
- Helper shopper who drops scores of unwanted but colorful items into your shopping cart
- Fashion plate who goes to restaurants only if she's wearing her tutu, red boots, and 10-gallon hat

Kids this age naturally want to do everything for themselves, even when they aren't always successful. And they want to do what you do because they think being an adult has more perks than being a kid. (Little do they know what's ahead!)

Do you want to discourage her unique behavior, so that you don't risk being labeled the most eccentric family in the neighborhood? No way! Any neighbor who doesn't understand the toddler desire for autonomy doesn't know toddlers — or isn't much fun with them.

The I-can-do-it-myself stage is the beginning of the drive, willingness to work, and optimism identified in Chapter 1 as characteristics of smarter kids. Properly managed, this stage helps her budding self-image turn into a can-do approach later in life.

So what's a parent to do when you're out of time and/or your child dawdles over tasks you'd rather finish yourself quickly. Do you have a choice when your child insists on performing an activity that's far too difficult for her? Here are some not-so-foolproof options to try:

- ✔ **Allow your child to tackle a difficult job, but stay close by.** If you see frustration building, ask whether she wants help. If the stars line up, she may permit your intervention, the task will be completed, and all will be well in Toddlerland.

- ✔ **Distract your child with a more pleasant assignment, so that you can handle the task at hand.** For example, offer your tot a chance to read a favorite book or hold her prized teddy while you tie her shoes.

- ✔ **Break down the tasks involved in what your child wants to accomplish.** Assign an appropriate task to her, and you do the hard stuff. Make sure your child knows that her part of the job is very important. For example, "Let's pour the juice together. You hold the cup very still, the hard part. I'll pour from the container."

- ✔ **Take the offending article along with you, if you're in a rush.** This gives you some extra time to work out a plan, one where you can complete the job without a violent response. There's no law that says your child has to wear shoes into the car or have a buttoned sweater before leaving the house. But do expect a few stares.

- ✔ **Arrange small jobs your child can do to work alongside you before a struggle develops.** Kids just want to play grownup. Give your youngster a dust rag. Buy her a pretend rug sweeper or small snow shovel or rake. Ask for her assistance making beds and setting the table. If you're brave and available for close supervision, give your child a few minutes of pushing the real vacuum, spraying the windows with cleaner, or smushing the polish on the table.

Don't expect perfection. And whatever you do, never redo anything your child has just done. Nothing deflates your child more than seeing someone adjust, pick at, or otherwise change something she worked so hard on. And that goes for children of any age and spouses, for that matter. If the job has to be done a certain way, don't give it to anyone else to do. Keep it to yourself, and assign a more workable but similar task for your child to do by your side. "Daddy slices the roast. But you can arrange the parsley on the serving platter."

✔ **Assign responsibilities your child can handle,** such as watching the baby on the rug or picking up toys. These seemingly little jobs give your child a chance to try out what being grownup is like.

✔ **Celebrate minor and major accomplishments.** Whoop and holler over staying dry at night, riding a tricycle for the first time, or putting on a coat like a big kid.

✔ **Point out how important certain objects are, such as nails that hold furniture and wall together or tiny serving spoons for ice cream.** This gives your child the message that she is important, too, even though she's little.

Respecting sane and silly fears and ideas

Kids respect parents who treat them fairly. And they find out how to treat others outside the home based on these early interactions. But toddler/preschool years are filled with imagination, fears, and sometimes plain silliness. These are the years of imaginary friends and monsters in the closet. In your busy concrete world, you may have difficulty understanding where ghosts and talking block figures fit into building a respectful relationship with your child.

What's the best way to show that you respect your child? Consider the following tips:

✔ **Listen to her.** If listening is difficult for you, read some hints from Chapter 7.

✔ **Reflect the feelings of what is happening to your child.** Provide feedback by saying what you hear in your own words. You're not saving your child from experiencing something that makes her feel badly. You're not passing judgment. You're simply showing that you care and understand.

For example, what would you say if your child came to you saying, "There's a monster in my room"? Perhaps your first reaction would be to check the closet and under the bed. Then you deem the room safe for sleeping.

You may allay fears for the night. But you wouldn't be acknowledging your child's feelings. You wouldn't be respecting her judgments, no matter how silly they are to your adult way of thinking. As a result, she may shut down her feelings. And if she keeps too many feelings bottled up, she may be unable to express them altogether. She may feel that no one cares about what she thinks and feels.

This may sound extreme for one night of monsters, but multiply this type of snuffing out of ideas, and your child may begin to feel that her thoughts don't count. That's not a good way to create a healthy view of herself or help her build relationships later in life.

What if you reflected what your child said, instead? What if you asked for more information to get at the heart of the problem? "There is a monster in your room? How do you feel about that? You seem worried (sad, scared)." Now your child knows she has been heard and accepted. If you continue to reflect her responses, she'll probably work through her feelings and slip off to sleep, her self-concept intact.

Rearranging Bedrooms for Growth and Learning

Many of the tidbits in Chapter 6 about decorating a baby's room apply to toddlers and preschoolers. But your tot is getting older now, and her interests and abilities are changing. Why not redecorate to emphasize your child's new-found independence?

✔ **Think about a big-kid bed after your child begins to crawl, climb, and walk.** If you worry about your thrasher falling out of bed, look for one that's not too high or has removable sides. Some parents merely skip buying a frame and leave the mattress on the floor.

If you want to know ahead of time when your child wishes to come in your room and invade your space, place a spring-loaded baby gate at the room's doorway. But smart kids eventually figure out how to climb over those.

✔ **Arrange your child's playthings and clothes within reach.** Lower the rods in her closets, so that your child can reach clothes to dress herself. And hang a nonbreakable mirror low for her to check her body while dressing. Affix hooks at pint-size height, so she can hang her own coat and PJs. Place a variety of favorite toys and books on lower shelves and drawers. These seemingly minor changes help your child grow more confident about what she can do and become more independent.

Be sure to switch items within reach regularly, so your child doesn't get bored. For example, every month take a couple stored toys, books, and puzzles off a high shelf and trade them for materials that have been eye level. Your child will play with them like they're brand new.

✔ **Hang new artwork that reflects your child's expanded interests.** What better way to support your child's interests than by displaying them? Pictures of family, animals, trucks, airplanes, trains, and cars may be big favorites at this age, but ask your tot to be sure what she likes. Hang a bulletin board or cork squares in one area for your child to display transitory treasures. You can also use plastic frames with cardboard box backings. That way, you can easily switch pictures as your child finds new special interests.

Frame your child's artwork. Nothing pleases your child more than seeing her productions displayed. One adult friend still has her first picture, all matted and framed from her childhood. She loves the tradition her mother started so much, she frames the first efforts of each of her children. After your child's art is safely tucked inside a frame, the creations look better than most modern art!

Use acid-free materials to protect the paper over time. If you can't find an inexpensive mat and frame and want to keep costs down, dry mount the picture on lightweight foam core at your local framer or have the art laminated in plastic, which protects art against sticky fingers, potentially damaging sunlight, and paper deterioration.

✔ **Consider more creative storage.** Remember to think horizontally rather than vertically. Your child can find items that are spread out more easily than trying to dig for objects buried on the bottom of a tall pile.

- Add a book shelf or two for toys and, of course, books, without worry about their toppling on your tot.

- Hang hooks on pieces of pegboard or on the wall for dress-up apparel, jump ropes, paint aprons, or other toys.

- Paint shelves or containers, each in a different color that goes with their contents. Color-coding helps your smart kid master colors, sort items, and put toys away at the end of the day. Of course, you can label containers with words, too.

- Store each puzzle in a different resealable bag or plastic container. Write a letter or number on the back of each piece, so you know which pieces go with the others. Nothing frustrates you and your child more at the end of a tiring day than trying to match pieces from a pile of different puzzles.

- Scour garage sales for a piano bench that's the perfect height for a work table, complete with a storage place inside the seat. Also look for old school desks and pint-sized kitchen and workbench equipment for a play corner.

✔ **Recycle baby stuff you aren't ready to dispose of.** That plastic baby tub makes a great boat, car, or storage bin. The bassinet stores toys, too, but it works for creative doll play.

✔ **Hang a chalkboard or markerboard at the child's level for free drawing.** As your tot ages, let her color on one wall but with the same strong stipulations. Just be adamant that, "This is the only wall you're allowed to paint or color. You may want to relegate wall-painting, if you like the idea at all, to a wall in an unfinished basement.

We let my daughter paint a wall in the basement. I painted, too, only my creations were more practical: the alphabet, numbers from one to ten, and so on. Every few days, often on rainy or otherwise boring days, we added more imaginary creatures. My daughter often invited friends to join her. And I repeated my mantra about how this was a special wall and they weren't to repeat this experience anywhere else. Only one family totally disapproved. Although their daughter and mine had been good playmates, after the parents saw them decorating a wall, my daughter never played with this buddy again outside of day care. But think of the fun of having a wall-sized easel at your disposal!

Trusting Toddlers and Their Preschool Partners in Crime

Smart older kids are safe kids. They know how to avoid dangerous situations. But even if she's so inclined, you can't count on your toddler/preschooler to understand danger yet. Kids this age are naturally erratic, excitable, and impatient, and that's a bad combination. They run into streets after balls. They hide inside clothing racks in stores. And they may go with a friendly adult they meet at the mall. Even when you plan on always staying together, your child may disappear when you turn your head or become involved in a conversation.

As a parent, you do the best you can. That involves beginning to train early for situations you hope will never happen. At this age, your child won't miraculously understand the first time around what throws you into a tailspin. In your child's egocentric manner (which is perfectly normal), she assumes you exist to serve and take care of her, keeping all harm away.

Therefore, you need a ton of patience, modeling (of proper behavior), and practice during this age. Given time, your child may adopt the same cautious philosophy you embrace. Just don't count on it happening too early!

You don't want to scare your little person so much she never leaves your side. But you can begin to work on the basics of who and what constitutes danger. Teach your child to:

✔ **Stay away from water's edge.** Review pool and beach rules before each outing.

✔ **Understand fire safety.** Check out the fire safety tips in the "Hot fire-safety tips for tots" sidebar.

✔ **Play where you can see her.** Make sure she knows to ask you or a care-giver before going somewhere or with someone else.

✔ **Pay attention when you talk.** Don't get in the habit of repeating what you want a dozen times until your child acts. She'll learn to tune you out. And safety-related directions usually need immediate responses. So make directions clear with understandable consequences for not responding after one time.

You can start by playing a stop-and-go game with your toddler. On *go* you both walk, run, hop, whatever. When you say *stop,* you both freeze. Repeat the game together and with you just giving verbal directions until your child acquires enough self-control to stop on command, kind of like Simon Says. Knowing how to respond to your simple words can save a lot of grief near streets, in parking lots, or racing through stores or poolside.

✔ **Talk with you about anyone who approaches her;** wants to give her something tempting, such as a puppy, money, or candy; offers her a ride; hangs around the playground; or asks her to keep a secret. Emphasize the importance of never getting close to someone else's car without per-mission, no matter how tempting.

✔ **Go to the nearest checkout counter, security officer, or lost and found if she gets separated** from you while shopping or in a public place. When going to a large store or mall, point out who your child can trust, should you get separated or an emergency occur. Take time for a couple run-throughs before heading off to do your chores together.

✔ **Practice street crossing together.** No way is your child ready for cross-ing independently yet. But you can begin pointing out the fine points of successful street crossing:

- Crossing at the corner.

- Looking both ways before leaving the curb.

- Knowing street light etiquette that says red means stop and green means go, although newer lighting systems show a character for walk and a hand for stop. This latter distinction is important in high-traffic areas that have confusing street lights with arrows for turning cars.

- Walking and riding bicycles on sidewalks only.

- Going places with a buddy.

✔ **Make sure your toddler/preschooler knows the following street-smart information:**

- Name (first and last), address, and phone number (with area code).

- Parent's names (first and last rather than Mommy and Daddy).

- Body parts. Stress that parts covered by a swimsuit are considered private. Talk about appropriate and inappropriate touching.

- That 911 is what you dial during an emergency. Make sure she knows how to use rotary and push-button telephones and can dial "0" for operator at a pay phone

Hot fire-safety tips for tots

Children under age 5 are at the greatest risk during fires. But fire safety takes practice. Start giving your preschooler the following fire safety messages now:

✔ Stay away from items that cause intense heat and flames, such as matches and candles.

✔ Always give matches and lighters you find to an adult.

✔ Never touch hot appliances, such as oven burners and space heaters.

✔ Practice fire drills that role-play two safe ways to leave the house.

✔ Know the sound of a smoke alarm and tell an adult if it rings. If fire or smoke block your way to an adult, leave the house.

✔ Keep a door closed that feels hot.

✔ Crawl on the floor where air is clearer of smoke.

✔ Never hide to get away from fire or smoke. Stay low to breathe easier but where fire-fighters can find you.

✔ Stop, drop, and roll to put out firey clothes.

✔ Know where to meet your family safely away from the house, such as under the side tree or behind the garage, and stay away from the burning building after you're out. Let fire-fighters retrieve the cat, if they can.

Chapter 9

You're Not Alone! Finding Help and Support

In This Chapter

▶ Exposing your kids to the bigger world

▶ Leaving your child with others

*P*arenting can be a lonely job. At first, you spend time with someone whose primary responses include flailing, blowing bubbles, and pooping. Then all you hear is, "no!" Just when you get a handle on one stage, your child switches gears. By the time your toddler starts telling you off, you may have experienced intermittent bouts of self-doubt. Who wouldn't?

The responsibility for another human being is awesome. But you don't have to do it alone. You can take your child with you to commune with other adults, and you can start thinking about finding someone else to take care of your child — not forever, but for limited periods of time. This chapter helps you discover ways to find answers for your parenting questions, get support for the job you're doing, and locate the best possible child care for your child.

Going Places with Your Little One

Time to get out and about. You're entitled — and your toddler appreciates the trip. But you may wonder where you can go where little ones are welcome.

Play groups

In a play group, you gather with other parents and kids on a regular basis for the express purpose of providing your child an opportunity to play. Play groups can meet at recreation areas or community or religious centers. Most often, you trade off holding play group meetings at the parents' homes.

Kids get the benefit of interacting with new kids, who often become fast friends. And while your tot plays, you get to ask questions, share information, and receive support from others who are going through the same good, bad, and messy times as you are.

Play groups give you perspective. They're not places to compare, because each child develops at their own speed. But if you haven't been around kids much, seeing how others about your child's age behave can be a real eye opener.

Find play groupies through parent or child-related organizations, community or religious centers, or your pediatrician's office. Ask if you can post a note on the office bulletin board or at the grocery, local preschool, library, or village hall. Then round up everyone, make a few decisions about ground rules and the frequency with which you'll meet, and have fun.

Co-op programs

Like-minded parents often get together and form a co-op program. With co-ops, each parent agrees to share babysitting time. You drop off your child, and then skip out to accomplish whatever you haven't done in ages, such as sleep, meet an old friend, shop, or catch up on letters.

Some co-op arrangements are extensions of play groups. Parents decide that their kids play together just as well without all the grown-ups around. They agree to watch each other's kids when the need arises.

Make sure everyone in the group understands the rules the co-op sets. Someone needs to keep a log of hours, so that one parent doesn't get more of a babysitting load than the others. And you want a clear understanding of what's allowed and what's not, including guidelines for what constitutes a sick kid.

Drop-in centers and resource centers

Drop-in centers and resource centers appear in more-populated areas. Most often, they're sponsored by colleges and universities, religious institutions, and not-for-profit organizations. The beauty of these centers is the much-needed break they offer you to recharge your parenting batteries.

Dropping in

Drop-in centers post certain hours when parents and their kids can do just what the name says: drop in. Usually, you must stay on the premises. But you can leave your child in a separate kid's room, complete with toys and supervision. Meanwhile, you meander into a parent's room, where you can veg-out or share childrearing tidbits with other parents and trained staff. Some drop-in centers allow drop-off, but time away from your child is limited.

Drop-in centers are great first steps toward you and your child separating. You remain nearby to catch a peak at how well he's doing and to be available when he needs you. Yet, you can put some space between you and your child for a little while.

Resource centers

Resource centers are places you can go to find out more about being the parent you dreamed of being. Some resource centers allow you to take out parenting books, children's books, and toys for your child to try. Others present programs for parents, parents and kids, and kids on their own.

The National Lekotek Center, 800-366-PLAY, sponsors a network of places with trained staff where kids can experiment with various toys and activities. *Lekotek* means play library, which means that your child can borrow materials to take home or drop-in for classes and summer-camp programs, some involving computers. The concept began in Europe for children with special needs. But many programs are for children with and without disabilities, a great learning experience for both groups.

Recreation classes

Be careful about enrolling your child in classes when he's too young. If you and your tot use a class as time together doing fun activities and meeting people, fine. Just don't expect to raise an Olympic swimmer, skater, or baby artist.

Your baby probably won't remember the class much after it's over. In fact, babies don't remember much until about 24 months. Even baby swimmers forget how to flap and kick later. And your child may not show the respect for routine that the class requires. But if you can follow your child's lead and be happy with however he chooses to participate, he'll remember the many times you two had fun together.

Dealing with Day Care

Finding quality child care isn't easy. In fact, I think lining up people and services for your child is one of the most frustrating parts about being a parent. Just going out for an evening often depends upon the whims of a teenager who won't give you a final answer until the last minute for fear something better may come along.

Ferreting out care for longer periods of time can be incredibly tough. But that doesn't mean you don't try, especially if you're the kind of person who functions better and is happier with dual lives in a career and as a parent. Whether you manage a family or add a job outside the home, too, you have to balance your child's needs and your needs with the type of child care available in your area. And then you want a place that maximizes the learning you've begun at home. Not an easy task. This section explores some options and offers suggestions for selecting the best match for your child.

Looking at the pros and cons of child care

A variety of reasons necessitate placing your child in day care. That's your call. Don't let anyone tell you otherwise.

Some high-minded folks may imply that you're the only choice for raising your child. They may suggest that you cause great harm to your baby's developing smarts and psyche by finding alternative care arrangements.

Yet, more than 50 percent of U. S. preschool kids receive regular care from someone other than their parents. Parents throughout time have always worked. On the farm. In the factory. Both my grandmothers worked outside the home. You're entitled to work, too, if a job and career make you a better parent for any reason.

If day care were that bad, people wouldn't drop off their kids and so many kids wouldn't grow up fine.

Sure, it's good for your child to spend his baby and preschool years with you. You're your child's best teacher. You know your child best, have the most investment in his well-being, and love him to bits. But that doesn't mean someone else can't pitch in for a while, especially if you carefully choose a situation in which he receives the kind of quality care and stimulation that helps him grow and learn.

Don't accept guilt-trips from others. You probably find the separation of day care difficult enough without feeling judged by someone else. Be assured of the following:

✔ You remain the most important influence in your child's life.

✔ Caregivers can never take over your role as parent.

✔ You and your child benefit from the break and change of pace.

✔ Your child interacts with other kids and begins to learn about a world outside your home, while being comforted by the fact that you return at the end of each session you're apart.

✔ Research shows that kids in quality child care are more verbal, independent, and open to new experiences.

Identifying the range of day-care situations

Creative minds have come up with several alternatives for care. Your child can receive:

✔ **In-home care by an individual caregiver.** This nanny, housekeeper, sitter, friend, or relative either lives with your family or lives outside the home but arrives at your door according to schedule. You may prefer in-home care if you have a young child who you believe does better in the security of your home. Or you may find in-home care cheaper and less cumbersome if you have several children on different schedules.

Current labor laws expect you to pay social security and unemployment for employees in your home.

You can get together with another family who lives nearby and hire someone together. Your child is assured of a friend to play with, and sharing costs saves money.

✔ **Family day care in someone else's home.** Here, too, the caretaker could be a friend, family member, or friendly stranger. With this setup, you bring your child to a home that has been modified for small groups of children. Most family day-care providers take children with similar ages so that they play together and require a similar setup. Many states limit the number of kids to six for a single caretaker. The benefits of family care include a homey setting and opportunity for your child to play with a few other kids without being overwhelmed.

✔ **Child-care center with several groups of children, each supervised by different caretakers.** Child-care centers provide day care for less than 10 children to more than 100 kids. This type of care runs the gamut in terms of programs, because age spans range from infants to after-school middle-graders. Centers are either run as businesses or organize through government programs, religious institutions, community organizations, employers, or unions. Because of larger numbers of participants, child-care centers are more plentiful in bigger towns or cities.

These settings tend to be less homey and more school-like. If you work outside the home, however, centers provide the security of knowing someone always arrives to take care of your child. If the primary care-taker gets sick, others whom your child already knows can cover for your child's adult buddy. More staff, space, and toys offer a diverse learning environment, and your toddler/preschooler can advance into higher level classes as he matures.

Finding a smart match

Age, personality, and activity level give you clues about the type of day-care situation to select for your child. This section gives you some general guidelines, but you're the best judge of what feels good for you and your child. Trust your instincts.

For infants and subdued toddlers

Look for low caregiver-child ratios in individual or small group settings. Infants are totally dependent, so you want an arrangement where your child receives good care — including lots of physical contact — from a loving provider. Beyond care, however, you charge this person with engaging your child in stimulating activities that build those baby brain cells.

An older, shy child needs lots of attention from someone who understands how to pace interactions. This person actively involves your cautious or quiet child in new, sensory-rich activities, making sure he tries developmentally appropriate toys and equipment. A low-key program sticks to routine, so that transitions are easier for your toddler to handle.

For active toddlers and preschoolers

Your active child doesn't want to miss out on anything. Switching activities and transitions? No problem. Lots of kids jockeying for toys and attention? Bring them on. If your child behaves like this, try to find a larger group setting that offers lots of opportunities for exploring and meeting new challenges. Be sure to find a program that allows for imagination and bursts of enthusiasm, along with caretakers who welcome curiosity, endless questions, and tons of energy.

For school-age children

If you work outside the home, you may need to find somewhere safe for your school-age child to go after school. Don't expect shouts of joy from your child on this one. But if you can find a place that offers a change of pace, fun with other kids, or a place to veg-out before hitting the books at home, perhaps your child will go willingly.

The same range of in-home or institution-based programming is available for after-school day care. Many communities provide bussing from school to the local community center or a centralized school where kids stay happily busy. These programs allow flexibility and independence, so kids can choose their level of involvement in activities. Day care for older kids provides a place to rest, snack, and receive homework assistance.

Choosing safe and stimulating child care

Plan on visiting several day care places before making your decision. You can find alternatives:

- ✔ Through ChildCare Aware, a nonprofit national resource and referral program, 1-800-424-2246, www.ChildCareAware.org, or the National Association for the Education of Young Children.

- ✔ Through your local school district, community service or child and family agencies, hospital, or religious institution. Some keep lists of good places to begin your search.

- ✔ By placing an ad for in-home sitting in your local newspaper or hanging a note on the grocery, library, or community center billboard.

Day-care facilities vary in quality from one region to another. You may be shocked to discover how little government regulates facilities for children, a national scandal.

Government licensing

State or local governing bodies require licenses or certificates for larger child-care centers and home care providers who manage several children. But these qualifications vary. Most merely cover the basics: adult-child ratio, facility size, food handling, and health and safety. A few locales require minimal child-care training and proof of appropriate play materials, but you don't want to assume your area does.

Association accreditation

Some programs voluntarily apply for accreditation through the National Association for the Education of Young Children, National Association of Child Care Resource and Referral Agencies, or other professional organizations. These may touch on programming or caretaker training, but so far, standards are uneven.

Licensing and accreditation standards are a beginning. But they tell you nothing about the quality of program or staff qualifications. You'll have to do most of the detective work yourself.

Your own assessment: Going on a day-care hunt

Be assertive in your investigative search for day care. Plan questions you want to ask before visiting. You may want to create a checklist, so that you can easily record responses that can be reviewed and compared after completing all your visits.

Don't rely on your memory, especially if accompanied by an active toddler. You may find a lot of emotion clouding what you remember, particularly if day care your the first long separation from your child. Your ability to make an informed choice influences the quality of care your child receives and your peace of mind.

Think about asking questions that tell you about the child-care providers, physical setting, and program. Observe for yourself whether the children look happy and content with their surroundings. Then adapt the responses to the needs of your child.

Do caregivers seem:

- ✔ Warm and friendly?

- ✔ Happy to work with children?

- ✔ Calm and relaxed?

- ✔ Plentiful enough for the number and ages of children?

- ✔ Involved in activities with children? If you're choosing an infant program, does the provider spend time holding and talking to the babies?

- ✔ Positive about what their charges do? Do they talk with children about their experiences and keep language flowing and in an upbeat tone?

- ✔ Trained to handle different situations? Ask about policies for handling behavior transgressions, anger, when a child disobeys, accidents, and sick children.

- ✔ Knowledgeable about stages of child development and what children need for growth? Do they treat each child as an individual?

✔ Informed about providing thought-provoking and stimulating activities? What are their thoughts about watching television, videos, or computers?

✔ Accepting and respectful of your cultural and parenting values?

✔ Physically fit, with up-to-date TB and other vaccines?

✔ Experienced with children or is this the first child-related job? Ask for references and call them, especially if you're investigating home care. You may want to do a background check through local authorities.

Does the home or center have:

✔ A welcoming and cozy atmosphere?

✔ Current licensing, if your town requires one?

✔ An open visitation policy? You have a right to know what happens to your child at day care, and these folks should have nothing to hide. This is your child!

✔ Enough space indoors for kids to move about, crawl, and explore freely?

✔ Play areas, such as for housekeeping, arts and crafts tables, block corner, sand and water play, carpentry, small construction toys, and dress-up?

✔ Enough safe and repaired child-sized furniture, including cots, cribs, or mats for naps?

✔ Enough safe and repaired equipment and toys that are suitable for the children involved?

✔ Child-proofed environment, including caps for outlets, radiator covers, strong screens or bars on windows, gates at each end of stairways?

✔ Healthy meals and snacks, rather than sugary or fatty junk foods?

✔ Sanitary bathrooms and changing areas? Is there a toilet training policy?

✔ Enough light, ventilation, and heat or air conditioning?

✔ Safe outdoor play area with mats or bark under climbing equipment to cushion inevitable falls?

✔ Areas for individual quiet, active, and group play?

Does the program provide:

✔ Well-supervised indoor and outdoor play?

✔ Enough staff to carry out activities with the number of children involved?

✔ A set but flexible schedule that alternates between indoor and outdoor and quiet and active play? (See the "Typical day-care day" sidebar.)

✔ Enough breaks for food, rest, and toileting?

✔ Age-appropriate toys for a variety of activities that suit the ages involved?

- Objects and toys to develop infant senses

- Toys and equipment for toddler imagination play

✔ Opportunity to practice skills, such as fine and gross motor, listening, music, and books for school-age kids?

✔ Communication with home? This can be tricky. You don't want a care-taker buried in paperwork devising clever notes for home and not paying attention to your kid. But you want a quick way to share what's going on at home and day care, be it verbal or written.

Be brave. Finding day care isn't easy. If you want another expert opinion, take someone else along, like your kid. Watch how your child reacts. How do care-takers react to your child?

Trust your gut feelings. If you sense all is not right in Playville, grab your tot and run.

Typical day-care day

The following is a common day-care schedule that providers may follow. Even if your provider veers from this schedule, look for a balanced mix of the following rest and play activities:

7:00–9:00	Arrival; free play
9:00–9:30	Breakfast snack; cleanup; bathroom
9:30–10:00	Circle time; sharing; music; finger plays
10:00–11:00	Outdoor play; indoor learning centers; art projects
11:00–12:00	Story time; bathroom; cleanup
12:00–12:30	Lunch
12:30–2:30	Nap
2:30–3:00	Bathroom, snack
3:00–4:30	Table activity; free play; cleanup
4:30–5:30	Outdoor play
5:30–6:00	Quiet activities

Attending Pint-Size School: Preschool

Today, the value of early education is a given. Every resource you consult tells you how crucial early education is for healthy development — and smart kids. Early stimulation and interaction with others lays the foundation for big-kid school, the serious stuff.

You may take this to mean your child must go to preschool, or nursery school, or early childhood school, or whatever early education is called where you live. You buy into the principle that organized learning is the best learning, which is not always the case.

If you talk with your child, sing with him, draw with him, and read to him, chances are he receives the best preparation to meet the challenge of kindergarten. You're not preordaining your child to life at the bottom of the class because you choose to monitor his experiences at home in a loving and responsive atmosphere.

Still, preschool does offer benefits, especially if your child seems ready for broader experiences and has few opportunities to socialize with kids his own age.

Unfortunately, preschool has become serious business for too many parents who value a smart path for their youngsters. In some areas, getting into the so-called best preschools produces the same anxiety as getting into Harvard. Some of the logic (if you can call it that) is that your child must get into the right preschool because it feeds into the right primary school, the best high school, and the most prestigious college. That's too much to worry about when your child is only 3 years old.

Don't let these *preschool ivys,* as educator Jonathon Kozol calls them, play on your desire to be the best parent. Resist the temptation to become caught up in an anxious frenzy of preschool protocols. Many preschool ivys require parent interviews and child play interviews. After the involved process ends, your child receives an acceptance or rejection, just like for college. Competition is so stiff some parents hire preschool interview coaches for 2½ year olds, so that they perform better. That's insane.

- Two-and-a-half-year-olds are at least six months too young to benefit from structured preschool.

- The rat-race puts too much needless pressure on your child and your family.

Knowing what to expect

Preschool's supposed to be fun. Keep repeating this mantra. Preschool's supposed to pump up your child so that he can't wait to learn more. For a couple of hours each day or a couple days a week, your child learns the fine points of singing, storytelling, playing games, talking, listening, and getting along with playmates without biting, pinching, or pulling hair.

Preschools, like daycare, vary greatly in terms of quality, orientation, and cost. The National Association for the Education of Young Children accredits preschools. But applying is voluntary. Less than ten percent U.S. preschools go through the process. So, you're on your own.

How do you find good choices? Ask around. Other parents, local schools, colleges, and religious and community centers each may keep lists or sponsor a preschool themselves.

If you suspect any kind of learning problem or difference, contact your local school district to evaluate your child. By law, public schools must provide early childhood testing and programs for all children 3 or older. In some states, programs for children with special needs begin earlier.

Go back to the section about characteristics of good day care because most apply to preschools. In addition, remember that:

- ✔ **Higher price tags don't necessarily mean better programs, no matter what your snooty neighbor says.** Better to find a cheerful, nonjudgmental environment with a loving, experienced teacher who can give your child a variety of activities geared to his interests and abilities.

    If you're lucky enough to live near a college or university, contact the education department for a referral. Chances are, the college sponsors a preschool. Colleges and universities are your best bet for consistently high-quality programs with staff either well-trained or supervised by trained professionals. And cost is usually fairer than with preschool ivys.

- ✔ **Program philosophies vary as to experiences and how they are presented.** You'll run into the deep divide between structured intellectual environment folks on one side and the touchy-feely emotional proponents on the other.

    At one end of the spectrum, intellectual programs concentrate on language, beginning math, and programs designed to teach young children to read. No wasted time here. The program is tightly accounted for with minimum time for free play and activities like finger painting and Play-Doh.

Touchy-feely proponents view this type of structure as robbing children of their childhood. They encourage an extension of the play and exploration begun at home or day care. Their curriculum concentrates on building, climbing, manipulating, drawing, and music.

Kids need preschools somewhere in the middle. Emotional readiness is important to school. But young minds work like sponges, soaking up whatever they're offered — if they're ready. There's nothing wrong in incorporating counting, letters, and concepts into preschool games, songs, and creative activities, as long as children aren't pushed to stressful levels. If one child reads, that's great. If not, he has plenty of time to acquire the skill. Meanwhile, he's learning to feel good about himself and his first encounter with school.

No conclusive evidence exists to indicate that very young children who read are any smarter than those who do not. They're merely on a different timetable.

Preparing for the first day of school

The first day of preschool signals a big change for your youngster. A new setting, new people, great toys: oh my!

Even though preschool is a fantastic new adventure, your tot may harbor conflicting feelings. Sure it's exciting. But it also triggers fear of the unknown and anxieties about adjusting, which may apply in a day-care situation, too. The following are some ways to ease the transition:

✔ **Talk about feelings before the first day.** Watch for changes in behavior that mean something is bothering your child. Expect some regression in behavior or toilet training as your child gets used to the idea of going to school. Investigate underlying feelings behind the actions. Does your child:

- View school as a punishment because you send him away?

- Feel jealous because a younger sibling gets to stay home with you?

- Worry he won't know anyone?

- Worry because he won't know what to do, where to store his prized possessions, or what happens should he need you?

✔ **Talk about what to expect.** Read aloud books about the first day of school.

Order the free pamphlet "When Your Child Goes to School," by sending a self-addressed, stamped business envelope to Mr. Rogers' Neighborhood, 4802 Fifth Avenue, Pittsburgh, PA 15213. Besides important information for you, the pamphlet has a great read-aloud introduction to preschool for your child.

✔ **Discuss your first day of school.** Recall the fears, what calmed you, what happened, and how well it worked out. It did work out, didn't it?

✔ **Visit the preschool ahead of time together.** Meet the teacher. Ask the teacher to show your child around the room and talk about what the day may be like. Make sure your child knows where the bathroom is and where favorite play areas are — the important information.

✔ **Walk or ride up and back to school with your child to familiarize him with the route.** Even though he won't be traveling on his own, review of the trip adds to your child's comfort level.

✔ **Arrange a play date with a friend or two who may be going to the same preschool.** A new experience is much more fun, and less intimidating, with a friend.

✔ **Prepare to meet a friend before going into preschool the first day, so that your child doesn't feel so alone.** If you don't know anyone who's going, arrive a few minutes early and talk with another parent and child. Even a brief meeting helps your child get a leg-up on making new play pals.

✔ **Maintain familiar routines and settings at home.** Routines provide comfort when your child thinks his world may be in turmoil.

✔ **Get something special, a new backpack or big-boy shirt, for preschool.** Your making a big deal puts a positive spin on the experience.

✔ **Allow enough time before school each day for leisurely going through usual routines.** Rushing creates tension that no one needs.

✔ **Reassure your child that you will return.** Acknowledge your child's misgivings about staying without you, if they surface. But reaffirm your going and his staying.

✔ **Never linger too long before leaving.** Your child may pick up your hesitation and think he should be upset about separating, even when he's not.

Similarly, never sneak away from your child without saying good-bye. You don't want him to feel abandoned. If the teacher thinks he's too upset for you to leave, stay until he gets settled into an activity. But leave the judgment call about your staying to the teacher, who has experience with teary separations.

Most often, dramatics are for your benefit. Crocodile tears disappear after you go out the door.

✔ **Leave your child on a cheerful and positive note.** Tell your child, "I know you'll have a fun day," or "I'll say good-bye because I see you want to play with those blocks." These send more encouraging messages than a tentative "Be good," or "Try to have a good day."

Remember to talk about your child's time at preschool when he arrives home.

Chapter 10

Preparing for Big-Kid School

In This Chapter

▶ Identifying what schools mean by *readiness*

▶ Creating a school-ready kid

▶ Planning to be your child's best advocate

*P*repare yourself. You aren't the only force in your little one's life anymore. School years bring other adults into your child's world. In their teacher-like way, these adults set different rules than yours. Often, to your child's utter surprise, they expect your child to follow them. And then they lay out new challenges for your child that test the learning foundation you built at home.

At times, these new expectations feel like a slap in your smart parenting face. Someone other than you supervises your child now. For the first time, you may find your parenting called into question, such as when the teacher reports that your child's pinching other butts or hopping down the hall aren't as cute as you thought.

Brief yourself and your child about this new school gig. Review what to expect and how to act before your child steps on the school bus. This doesn't mean your child behaves perfectly from day one, because she's still very much a work-in-progress. But you can check out this chapter for ways to complement your child's formal education while keeping your finger on the pulse of learning that beats at home.

Positioning School As Number One

Send the message loud and clear early-on. From now on, your child's primary job is going to school. And during the school week, schooling will be the family's number one priority, within reason, of course.

Meanwhile, keep up the great work you've already begun. Keep teaching your child at home through family and everyday experiences. Build on your child's curiosity. Instill the love of learning, making learning so much fun that your child can't wait to go to school.

Studies show that academic success stories come from families who put a high price on the value of all learning, not just the high-tech or scientific stuff. And this holds true for every socioeconomic group.

Supporting school efforts beginning with kindergarten contributes to your child's success more than any other family quality. Your attitude and expectations about school make a gigantic difference in how your child adjusts and performs.

Building Readiness for School

Teachers vary in what they expect of incoming kindergarten students. Some emphasize students knowing how to take care of themselves. So your child better master the intricacies of toileting, putting on a coat, and behaving. Other kindergarten teachers believe kids should come to class knowing numbers and letters. How is a parent to know?

Call ahead to check what the school expects. Ask to talk with a kindergarten teacher, if this person is available and has time. Think of making your call a year or two in advance. You probably won't do anything different in the way you hug and play with your child, but the guidance may give you confidence that you're on the right path in preparing your child for kindergarten.

Children come to school with varying degrees of readiness, and so will your child. Most 5-year-olds aren't developmentally ready to sit at desks hours at a time to learn. Nor can they decode in a way that leads to instant reading. Don't let anyone tell you your child has a problem simply because she finds these areas difficult. If you, your child's teacher, and eventually your child fixate on these normal areas as weak spots, your child may start to dislike school. That's not exactly what you want to occur.

This section examines the range of skills and behaviors that encompass school readiness. The lists serve as guidelines to help you prepare your child for big-kid school. They're not meant to cause hysteria if your child doesn't perform this or that task. With time, your child will accomplish most of these items by practicing them naturally during school and during your regular family activities.

What you must know before kindergarten

The more informed you and your child are about new settings, the easier the transition will be. Start way in advance of kindergarten to find out:

✔ When to register for kindergarten

✔ Which forms need completion before school starts

✔ When to bring your child for early childhood screening

✔ Which immunizations are necessary for school entry

✔ How your child best prepares for kindergarten

✔ Who handles transportation and making arrangements

✔ What food service plans need to be made

✔ What the kindergarten program is like

✔ Who the principal is

✔ What the school calendar and daily schedule are

✔ When to bring your child to get acquainted with the new setting and teacher

Recognizing social skills that smart preschoolers need

Kindergarten teachers don't expect perfect behavior, which is a boon for 99.9 percent of families. But the more your child can get along with others and follow rules, the easier the transition to a more structured setting will be.

To learn these skills, expose your child early and often to similar-age buddies. Arrange for meeting other kids at the playground, in the neighborhood, on play dates, at day care, or at preschool. Encourage your child to acquire at least rudimentary knowledge of these 12 important social skills:

✔ Separating from you and home without getting bent out of shape

✔ Recognizing that different people and places have different rules

✔ Following rules at home and at other places

✔ Listening quietly and paying attention

✔ Playing and working as part of a group

✔ Understanding that others have feelings and rights

✔ Taking turns

✔ Respecting what belongs to someone else

✔ Sharing

✔ Controlling impulses, such as temper outbursts or hitting

✔ Delaying gratification, such as waiting for snack or outdoor time

✔ Liking or acting curious about new experiences and having the confidence to explore them

Taking care of personal business

By now, your child handles many of life's details independently. And more will come as she matures and continues through school. To better prepare for kindergarten, encourage your child to:

✔ **Manage basic eating routines by herself.** Bring on the chores here. Besides eating with a spoon and fork, give your child practice in pouring water into a glass, spreading peanut butter and jelly, carrying food and drinks without spilling, and cleaning up after herself. Here again, neither you nor a teacher expect perfection. But the opportunity to complete a task and take care of herself builds confidence and makes life much easier for you and the busy kindergarten teacher.

✔ **Master toileting and washing.** Give your child practice going to the bathroom in public places, so that the school bathroom won't intimidate her. Make sure your child knows the entire routine: taking down and pulling up clothes, wiping afterwards, flushing the toilet, and washing afterward. Add some urinal practice for your son.

✔ **Conquer the ins and outs of dressing.** Remember to practice zippers, buttons, and testy boots. The ability to tie shoe laces is great, but that skill may be difficult for little fingers now. If being unable to tie shoe laces bothers your child, find shoes with Velcro fasteners. And one-zip, one-piece clothing often simplifies the dressing process.

If you live in snowy territory, teach your youngster to place a plastic bag over each shoe before inserting it into a snug boot. The shoe slides in without all those pulls and tugs that drive kids and teachers crazy.

✔ **Know the basics about herself and her family.** Practice with your child to ensure she knows her full name, address, telephone number, age, gender, and body parts. Make sure she knows the names of family members and the fact that the dog isn't really a sibling, no matter how close they are. Some teachers lack a sense of humor.

Getting specific with academic readiness

So many rudimentary concepts go into learning the core subjects of reading, writing, math, and science that it's difficult to pinpoint them all. Check Table 10-1 for the basics. Then consider incorporating them into your general activities at home:

- **Keep communication flowing with your child.** Ask questions as you travel about. Point out words on signs and buildings. Make up stories together about what you see.

  Listen as your child talks about what you read together. Reinforce that reading is talking — just written down. Also discuss that letters make words, and words are what you're reading to make stories. Read lists of activities so that your child gets the idea that reading and writing are connected and practical for daily life.

- **Name, sort, and match as you finish chores together.** Same and different are important concepts for learning about letters and numbers. Think about sorting laundry, eating utensils, and toys as you put them away. Look for what's tall and short, big or little, and soft and hard.

- **Listen to music and sing songs together.** Besides your child's name and vital statistics, pair words for concepts you want your child to remember with common tunes. Music helps your child differentiate sounds in a fun way. Hearing different sounds is important for reading, spelling, and writing letters and words.

- **Count items as you use them.** Use blocks, chips, cards, clothing, toys, or whatever is part of your day. Show that math has a purpose.

- **Give your child a regular allowance.** Name the coins and count them. Point out price tags on items that indicate cost. Instill the idea of saving to buy something special.

- **Play games that involve numbers and letters.** Inexpensive bingo (lotto), CandyLand, junior Scrabble, and memory games emphasize matching colors, pictures, numbers, and letters. And they're good family fun, too.

- **Keep a supply of paper, glue, paste, scissors, crayons, and paints.** Make collages from torn paper, old magazines, or different foods and spices from your pantry.

- **Remember that dramatic play isn't just for fun and enrichment.** Acting out life and imaginary tales contributes to literacy skills in young children in ways paper and pencil book learning do not.

Readiness involves every aspect of development. In the olden days, the skills in Table 10-1 were lumped under the single heading called *reading readiness*.

That's because reading is the soul of education. Today, you find teachers invoking that term or talking about general readiness for school.

Table 10-1	The Scoop on Readiness Skills	
Reading	*Fine and Large Motor*	*Math/Science*
Knows what letters are	Draws, scribbles with crayons	Counts from 1 to 10
Names alphabet	Buttons, snaps, zips	Counts some objects
Recognizes name	Assembles easy puzzles	Matches by color, shape, size
Identifies colors	Cuts with rounded scissors	Names basic shapes
Recounts stories	Laces, strings beads	Sorts by color, shape, size
Identifies rhymes	Copies simple shapes, letters	Knows money buys things
Asks questions	Pedals a tricycle	Knows position concepts (up, down, under, over)
Makes up stories	Hops on one foot briefly	Knows quality concepts (hot, cold, hard, soft)
Follows three-step directions	Alternates feet on stairs	Grasps idea of time (night, day, today, tomorrow, now, later)
Names common animals	Pastes, models clay	Appreciates nature
Enjoys stories and books	Throws, catches, kicks a ball	Knows full and empty

Teaching street smarts

You aren't always going to be with your child anymore. Time to build on the smart safety basics introduced in Chapter 8.

> ✔ **Teach your child that danger comes in all kinds of people.** Saying "never talk with strangers" isn't practical because your child may need

to get help or ask directions from an unfamiliar person. And not all predators look scruffy or weird. Role play what situations may feel uncomfortable and how to get out of them. For example, if a car honks and stops nearby your child, and then someone walks toward her quickly, she needs to take off and find another adult.

Make sure your child understands that certain situations can bring trouble, rather than people.

✔ **Develop a catchy way of reinforcing stranger danger,** similar to the fire safety "stop, drop, and roll." One suggestion is "yell, run, and tell." Ask the school if they address dangerous situations with such phrases for kids, or if the local police or sheriff's office sends trainers to schools. Coordinate your teaching efforts and reinforce what the pros say.

All kids need a mental plan. Reinforce actions, not fears.

✔ **Review after-school rules with your child.** Tell your child you always want to know where she is. Discuss where she can go and how you want to be notified. Emphasize that changes in routine must be cleared before they occur, so that you can okay who your child goes with and where.

✔ **Discuss different ways to say "no."** Role play situations when being firm can be life-saving, such as when a creepy neighbor invites your child into the house or a motorist beckons your child close to the car to ask directions or see a pet. Instruct your child to always stay beyond arm's length when talking to unfamiliar adults on the street, and to scream, scratch, bite, kick, and run like heck if someone reaches for her.

✔ **Establish a family code word** for times when a trusted friend picks up your child, should you be unable to come.

✔ **Review information about preparing for the first day of school in Chapter 9.** Most of the first-day-of-school suggestions apply to kindergarten.

✔ **Talk about what to do if you and your child become separated.** Your first choice is that your child stays within eye-sight of you. But if laying down the law fails, point out a realistic meeting place.

✔ **Prepare your child for who is a safer bet to approach if lost.** A low-risk adult is someone in a store who wears a uniform and name badge and is behind a counter. Otherwise, look for a woman. This is the only place I get sexist in this book. The reason is because women are statistically safer bets than men, when looking at child-abduction cases.

Practice dialing 911 or 0, which is free on a pay phone, and looking for phones in stores and malls.

✔ **Get your child in the habit of traveling with a buddy.** Arrange for her to go and come with someone from school and for after-school activities.

You may need to think about preparing your child for being alone after school, too. As with any safety advice, the best training is prevention. Smart kids who come home to an empty house and stay alone need to know the following.

✔ **Teach telephone etiquette.** Your child of any age at any time should never say you're out and she is alone. Train your child to say, "My mom/dad is busy." As your child ages, you can direct her to ask for the caller's name and number, and to say she/he will call you back soon.

✔ **Train your child to never let people in the house or open the door when you're not home.** Role play what to do and say should someone ring the bell. Similar to telephone awareness, train your child to say, "My mom/dad is busy now and can't come to the door. Leave a note about what you want in the mailbox, and he/she will get back to you."

A good-sized dog keeps kids company and provides some protection.

✔ **Check in when they arrive home.** Make calling you or your spouse a hard and fast rule. Be sure your child knows to come home unless an excursion elsewhere has been cleared with you beforehand.

✔ **Establish and maintain a routine.** Kids feel safer, more in control, and less lonesome if they know how to keep busy. An agreed-upon routine helps your child know exactly what she can and cannot do. Her routine may include calling you, getting an after-school snack, doing homework, or some other routine you establish.

Leave a choice of snacks that don't require cooking or other intricate preparation, so that your child isn't using sharp knives or a hot oven. For more on how to keep kids safe in the kitchen, check out *Cooking with Kids For Dummies* by Kate Heyhoe (Wiley Publishing, Inc.).

✔ **Understand basic first aid and when to call for more help.** Keep a first-aid kit handy. Show your child each item, identifying how and when to use it. Then review emergency numbers or which neighbor to run to, should an emergency happen. If your child doesn't leave your sight after school, save the first-aid kit for a couple years later. But at a young age, begin encouraging an emergency plan for when you step out briefly.

Assigning chores that build smarts

Time to delegate a few regular chores that match your child's abilities. By assigning chores early, you teach your child that working together is a natural a part of belonging to your family. Everyone contributes, and your child should, too.

As you increase responsibilities for your child, she gains competence and a sense of discipline. She takes pride in a job well done. She learns how to be responsible, dependable, and thorough, and she acquires much-needed skills for eventually taking care of herself. These attributes build character. And they carry over into schoolwork and relationships.

Recognizing the value of pets

I know that pets aren't for every household, but nothing keeps a child who is home alone company and instills responsibility better than owning a pet. Even a fish brings joy, although not as much as something you can hold and dress up in doll clothes. Pets bring the pride of ownership, regular feeding and cleaning, caring for another living creature, and as an added bonus, fewer allergies and greater resistance to disease.

Best of all, though, you'll probably notice that after a pet joins your family, your child becomes more compassionate, caring, and able to follow through with routines. And who provides much-needed solace better than a cat to cuddle with or a dog to lick wounds, both physical and psychological? Taking care of a pet gives your child the confidence and structure that translates into participating in school activities.

Pets are cheaper than therapy.

Getting a Leg-up: Kindergarten Retention

For quite a few years now, trendy teachers and anxious parents have advocated keeping kindergarten-age kids back so that she goes to first grade a year older than she would otherwise. *Kindergarten retention,* as the policy is called, is different from academic retention of older students discussed in Chapter 14. With kindergarten retention, or *red-shirting,* either you start your child later than your district allows or keep your child in kindergarten a second year. The extra time buys your child some development time to prepare her for the competitive school world.

Some districts open separate classrooms, called *developmental classes,* as transition placement, instead of asking kids to repeat kindergarten or start later. Developmental classes provide a place for kids who need to spruce up their readiness skills either before kindergarten or after. But the end result is the same: another year of school tacked onto the elementary years.

You may mean well, if you're considering holding your 5- to 6-year-old back. Your child receives an extra year to mature. And because she's one of the older kids the next year, she rises to the top of her class, thereby getting a leg-up on this high-achievement insanity. Sounds logical, but the system lacks credibility.

Being alert to harmful trends

The fad has gotten so out of hand that your child's kindergarten teacher may request to keep back your darling merely because her birth date falls within the second half of the school year, making her one of the youngest kids in class, which I guess isn't supposed to be good. The weird point about this reasoning is there will always be someone who's youngest, right?

The request for retention may also derive from the teacher's falsely deeming your child unprepared to progress and in need of extra time to catch up. Similarly, you may think staying in preschool gives your child extra time to develop better learning readiness skills, which will help her shine in kindergarten. But you already know that kids progress at different rates. Who knows what your child will be like next year?

Be forewarned. None of the preceding assumptions hold true, not with researchers, not with educators in the know, and, most importantly, not with kids who've traveled the retention road. Findings show that:

✔ **Kindergarten retention makes no lasting difference in improving skills.** Even in studies that claim some readiness skill gains in children, long-term results find the gains disappear into the next grade. Eventually, kids who've been held back and kids who haven't score the same on standardized tests.

✔ **Kindergarten retention cannot alleviate specific learning difficulties.** Only individualized instruction that suits your child's needs can ease or correct disabilities.

✔ **Kindergarten retention plays havoc on a child's self-concept.** Kids know when they are the oldest, and possibly biggest, in class. For years afterward, they feel funny about needing an extra year, wherever they spend it. For some kids, the stress of seeing their buddies move into another grade affects their behavior and attitude toward school, which you don't want to encourage at this tender age. Kids find enough issues with school to grouse about later. No need to encourage negatives now.

Bucking trends

Better to seek out other alternatives, if you find your child has some grow-ing up to do. Instead of holding your child back, try to find settings that emphasize:

- **Individualized instruction:** Teachers who believe in looking at each child's strengths tailor activities to meet individual student needs, no matter how uneven they may be.

- **All-day kindergarten:** A longer day gives your child extra time in class without adding another year to elementary school.

- **Mixed ages and skills:** Classes that aren't supposed to have all students at the same level usually offer more opportunities for kids to mature at their own rates.

- **Smaller class sizes:** Reduced class size gives teachers more time for individualized instruction.

- **Your involvement:** Your working with the school gives you the tools to help your child gain the needed classroom skills. You can give your child assistance in class and refocus some of your home time with your child to practice school work and behavior.

A wise kindergarten teacher offered a good way to judge whether repeating kindergarten benefits your child. If playing rather than conforming is your child's thing, perhaps she is immature enough to not mind another year in a less-structured setting. In other words, if your child won't notice staying behind, consider the option. Otherwise, buck the system and move her along. She'll probably do just fine.

Advocating for Your Child

The principal at my daughter's school told me, "Always be your child's advo-cate." I take his words to heart, and you should, too. As far as my daughter and I are concerned, no system is too big for momma bear to take on when it involves her cub. And that includes the schools.

When raising a smart child, you need to be on the front lines. Unlike preschool or day care, you usually don't get your choice of setting unless you go the private route. Even then, you can't choose your child's teacher or class. You have to make an effort to keep on top of your child's education.

Schools may try to keep you at arms length baking cookies and collecting lunch money. Administrators may tell you to leave book-learning to professionals. But it doesn't take a Ph.D. in education to assess whether the school is doing a good job with your child.

You're your child's most qualified advocate. You understand your child's strengths and weaknesses. You maintain the greatest investment in your child's success. And you hold the power to influence your child's future. To advocate for your smart kid:

- **Stay informed.** Keep up with your child's life and the people who work and play with her. Learn about lessons and teaching methods used in your child's classroom. Understand education jargon, so that you overcome intimidation from professionals who assume their titles grant them the right to make decisions about your child. And know the enemy, in case your child hangs out with the most troubled and troublesome kid in class — from your perspective, of course.

- **Ask questions,** especially if the school isn't serving your child's needs. Work with the teacher to change approaches that aren't effective with your child. Talk with administrators, should your child's teacher be unresponsive.

- **Trust your judgment.** You don't have to be an educator to determine whether your child is learning. Challenge ideas and strategies you believe run counter to your child achieving a good education.

- **Understand that you always have options.** Work within the school community first. But if improvement never comes, weigh other alternatives, such as those mentioned in Chapter 16.

Part III
The Eager-to-Learn Years:

The 5th Wave
By Rich Tennant

"I don't mean to hinder your quest for knowledge, however it's not generally a good idea to try and download the entire Internet."

In this part . . .

*T*hought your work would be through as soon as your child entered school? Guess again. As with each important stage your child experiences, your job is only beginning.

This part takes you on a romp through your child's elementary school years. Along the way, you examine how to produce offspring who are smart in and out of school. In this part, you get tips for evaluating school readiness, ways to enhance learning at home, ideas for using media wisely, and techniques for improving time for homework.

Chapter 11

Nurturing Your Smart Student at Home

*Y*our child has officially launched into elementary school, sailing from one grade to another. Before you can say, "I hate bake sales," the years whiz by. Each transition brings exhilaration, frustration, and maybe a few tears — possibly yours. This chapter helps you make the most of the school years while keeping the thrill of learning alive for your child after hours of studying, dioramas, and toothpick constructions.

Becoming Too Intense about Smartness

One distraught student refused to believe that no one would care what she received on a second-grade math test after she had moved on to college. In her mind, at that moment, the math test was a future-breaker.

If your child reacts like this, make sure that you counsel him to get a grip. School success is more than top grades on math tests, book reports, and timelines. True success is about developing a lifelong hunger for learning and enjoying the socialization a classroom brings.

Now, I'm not naïve enough to say that grades don't count, because you know that they do. But try to offer your child a more balanced perspective during activities you do together at home:

- ✔ **Connect learning at home to school, but don't make it schoolwork.** Your child needs different ways to say, "I can do it!" that may eventually help with class work.

- ✔ **Keep family learning activities simple.** Read the hints for organizing learning in Chapter 3. They really work.

- ✔ **Plan activities so that everyone can succeed, including yourself.** You may suggest activities that center around a theme, such as animals or food groups, or that capitalize on the approaching holidays. Don't pack in more than your time, budget, and innate teaching skills can handle.

  Not everyone is a born teacher, so don't force that role, if being teacher isn't a comfortable fit. Being an attentive and loving parent who's a naturally good person is more than enough.

- ✔ **Build on your child's interests and talents.**

Exercising Your Child's Brain

To be honest, I'm a little worried about this section. On one hand, I know you want fun ideas to do with your child that contribute to school learning. On the other, I worry that you'll take these suggestions as a green light to constantly work on the *academic* part of raising your smart kid.

Even worse, I worry about you and your child getting a bad case of the *overs:* over-programming, over-extending, and generally over-doing. When your family gets like this, you feel the need to constantly produce. You must achieve something with whatever you do, or you feel guilty or that the time is wasted.

Therefore, I give you permission to skip this section. Take a break from arranging learning activities. Move on to the next section or until your overs blow over.

But if you feel that you can handle tailoring your family time to specific school subjects without going overboard, check out the following activities.

Reading together

The more your child reads, the easier reading becomes. Continue to read aloud together, even after your child learns to read independently.

Don't give up just because your child claims you're the last parent on the planet to read aloud to their older school-age kid. Trust me, you're not. At our house, read-alouds went through junior high, and some families report reading together well into teenage years and at all-adult gatherings.

Deep down, your child likes read-aloud time together. After all, the setting provides uninterrupted cuddle time with you but without your harping on homework or undone chores.

If your child absolutely refuses to be read to, schedule a regular session when everyone reads independently. Your child sees you read. This vision of bliss makes him more likely to become a reader, if not now, then later, when you're not watching.

Keep the attitude about reading light. Reinforce that reading is fun as well as practical. Never pound your child over the head with how good it is or what a great learning experience it is for him, which is a definite turnoff.

Finding tricks for reading together

Think about proposing the following ideas to cultivate a reading environment at home:

- **Make reading books so special that your child clamors for more.** Give new books as rewards. Take surprise trips to the bookstore for a rainy-day outing.

- **Suggest that your fidgeter do something while listening.** For example, your child may sit better if he doodles or scribbles as you read aloud. Or he may prefer hugging a favorite stuffed buddy or the dog, who may also like to hear a good story. After all, this isn't school. The idea is to enjoy the story.

- **Take some audio books out of the library.** Listen to the story together, at home or in the car. Your child can follow along and turn the pages. Offer a flashlight to use as a cursor or a ruler to help focus on following the words.

  Find a book on tape that the entire family can enjoy and listen to in the car on your next trip. You'd be surprised how calming the experience can be. Plus, you hear a great story. Your librarian can suggest a few good ones for the whole family.

- **Take turns reading a story into a tape recorder.** What fun to listen to yourselves later! And your taped voice can reassure your child when you leave and the babysitter arrives.

✔ **Suggest that your child keep a reading journal.** A diary or journal is a great way to remember names of books, authors, and something about the story, such as whether your child liked it.

Watch patterns emerge. Track how interests change. Even in early grades, your child will identify favorite authors and types of stories. Applaud the list as it grows. Make sure to save the journal as a keepsake.

✔ **Give your child a shelf or bookcase to store books safely.** He's out of the gnawing-books stage by now, or at least he should be. So teach him to show a little respect for these important printed possessions.

Put library books in a special bag or in a designated corner on a shelf, so that they don't get misplaced or mixed up with household books.

✔ **Read books your child reads, so that you can discuss them.** Another idea is to choose a book for the entire family to read. Then talk about it. For casual discussion starters, ask:

- What did you like or dislike about the book?

- Who was your favorite character? Least favorite? Why?

- What was your favorite/tensest/happiest/saddest part of the story?

- Why do you think the ending did or didn't work?

- When and where did the story take place? How could you tell?

✔ **Involve your child when you read aloud.** Ask him to point to different characters or actions in the pictures, guess what may happen next, summarize what just happened, or identify the main character's thoughts or emotions about what just occurred. But don't make this exercise like school!

✔ **Think about reading longer, more difficult books aloud as your child's attention span lengthens.** Reading a chapter a night in a long book builds excitement for more. Books like the *Harry Potter* series, the *Redwall* series, *Matilda,* and *Charlotte's Web* hold young kids' attention even without pictures and with difficult words. And they're fun for the entire family to hear.

Your child will understand more than he can read or write. So you're really expanding his language base and ideas about sentence structure by reading books that are understandable but above his reading level.

✔ **Allow your child to choose books that you think are too hard or too easy for him, if he's interested in them.** Showing off with an easy book builds confidence. And an intense interest in something, such as railroads, bugs, or soccer, overcomes a few difficult words.

If you find your child really struggling, suggest another trip to the library for alternative books or make your child's selection a family read-aloud.

✔ **Encourage your child to participate in library and bookstore programs.** Both probably schedule author/illustrator presentations and birthday parties, book-character parties, book-reading competitions, and book clubs based on particular interests.

Don't push. Some kids gravitate to anything with books. Others prefer to keep their reading private or want to keep rereading what they find interesting and comforting. Or they find group reading uncool. Your child's not agreeing with your reading choices and activities is okay, as long as he reads something, somewhere.

✔ **Keep up with what the school requires your child to read.** Look at your child's reading assignments. Evaluate them. Discuss them together. Find out what your child likes and dislikes about these must-reads. Based on these discussions, suggest stories and books you think your child may like on a similar subject.

Never say "Read this" and expect your child to jump for joy at the prospect. Give your child a reason to read your suggestion. The best reason is you knowing your kid's interest in the article's or book's subject. Be your child's filter to review what's appropriate, fun to read, and good literature.

Deciding what's good literature

Sure, learning to read is important. But so is what your child reads.

How do you know what's good children's literature? Chapter 7 suggests what to look for in books for younger readers and Chapter 21 gives you a head start list of book and magazine suggestions. But you'll want to make your own choices at some point. Here are some questions to ask yourself when evaluating books for your older reader:

✔ **Is this book interesting to me?** Good kiddie lit grabs a reader of any age. It has a dynamic story, rich language, and appealing characters. You identify with the main character's problems. You want the *Runaway Bunny* to be found and Nancy Drew to save the day.

✔ **Does this book have staying power?** Good kid's stories bear repeating — again and again without you or your child getting bored. And the stories stay around for years, sometimes generations. When you find a book you read as a child and want to share with your offspring, you've discovered a classic, a keeper.

✔ **Will my child come away with an important message from this book?**
Will he discover what telling the truth means from reading about
Pinocchio or the value of curiosity in *Alice in Wonderland?* Will he
learn to be true to himself?

Watch out for preachy tales that talk down to readers. All kids are smart
enough to pick up that annoying adult voice in their books. Subtle messages that spring from the main character are much more palatable.

✔ **Does this book or article expand my child's natural interests?** Keep
looking for a hook that will lure your child into reading. Your athlete may
want to read articles about "the acoustics of baseball," or "the science of
super-soakers." Your artist may want to read how to create a certain
visual effect or a biography of a favorite painter. Even recipes and
instructions count as reading.

Buy a book at those greedy museum gift shops to reinforce the fascinat-
ing exhibit your child just saw. Or go to the library to find out more about
the topic. Connecting what your child experiences with what he reads
gives the experience authenticity and makes the information come alive.

Encourage nonfiction as well as fiction reading. Kids like to read about
what they do and are interested in. Most adults, teachers, and parents
think of novels and fiction when they think of curling up with a good
book. Yet, these same people probably devour newspapers, magazines,
and how-to books. Go figure!

Writing for the fun of it

How do you boost writing skills, chase away writer's block, and develop a
love of playing with words? By writing, of course. Similar to reading, the more
your child puts letters and words together in sentences that make sense, the
easier writing becomes. Help the process along by suggesting that your child:

✔ **Keep a journal.** If your child can't write yet, take dictation. Your writing
reinforces that idea that writing is talk written down, a simple but often
overlooked concept that makes writing less scary. Preserve the stories
in a notebook with a binding, so that pages don't fly around.

After your child writes independently, invest in a journal or diary with a
lock. Never allow anyone in the house to read it without permission and
never ask to yourself. Journals give your child a private place to record
ideas, feelings, and whatever springs to mind about the day's events.
Equally important, journal writing keeps the flow of words coming.
What's important is that your child writes every day.

✔ **Create a book.** Fold papers and tape or staple them into a book. You can also fix pages together inexpensively on a plastic binding machine at an office supply or teacher store. Or, if you want a more polished look, buy prepared books with blank pages. Either way, your child does the work of writing the story and drawing pictures.

Shower the finished product with accolades. After all, your kid's a real author now!

✔ **Write thank-you notes, which are becoming a lost art.** Your child practices formal letter writing, and your friends and family learn you're not raising an ungrateful Neanderthal.

✔ **Pound on the old typewriter gathering dust in your attic.** Move it to a central location, and let your child hammer away. Some authors like the feel of writing with clicking keys that a typewriter offers.

✔ **Report in the family newspaper.** The entire family plays reporter, writing short articles and illustrating the stories. Running accounts can be easily put into the computer and e-mailed or printed for distribution, say to grandparents or out-of-town aunts and uncles.

✔ **Turn dramatic play and dress-up into written-down plays.** This reinforces the idea that writing involves spoken words written down.

✔ **Encourage letter writing to friends and out-of-town family.** I know the computer saves time and energy. But e-mail rules never contribute to good writing, spelling, and grammar. Once in a while, coax your child into sharpening writing skills by sending a hand-written paper and pencil note in an addressed envelope by snail-mail.

✔ **Send letters to the editors of local papers and to special interest groups.** Encourage your child to write when something concerns him or when he has a question. Explain the power of the written word. Does your child disapprove of the new earlier school opening hours? Does he want healthier desserts in the cafeteria? Your child has a right to express opinions. All the better to put them in writing and, potentially, see them in print.

✔ **Emphasize that writing is practical.** Have your child write the grocery list while you dictate. Practice writing with name tags, invitations, labels, and place cards. Everything counts in the writing game.

✔ **Play word games, such as Scrabble, Perquacky, or spelling bees.**

✔ **Participate in free-writing family time.** Sometimes, your child finds that writing whatever he wants can be fun: no grades, no school topic, and definitely no correcting. Keep comments about your child's spelling and grammar errors for schoolwork. Creativity and flow of words are what's important here.

Coaxing the writing muse

Your child may need some ideas to stimulate creative juices. Writing may begin with responses to:

- ✔ "What if . . . (my sister turned into an alien? I collected 1 million bottle caps? the cake I made oozed from the oven? I opened a lemonade stand along the bicycle path?)

- ✔ "One gray and rainy day . . . (a talking toad jumped into my lunch box; lightening opened a secret stairway into the ground; the lights went out)

- ✔ "The wacky animals I met . . . (the orangutan that does needlepoint; the porcupine that jumps rope; the talking coyote)

- ✔ "I couldn't believe my eyes . . . (when dad turned into a gorilla; when my sister's tongue got stuck to the railing; when my dog ran away to join the circus)

You may hear, "I don't know what to write." Perhaps you feel that way yourself. Do your child and yourself a gigantic favor by reinforcing that anything, yes anything, can be the subject of a story. Talk about current events, friends, what happened that day, sibling battles, a favorite article of clothing, or the fact that the dog steals your slippers each night. If that doesn't work, use some suggestions from the "Coaxing the writing muse" sidebar.

If brainstorming ideas doesn't work, find a copy of *A Writer's Notebook: Unlocking the Writer within You* by Ralph Fletcher (Avon) for your child. The text is chatty, easy-to-read, and packed with ideas to spark writing creativity. If your child wants to investigate more about the craft of writing, point him to www.smartwriters.com online for a ton of Web sites, chat rooms, publications about writing, and contests to win with those polished pieces.

Managing math wizards

You say you're math phobic and that you'd best to leave this subject to the pro? Think again. Math is part of life. The sooner your child gets comfy with numbers, the easier life will be. Bring math into your home.

Number-crunchers consider mathematics the epitome of smarts, the path to higher education. These folks truly believe math is a great learning adventure. Grade-school math lays the groundwork for high school math courses and a wide range of college majors.

- ✔ More jobs depend on math than ever before.

- ✔ Life depends upon math. Try calculating discounts at a sale without it.

✔ Western culture quantifies everything: problems and solutions, trends, and explorations that tackle the shape of a snowflake and DNA decoding.

In other words, math is here to stay. Even if you're math-challenged, your child needs to feel more comfortable with numbers and number concepts. So make math relevant at home, and make it fun. You don't want to raise a math-phobic kid.

One source of direction for you is the book *Family Math* by Jean Stenmark and her number-savant friends at the University of California in Berkeley (Family Math Program, `equals@ucling.berkeley.edu`, 510-642-1823). The book covers over 300 pages of math activities to do at home.

If buying yet another book seems a bit intense, try some of these family-friendly math ideas to fortify your child's math comfort zone:

✔ **Perform a house audit.** You may be surprised the math concepts that help you run the house. Involve your child in figuring out how to:

- Double or divide recipes (fractions); apportion tablespoons, ounces, cups, pints, gallons, or liter equivalents; under- or over-baking (measurements)

- Evaluate how much groceries cost (addition)

- Calculate discounts from newspaper ads (percentages)

- Find out if you gave the correct allowance (money sense)

- Count days until a birthday; in fact, count everything as you use it (counting, addition)

- Mark the wall for height and weight, if you're brave (measurements)

- Note different times of day (telling time)

- Estimate what part of the cake you each ate (fractions)

- Set the table, adding how many plates to put out or how many spoons to take away (matching, addition, subtraction)

- Prepare lunch or a snack, counting and measuring each ingredient; calculate what percentage one bite is or the fraction of a sandwich the dog stole (measurement, fractions, percentages)

- Investigate numbers in newspapers: sports statistics (batting averages, team scores, leading teams); following an easily identifiable stock, such as Wendy's or Nike, on the stock market (percentages, decimals)

- Measure the cat's food; decide how many servings before you need to buy more (measurement, multiplication)

✔ **Talk about how math helps you work.** Show your child how you balance a checkbook. Point out computer spreadsheets or how you calculate enlarging or reducing photos.

✔ **Keep suggestions for your child's math concrete and visual.** Your child will understand math applications much easier if he visualizes fractions by folding napkins into equal parts or masters multiplication by sorting raisins into equal piles and adding/multiplying the piles.

✔ **Find math concepts on the road.**

- Count cars. Count cars of different colors. Add up totals. Calculate percentages of each color compared with the total.

- Figure the miles to your next destination and how long it will take. Your days of, "When will we get there?" are over.

- Play adding, multiplying, subtracting, and dividing games with license plate numbers. Identify numbers on a plate, pose a problem, and have your child locate another plate with numbers that solve the problem.

✔ **Play games that involve numbers.** Try Dominoes, Monopoly, hopscotch, bingo, lotto, card games (remember crazy eights, go fish, rummy, canasta, bridge, pinochle, poker), darts, bowling, or any game that requires points and keeping score.

✔ **Suggest that your child check out** www.coolmath.com. The Web site for kids ages 13 to 100 has fun math activities and games for the whole family.

Math avoidance is one characteristic of yours you never want your smart kid to model.

Thinking like a scientist

To be well-rounded, your child needs a solid grounding in science, regardless of his eventual choice of occupation. To encourage scientific inquiry:

✔ **Observe together.** Notice leaves falling, the brightest star, the difference in growth between your two tomato plants. Suggest that your child keep a log of interesting observations, either in writing or drawings.

✔ **Encourage collections.** Your child can compare and contrast the items or investigate other information, such as origins, of each. Anything goes for collections, whether they include rocks, shells (wash smelly ones), leaves, erasers, or sponges.

REMEMBER

✔ **Ask questions together.** Why is the sky blue? What makes fireflies light up? Why do two magnets repel each other? Give your child a notebook to fill with burning questions. Discuss possible answers. Test hypotheses by visiting a museum or researching online or in books at the library.

Get in the habit of seeking answers to questions as they arise to keep the investigative spirit alive.

✔ **Experiment together.** Experiments create a hint of magic. They're hands-on, which often scares parents. They become great learning experiences without the tedium of memorizing. With experience, your mad scientist takes a question, plans an investigation to find the answer, and analyzes what happens, just like grown-up scientists do.

Simple science supplies

Most of what a budding scientist needs is inborn: some creativity, the ability to observe surroundings, and a ton of inquisitiveness. The rest you can supply. Keep a storehouse of the following supplies:

✔ Alcohol

✔ Baking soda

✔ Balance scale

✔ Batteries

✔ Binoculars

✔ Bottles, beakers, jars

✔ Bug box and net

✔ Carbonated water

✔ Compass

✔ Containers of various sizes

✔ Cotton balls

✔ Eyedroppers

✔ Flashlight

✔ Fruit/vegetable seeds

✔ Insulated wires

✔ Magnets

✔ Magnifying glass

✔ Measuring utensils

✔ Microscope

✔ Mirror

✔ Paper pads and pencils

✔ Petri dish

✔ Ph paper

✔ Prism

✔ Spoons

✔ Stopwatch

✔ Thermometer

✔ Tweezers

Need more science stuff? Buy supplies at hobby shops, hardware stores, or specialty shops, such as rock shops or electronics stores. Order math and science items from American Science and Surplus (1-847-647-0011), or Carolina Biological Supply Company (1-800-334-5551).

Check out of the library fun children's books with simple experiments, such as *Science Experiments You Can Eat* by Vicki Cobb (HarperTrophy). Acquire a chemistry set, telescope, microscope, or magic kit, if that's your kid's thing. Or get creative juices flowing with these home-grown experiments:

- Identify which of two or three foods your dog prefers. Does he naturally choose nutritious or junk food?

- Watch bacteria grow. Tell your child to wash hands and make a fingerprint on a petri dish. Have him pet the dog or toys or other objects and do the same thing. Put the dishes in a warm place, and in time gross stuff appears.

- Collect a water sample from a lake, stream, or river to look at under the microscope.

- Use a magnifying glass to see fingerprints. Press fingers on a dark surface. Then sprinkle them with talc powder to make the prints show up.

- Plant lima beans in a glass container. See how they split and sprout in two directions. Plant other seeds in a garden.

- Find a cocoon, keep it safe, and watch the beautiful moth appear.

- View a drop of blood, hair, or various home products under the microscope, and talk about what your child sees.

Exploring history and geography from home

History and geography provide valuable information to your child about who he is and where he comes from. Through history your child learns what good citizenship means. You can help your child identify places and events that are key to your family, community, and the world through some of the following activities.

Going places

Travel is exciting. Kick-start your child's sense of adventure with the following:

- **Buy map puzzles and placemats with the world and United States.** Identify countries and the different states.

- **Draw a map of your child's room.** Have him locate furniture and treasures by filling in the map.

✔ **Own an atlas and globe.** Young kids like inflatable globes to toss around. Reach for these geography tools whenever you talk about going somewhere.

✔ **Spice up car travel by assigning your child the navigator job, complete with maps.** Play car bingo, which involves spotting specific signs and landmarks along the way.

✔ **Hang maps and pictures of exciting places on walls.** Stick tacks to identify the family travels.

✔ **Investigate other cultures.** Eat at ethnic restaurants. Prepare various ethnic foods at home. Start a foreign coin and stamp collection. Experience music and art from different lands. Find your child a pen pal from another country. (See the "Encouraging foreign-language study" section.)

Don't forget the myriad books, magazines, computer games, and Web sites that provide history and geography fun.

Going back in time

Kids like to think life forms didn't exist before them, except for dinosaurs (and, of course, kids' own dinosaur-like parents). Give your child some idea of what life was like before their memory kicked in by following these guidelines.

✔ **Pay attention to relatives.**

- Prepare a family tree and timeline. Give your child a sense of family history by talking about each generation. Explore what life may have been like for these people. Compare clothes, hobbies, work, or anything that interests your child today.

- Investigate places where family members grew up. Compare these settings with your home and community.

- Look at old family photos, letters, and treasures.

- Encourage your child to be a history detective. Have him ask older relatives about what life was like for them.

✔ **Pay attention to your neighborhood.** Life wasn't always the same where you live. Explore the origins of specific blocks, buildings, or monuments. Go to the local library, town hall, or historical museum. Help your child get a sense of history by observing that neighborhoods aren't always what they seem.

✔ **Pay attention to special events.** Celebrate birthdays and holidays by filling a time capsule. Hide a box or jar filled with treasures. Include some photos, newspaper headlines, a letter about the day that includes what's hot, such as hit songs and movies, and an audiotape. Remember to dig it up a few years later.

✔ **Pay attention to current events.** Read magazines and newspapers. Point out articles that may interest your child.

Ask your child what he thinks about an issue. Keep the question simple and age-appropriate. Most kids are pretty egocentric, but they have opinions.

Discovering the arts together

Lay out newspaper to protect your rugs from drippy paper maché. Stuff cotton into your ears during violin lessons. Smart kids need the arts in their lives. Music, painting, drama, and dance all delight the senses. They expand your child's world beyond what's measured on tests. Exposure and lessons in the arts:

✔ **Offer your child different forms of expression.** Let your child pound drums, belt out a song, or act out grandma's reaction to losing her dentures. The arts provide a source of release for those good, bad, and ugly feelings.

✔ **Permit your child to meet great artists and appreciate their work.** Their masterpieces enrich the mind. Initiation into fine art allows your child to gain an appreciation for beauty.

✔ **Take your child on a trip around the world and through history without tests or book-learning.** The arts give clues about what values and customs different societies hold dear.

✔ **Give your child a sense of success outside of the three Rs.** Creativity soars with the arts, unlike with some core subjects. Molding a sculpture or strumming a guitar can turn into a satisfying hobby. These and similar experiences in the arts ultimately reinforce academic skills because of the expression they allow and feelings of success they create.

You'd think with all these bonuses, schools would set aside large amounts of time and money for arts programs. Wrong! When district budgets deflate, the first programs to go are art and music. What some kids view as a lifeline to school, powers-that-be regard as frills.

That leaves you to open your child's eyes and ears to the wonder of art appreciation. Your child can either be a doer or an observer with you or alone.

You say you're not an artist. No problem. The beauty of the arts are the great togetherness opportunities they provide. The following sections give you some suggestions for making fine art part of your family's activities.

Music

Music calms the spirits and inspires creativity. Introduce your child to any or all of the following activities:

- ✔ **Listen to different kinds of music.** Play music in the background as your family completes chores or eats together. Switch to a variety of stations in the car. Discover classical, jazz, blues, folk, country, gospel, and rock. If someone likes or dislikes a type of music, explore why.

  If battles erupt over which type of music to listen to, institute a policy of taking turns. Set a time limit and switch when time's up. Who knows? You may get to like each other's music.

- ✔ **Attend music performances together.** Check out children's performances and musicals. Go to school concerts. Meander over to outdoor concerts in warm weather. These introduce young kids to music without their having to sit still.

- ✔ **Keep instruments accessible, just in case the musical muse hits.** Playing music doesn't have to be expensive. Young children enjoy bells, tambourines, drums, woodblocks, and recorders or harmonicas. You can *rent* expensive instruments to test interests.

- ✔ **Enroll your child in lessons or group classes, if he expresses any interest.** Encourage joining the school choir or band. Playing an instrument contributes to growing a well-rounded kid. Your child assumes responsibility to practice, which is no easy feat.

  Don't expect a virtuoso. But do know that if you can afford an instrument and lessons, your child gains more than playing a few tunes.

- ✔ **Sing together.** Singing lifts spirits, helps chores go quicker, and warms the heart.

Visual art

Creating art and craft projects is one of the best ways to veg-out. Nothing makes spirits soar with pride like finishing a picture or sculpture. Here are a few suggestions for getting your child started on the road to Picassoland.

- ✔ **Welcome art projects at home.** Keep a supply of art supplies in case the creative muse hits. Review the list of basic supplies from Chapter 7. Then add this fun stuff to your craft corner:

- Beads
- Bottle caps
- Buttons
- Chalk
- Corks
- Doilies
- Egg cartons
- Fabric scraps
- Feathers
- Glitter
- Papers/magazines
- Pint berry boxes
- Pipe cleaners
- Ribbons
- Sequins
- Spools
- Styrofoam grocery trays
- Watercolor paints
- Yarn

Store felt-tip pens in a sealed plastic bag or jar to limit their drying out. Restore dry markers by dipping them in nail polish remover and recapping for a couple hours before using again.

✔ **Display your child's drawings.** Hang them on bulletin boards, the refrigerator door, or in a frame on any wall. Show you are proud of your child's artistic attempts, no matter how primitive they look.

Remember to hang art throughout your home. Artwork doesn't have to be expensive. You can clip pictures from magazines and frame family photos. Museum shops sell inexpensive reproductions as posters and postcards. Whatever pleases your eye counts.

✔ **Visit art together.** Walk through museums and attend local art center events. Stop and look at displays your library may have. Point out art on walls and talk about what you find wonderful, or not, and why.

✔ **Enroll your child in art classes, if your child likes this idea.** Community centers, children's museums, art museums, and local colleges offer classes or workshops in various media.

Drama and dance

Rhythmic movement is healthy for body and mind. Add a little role playing, and you have great opportunities for creative expression that carry over into academic and social successes. Encourage your child to act and dance with the following activities:

- ✔ **Attend dance concerts and age-appropriate plays and movies.**

- ✔ **Dance together to the radio or CDs.** Encourage movement to different types of music: tango, cha-cha, waltz. Nothing loosens everyone up like seeing a parent frolic around the living room.

- ✔ **Play movement games,** such as:

  - Statue: Stop music and everyone freezes, often in unusual positions. Keep starting and stopping the music.

  - Musical chairs: Same idea, only your family walks around chairs. When the music stops, they scurry for a chair. Because you put out one less chair than number of people, the one without the chair is out.

- ✔ **Keep full a box of costumes and old clothes.** You'd be surprised to know that older kids still love to dress up.

- ✔ **Encourage your child to put on skits for friends.** Presenting is a great way to grow comfortable in front of strangers.

  Watch amateur theatrics when invited, no matter how inconvenient the timing. Thrill to the silliness. Provide considerable applause for a job well done.

- ✔ **Act out your favorite stories together.** Ask your child to tell the story first and direct who does what. Pantomime stories, emotions, and everyday activities.

- ✔ **Videotape your little drama queen or king.** Tape-record silly voices.

  Don't forget all the wonderful kid's books about art and famous artists that you and your child can find at the library or bookstore.

Taking lessons and extra classes

Don't panic. I'm not really suggesting that you pile on more school and classes. But I wanted to mention a couple extracurricular alternatives your child may like. Each is something many kids (including smart ones) like to do, and each has been linked to improvement in specific skills.

Encouraging foreign-language study

Remember verb conjugation and vocabulary lists? That's not what the pros mean when they advocate that your young child learns a foreign language.

Pro-language folks want you to expose your child to a second language even before speaking the first. They claim young kids:

- ✔ Possess a natural ability to hear and reproduce sounds, intonation patterns, and phrase structures. Their elastic brains allow them to develop abilities in two languages at the same time.

- ✔ Improve English language and other analytical skills, including math, as a result of foreign-language learning. Your child understands early that he can approach a concept in more than one way, and this leads to more effective problem-solving.

- ✔ Obtain greater fluency in other languages later after learning a foreign language at a young age. Knowing other languages increases your child's sensitivity to other cultures and international awareness.

If your child continues along the language-learning path and retains what he learns, years later he'll be worth more in the global marketplace. Don't force-feed it, of course: Keep it fun!

How can you interject language into your family life? The easiest way is to coax your school district into offering classes. If the school can't afford foreign language or they claim the curriculum is too packed, you can suggest that the parent's organization arrange for classes that you pay for and hold before or after school.

The major problem with starting foreign language too early is retention. Sure, younger kids learn easier with their spongelike brains, and learning anything that's mind-expanding and fun is good for them. But don't expect a teenage or adult linguist unless you plan on continuing exposure to language in some way for years to come. And some kids get a bad case of the grumps waking up early for what appears to be more school.

Should your child balk at a class to learn another language, don't despair. The following informal opportunities offer your child the chance to branch out language-wise:

- ✔ **Listen or watch foreign language television and audiocassettes, CDs, software, and videotapes.** Surf the net to find different age-appropriate options through Amazon.com, www.bookswithoutborders.com, and www.bn.com.

The Web site www.edutainingkids.com rates and evaluates foreign-language software, music, toys, and books for different age children.

✔ **Buy foreign-language picture dictionaries and children's books.** Many of your kid's favorite stories are also in French or Spanish and can be purchased through Web sites I just mentioned.

✔ **Subscribe to a foreign language newspaper, or pick one up occasionally.** Besides picking out individual words, your child sees the written language and grammar at work.

You can find foreign newspapers at www.onlinenewspapers.com, which provides links to thousands of papers worldwide.

✔ **Visit local centers, festivals, and museums that highlight a particular culture.** Use the opportunity to launch learning about another ethnic group that may include language.

✔ **Arrange for your child to write to a foreign pen pal** through www.penpals.com or www.epals.com. If you are wary of your child corresponding with a stranger, suggest to the teacher that the class embark on a cross-cultural pen-pal project.

An alternative to establishing a pen-pal relationship is locating an international chat room with your chosen language. Most Web browsers offer entry to foreign chat rooms. For example, chat.yahoo.com links with international chat rooms from Western Europe, the Pacific Rim, and Latin America.

✔ **Send your child to a daily, weekend, or overnight foreign-language summer camp.** Some camps exist for the main purpose of language immersion. But kids experience fun activities, too. Concordia College, www.concordialanguagevillages.org, runs several programs for junior high and high school kids on campus in Moorhead, Minnesota.

✔ **Hire a babysitter or au pair who speaks another language.** Start your search with the International Au Pair Association at www.iapa.org, which is the trade association for most au pair agencies and organizations worldwide. Or post a note on bulletin boards of local cultural institutions.

✔ **Participate in an exchange program.** With an exchange program, you either host a foreign student or send your child to another country to live with a family. Two popular exchange student organizations for high schoolers are the American Field Services (AFS) at www.AFS.org and Youth for Understanding at www.youthforunderstanding.org, but many more exist.

✔ **Travel together.** If you can afford vacations, go to South America, French-speaking Canada, or Europe. Make learning a foreign language meaningful by being able to speak to locals. Order food, buy trinkets, and take buses. Nothing contributes to learning a language more than needing a restroom or getting the wrong change for a purchase. And the time together is priceless.

Moving pieces on a chess board

Chess involves more than pushing little figures on a checkerboard. Chess is a sport with its own language and rules. Only these rules are brain food for improved grades and self-esteem. Many folks believe that chess and smart go together. So why not play chess in your home?

Through chess, your child:

✔ Sits long enough to analyze a situation

✔ Focuses on what's important and disregards what's not

✔ Integrates logical and creative plans to solve problems

✔ Devises creative solutions and puts them into action

✔ Learns to think coolly and objectively under pressure

✔ Builds self-esteem even in the face of defeat

Teachers usually like chess because the game is a great equalizer. Girls and boys from every background can compete on equal terms. That's one reason why the U.S. Chess Federation sponsors a Chess in the Schools program around the country.

To bring chess into your child's school, contact the federation at 1-800-388-5464; or 3054 NYS Route 9W, New Windsor, NY 12553; or if your child really likes the game, order the magazine *School Mates*. The publication is chock full of tips to play better chess and articles about other young chess enthusiasts.

Play chess as one of your family activities. The concentration the game requires relieves stress, probably from doing this smart thing.

Chapter 12

Monitoring Media

Computers, video games, movies — oh, my! So many ways to entice your child with creative learning options, yet, so many anti-smart possibilities, too.

Read this chapter to heighten your parental awareness of what media means for raising a high-achieving kid. Decide for yourself when and if television, video games, and the Internet have a place in your child's educational plan and discover how to control media you choose not to let in your home.

Choosing Smart Electronic Media

Don't get me wrong. I'm not against movies, television, radio, video games, or computer games. Media can be fun and entertaining. At times, programs offer enlightening information and in lively and absorbing ways. With the variety of formats and visual effects available nowadays, you can understand why kids find media so appealing.

But beware. Media present several drawbacks that interfere with raising a smart kid.

Understanding media imperfections

The gravest problem with media is content that's unsuitable for smart kids; actually, for any kid. In addition, media gobbles up your child's precious play and study hours.

In addition, kids who watch too much television or play too many video games:

✔ **Show more verbal and physical aggression** than their media-deprived friends because they see violence and anger on the screen as the best way to resolve conflicts.

✔ **Bulk up with more body fat** than those who refuse to be couch potatoes. Moving thumbs to press video game buttons doesn't count as physical activity.

✔ **See too many images of inappropriate body-image and sex-role stereotypes** that pervade many programs.

✔ **Are less creative** because media imagines for them. Passively watching characters jump around isn't the same as experiencing the world yourself. Excessive television viewing teaches kids to watch without really paying attention.

✔ **Sympathize less with other's pain and suffering.** Kids see so much of it on shows and games they become desensitized. How sad!

✔ **View the world as a dangerous place** because they witness so many random acts of violence and out-of-control people. Watch a couple hours of television and count the hostile interactions, and you'll understand what I mean.

Knowing when your family watches too much television

You know too much television-watching goes on in your house when your child:

✔ Bops friends over the head, *Three Stooges*–style.

✔ Stares at the screen, zombie-like.

✔ Fights turning the set off yet flicks from one show to another without a preferred choice.

✔ Suggests watching television rather than playing when friends visit.

✔ Eats meals in front of the television.

✔ Wears Barney purple; Britney Spears scant, even though she's so yesterday; or Batman pajamas all day.

✔ **Achieve less** because they are too busy being glued to a screen. One report claims that many kids spend up to 40 hours per week in front of some sort of screen. Imagine the projects, sports, books, and family outings your child can experience in that amount of time. Imagine, too, if that time were spent studying! Several studies conclude that kids who spend this kind of time in front of a screen earn lower grades. Subjects of most media products aren't exactly brain-cell builders either, with sitcoms and violent and sexy programs filling the airwaves. Too much media wastes valuable time better spent learning and socializing.

Limiting the TV monster

Admit it. Sometimes, television and video games function as a babysitter. Or they calm family beasts like a tranquilizer. No one says you have to pull the plug altogether, although going cold turkey isn't a bad idea. But limits are in order.

If you want a smarter child who's fun to be around, reign in what your child watches and for how long.

This section shares some suggestions for helping your child control the media monster.

Put the family on a television diet

Budget the time everyone — including you — watches TV. The American Academy of pediatrics suggests limiting viewing to no television for anyone under two, half-hour increments until starting school, and at most two hours a day for elementary-age kids.

To make everyone happy, read a TV magazine together. Plan which shows to watch during permitted viewing times. Identifying shows your child likes is more satisfying than watching whatever appears.

Place toys, puzzles, games, and art materials near the television to involve bored kids who normally grab the remote. Suggest alternative activities, such as reading, writing in a journal, or family games. Sometimes, limiting media is merely a matter of breaking lazy, less smart habits.

Set rules for media

Agree on basic rules, and stick to them.

✔ No media of any kind before bed.

✔ No television, video games, or Internet chats on school nights unless homework is finished or you agree beforehand on a brief after-school break.

✔ Definitely, no television during meals together.

Place the television away from the center of family activity

Out of sight, out of mind works here. But make sure that the TV stays within earshot or eyeshot, so that you monitor what and when your child watches.

Never put a TV in your child's room. That's the best way to give up control of what she watches and when she sees it.

Watch television and videos together

Know what's on your child's video games. This comes under the headings of "know the enemy" and "I prefer my child get involved with activities that build, not destroy, brain cells." If you feel uncomfortable about what you see, don't hesitate to turn it off. Chances are, your child feels the same way about the program.

If you see something that offends your values or reinforces dumb habits, discuss it with your child. Ask for her version of what's happening onscreen. You may be surprised at the different interpretation from what you observe. Discuss different ways to handle problems you see on the screen. Explain why you disapprove of preteen stalkers or scary killer bee movies that may keep you both awake at night.

Don't forget to stay for the cloying commercials. Your child does. Explain that advertisers are out to make money off viewers, so they tend to exaggerate or make false claims. Part of being street smart is having the ability to differentiate the real from hype and not be sucked in by advertising.

Choose educational shows when you can get away with it

Expose your preschooler to good educational programs, like *Sesame Street* and *Reading Rainbow,* that have been proven to increase vocabulary and improve skills. For your older kid, choose shows that build on interests and curiosity. Check out varied music, art, and science shows.

Try programs that represent other cultures and viewpoints realistically, rather than promote lowest common denominator stereotypes. Look for family programs without kids who act surly or sarcastic, talk back, or fight first and communicate later. If you're lucky, you may find one or two good role models who value education and smart thinking .

For great ideas about media and software products, go online to www.edutainingkids.com.

Deciding whether to buy the must-have video game

Would you knowingly advocate that your child shoot another person? How about stealing a car? Or ogling tightly-clad voluptuous women for the sake of dismembering them? I hope not.

Then why would you permit these sorts of terrible role models in your home? They detract from the high achieving, academically successful vision you have for your child. If you oppose guns and smoking, you don't bring them into the house. So why let brawling, brainless action figures into your child's life? Who's the parent here?

Discovering the down side of video games

Unlike movies and television, video games are interactive. You lack time to mull over the virtues of gore and violence like when you watch a movie together. Suddenly, your sweet child shoots people. Blood spurts out. Body parts fly off. Your previously nonviolent child mows down pretend enemies in a box solely because she wants to reach a higher level of play or score points. Not smart.

You may think these are only games, but most video games emphasize violence, and almost one-third spotlight aggression against women. Any amount of violence in video games should disturb you.

What's worse, playing video games is addictive. Some kids spend hour after hour fixated on impulsive, negative, and sexist entertainment, seeing the same images repeatedly. If their brains function at all, after awhile they becomes numb to the violence. And the amount of time spent satisfying this addiction takes away from time that could go for studying, involvement in activities that strengthen your kid's body and mind, and reading.

Finding the courage to say "no"

What's a well-meaning, success-oriented parent to do? Suggest renting the must-have game first. Notice the rating, paying attention to matching the code with your child's age. Then preview all levels of the game before your child does. Violence usually escalates with each subsequent level.

If the game proves destructive to your child's emotional health, refuse to keep it in your house. Definitely don't cave on this one.

Refusing to buy an offensive video game isn't the time to dredge up every bad decision your child has ever made. "You always choose the worst games/music/hairdos or whatever." Putdowns get you nowhere except increasing the black hole in your parent-child relationship. Better to:

- ✔ Say something like, "We won't spend money on this video game because I don't want violent and sexist images in our home."

- ✔ Acknowledge that your child will most likely play the game at a friend's home. But caution her to be reasonable about what she does away from home. This message lets your child know you aren't a hayseed — just a concerned parent who trusts her own judgment and sanity. Usually.

- ✔ Discuss the offensive game together. Listen to why your child likes it. Exchange views about the game. Come to a meeting of the minds, even though you won't change your mind for x-y-z reasons. You don't want a game to interfere with good family communication.

Using the Internet: The Good, the Bad, — and What to Do about It

No doubt about it: Computers are here to stay. With each new technological advance, computers reach farther into the information world. By inputting a subject into a search engine, a host of Web sites appear for exploration. Your child can research organizations and libraries across the nation. She can travel to other countries with a few clicks on the keyboard.

The potential for computers as an educational tool is limitless. Computer games can build on your child's basic skills and enhance her knowledge base. For example, *Richard Rabbit* teaches reading readiness, and *Carmen Sandiego* takes kids around the world to learn countries and states, their whereabouts, and the flags that represent these places. And sites such as these provide accurate, mind-broadening information:

- ✔ Most state Web sites contain kid-friendly sections that discuss state history, geography, economy, special sights, and types of people and where they live.

- ✔ Most museums, historical sites, and zoos offer well-researched and accurate information online about the theme they cover.

- ✔ Local public and university libraries either display kid-related sites or can direct young researchers to credible sources online.

But is computer literacy as necessary for academically successful kids as marketers want us to believe? Understanding the technology, knowing how to locate information online, and feeling comfortable with the process is necessary to succeed in the modern world. Many knowing teachers, however, specify that students find information other than what they need for projects on the Internet. Why? Because other than the Web sites I just mentioned, few are monitored. Anyone can put anything online. Your child may not be able to discern what's true and what's not. And too many kids think the Internet is a cheating tool — meant for copying information without penalty.

In 2002, half a class in Kansas downloaded information from a Web site and inserted the information into their assignment papers word for word, without giving credit. The teacher caught them and gave each student an F, which was half of the grade for the semester. So A students received Cs and Ds for the semester. The parents stormed the school board, claiming their darlings had no idea they were cheating. Oddly enough, the school board sided with the students and parents, and the teacher quit. Your smart kid needs to know she can't count on being treated like these students.

More often, print information is targeted for your child's age and skill levels and is usually monitored for accuracy. The Internet is generally not.

Before the computer worms its way into the heart of your smart kid, review Table 12-1. Evaluate the pros and cons of allowing too much unchecked technology into your home too early.

Table 12-1	Pros and Cons of Computers for Smarter Kids
Pros	**Cons**
Widens access to increased body of information	Easy access to information you may not appreciate; exposes kids to vast pools of Internet marketers.
Eases homework writing and rewriting	Current e-mail etiquette worsens grammar skills.
Enhances the look of finished products	Spell check reduces the ability to spell generally.
Simplifies research	Internet resources are not always accurate and up-to-date. They make those who rely solely on Web sources lazy researchers.

(continued)

Table 12-1 *(continued)*

Pros	Cons
Provides quick access to information	Speedy responses contribute to your child expecting unrealistic instant gratification. Focusing visually on a screen lessens development of other senses.
Allows kids to stay in touch and meet new people	Sexual predators prey on kids who chat online. Chatting online with unseen folks interferes with your child developing the emotions and listening skills that accompany face-to-face interactions. Kids need human contact to develop socially and emotionally.
Graphics and special effects hold interest	Constant bombardment of disorganized choices increases hyperactivity and poor attention span, especially for step-by-step problem solving. Addictive games rob kids of valuable play and reading time.
Costs pennies to communicate and research	E-mail and chat rooms eat up time. Keeping up with new technology and games costs a bundle.

Don't feel pressured that your tot will fall behind in the academic race without computer skills. Research shows that kids pick up computer skills easily at any age — ind of like programming the VCR.

Getting conned by chat room users

E-mail. Instant messaging. Expect your child to rely on the Internet to communicate with friends as much or more than you used the telephone at her age and definitely more than for schoolwork. If you're anything like some of my childhood friends, that's probably a lot.

These communication avenues wind up being more than simple chats with friends. According to one study of preteen girls:

✔ Talking online allows them to speak freer, especially about emotionally-charged issues. (Enhancing communication skills is good news.)

Smart computer shopping

New computer equipment (hardware) and programs (software) come out about every six months. Companies figure that after you're hooked on computers, you'll keep buying updates. But you don't need to buy the most expensive gear or keep up with the neighbors, computer-wise. Instead, evaluate your family needs and shop for the lowest prices. Here are some computer shopping hints:

✔ Decide what family members will be doing: word processing, spreadsheets, graphics, downloading music, playing games.

✔ Choose a computer with enough RAM, or memory, to handle the programs. Multiple programs require at least 256MB of RAM, at least at this writing. You can usually add RAM inexpensively as needs change without buying a new computer.

✔ Find a hard drive with large amounts of hard drive space (GB for Gigabytes) to store multiple program files, images, music, and video. If you expect to store ordinary files, 20 to 40GB will do. Otherwise, go for 60GB or more. Similar to RAM, extra space can be purchased later.

✔ Select a way to access the Internet (by modem or by faster but more expensive and complicated DSL or cable modem connections) for information. Remember to factor in the monthly cost for a server company that connects you to the Internet, although some free services, such as hotmail, still exist.

✔ Consider whether you need USB ports to add other capabilities; CD-RW (burners) to download music files and back up files; a DVD drive to play DVD movies on the computer; video graphics cards to run the latest 3-D games; and a color monitor to display games. Only some of these are necessary for smart kids. Decide what's fluff.

✔ Shop around. After you decide which features you need, read current computer magazines. Go to several stores because prices vary greatly, even with the same brand. Ask about free backup support. Chances are, you'll need help with the installation of the computer or with which add-on products to buy.

✔ Buy last year's model or buy an upgraded used computer to save money. If cost is still too high, send your child to the library. Most have free computer usage and Internet connections, so your child can gain experience with both without your spending a dime.

✔ Choose software programs that are age appropriate. Think about buying a typing program first. This helps your child master the keyboard. Look into buying software that filters incoming messages and your child's access to certain types of Web sites and chat rooms you may find objectionable.

✔ Check out the Computer Learning Foundation online at www.computer-learning.org or by calling 415-327-3347 or writing P.O. Box 60007, Palo Alto, CA 94306 for recommendations about ways to integrate computers into a smart kid's life. The nonprofit organization reviews and recommends software and safe Web sites by age. Their references include homework help and access to museum Web sites.

✔ Communicating online rather than seeing each other face-to-face bolsters confidence when talking to guys. For some reason, boys online seem sweeter than those who snap bra straps and pull hair in school. At least, that's what they want these girls online to think. (This news could go either way. Added confidence is always a good thing. But who wants their precious child interacting with the opposite gender outside of school?)

✔ Booting up brings an avalanche of porn. (That's terrible and creepy news that cuts into the information sharing of chat rooms.)

What does all this mean? That you need to be vigilant about monitoring what your child does with the computer.

Using computer common sense

An easy-to-understand book about net surfing for kids and unenlightened adults is *Homework Busters: How to Have A+ Grades* by Bill Thompson (Big Fish). The book covers how to make the best use of the Internet as a great learning tool.

What the book doesn't cover is the bad stuff that comes from the most benign Internet surfing: advertising scams, foul language e-mails, porn, and viruses that destroy your hard drive, coop your Internet address book, and expose your child to not-so-smart stuff. The good news is the Internet takes your child anywhere. The bad part is the possibility that your child can be lured anywhere by a stranger met online.

Safeguard your child by instituting a few preventive safety measures:

✔ **Know how to use the computer and navigate online yourself.** You need to be computer literate to understand how to best help your child use the Internet effectively and wisely. Protect your password, so that your child can't change settings, especially ones that block what kids shouldn't get into.

✔ **Keep the computer in a central location, so that you can see the screen.** Don't lull yourself into thinking that because the computer is in your home, your child is safe.

✔ **Monitor your child's Internet use.** Supervise forays online, especially if your child is young and new to the Internet. Oversee which sites your child visits and what she downloads. Bookmark good sites for repeat visits.

Review your child's buddy list and address book. Check her profile and how she introduces herself. Delete people your child doesn't know. Help her clean out files and e-mail regularly.

Make going online a safe, informative, and fun family affair.

✔ **Set ironclad rules about sharing personal information online.** Caution your child *never* to send family names (including her own) or anaddress, telephone number, school name, photo, or credit card information to strangers online.

Make sure your child understands that strangers who have this information can use it to send unwanted garbage, known as *spam,* or to harm her. If your child wants to communicate with someone she meets online, a safer choice is to give an e-mail address only.

✔ **Warn your child not to respond but to always let you know when someone online:**

- Writes in a way that makes her feel uncomfortable

- Wants to meet her face-to-face without telling a parent

- Says statements against her family, friends, ethnic group, or religion

- Leaves messages that are threatening, sexually explicit, or refer to cults or violent acts

Chapter 13

Launching Lifelong Study Habits

In This Chapter

▷ Making homework and studying top priorities

▷ Organizing homework-friendly environments

▷ Understanding what produces smarter homework

▷ Studying for tests

*B*e forewarned. If you haven't experienced the rigors of homework and tests, they're on the way, as are worksheets, dioramas, reports, science projects, and posters. Completing homework and studying (the activities your kids usually gripe about under your tutelage) are critical to their being smart students.

Homework routines help smart learners establish the foundation for organizing themselves and managing time. By finishing homework and studying for tests, your kids learn responsibility for life. This chapter prepares you to help your smart kids make the most of homework.

Positioning Schoolwork as Number One at Home

Time to forget negative feelings left over from your days of school and homework. Dismiss the sink-or-swim attitude your parents may have followed when they left you tread murky homework waters by yourself. Homework in the 21st century must be a family affair in order to raise smarter students. The sooner you accept this notion, the better you can motivate your offspring.

Kids are clever. If your child sees that you pay more attention to football games or PTA bake sales than to schoolwork, she'll put less effort into homework. The more heartfelt interest you show in studying and homework, the more successful your student will be. Here are some ways to show you care about your kids and their doing their best work:

✔ **Talk to your kids about how important homework is for learning.** Don't lecture, which will cause your kids' eyes to glaze over, especially older kids. Just matter-of-factly reinforce that homework is their work. Say how you expect them to do their best with homework as with everything. You want to keep family expectations high, while recognizing sincere efforts, of course.

✔ **Make a point of asking about homework at dinner or whenever your family gathers.** You talk about your work. Why not do the same for your kids? Avoid the rhetorical yes-or-no-answer questions that tend to stop conversations dead. "Do you have much homework today?" Better ways to show interest: "Let's look at your homework together." "Tell me the most interesting tidbits you learned from the history chapter you just read." "Where did you get such clever ideas for the story you wrote?"

✔ **Bring up longer projects for mealtime discussion.** Everyone can contribute ideas, if your child welcomes them. Through casual discussion, you can slyly monitor how the project's coming. And your hard worker feels that you value his efforts.

If you care about homework, so will your kids.

Devising a Homework-Friendly Environment

One way to show you expect tip-top homework is to designate a work-friendly area. The best place for homework is anywhere that promotes studying and lets your child know that this place means serious business. No sock fights. No computer games. Just homework.

But beware. Kids differ in where they work best, and that's okay.

I have friends who tried to create the perfect work atmosphere for their son. They bought a desk and comfy chair and hung book shelves in his bedroom. They thought the room ideal for studying because it was away from the main household activity. But each day before dinner, their son collected his books and papers and pencils and plopped himself at the kitchen table. He preferred to stay close to his mother while she cooked. He liked activity around him while he worked and wanted someone nearby to answer questions. The pluses his parents deemed crucial for homework success turned into negatives for their son.

What does this mean for you and your studying offspring? Stay sensitive to your child's work style, even if it differs from yours. Admit that some kids work better in a cave with blinders on, while others crave a Fourth of July parade around them.

Another factor to consider is how available you want to be for questions and problems. Working near your child allows you to be accessible. The important point is to find one well-lit place that signals to your child that work goes on here, whether it be in the bedroom, kitchen, or basement at a desk, table, or hard-top cushion.

Same differences apply to noise levels. I know kids who need padded cells to concentrate. I've also watched kids with headsets work in crowded cafeterias. And don't forget students who watch TV while finishing their homework. Never feel you've failed because your study bug does homework with CDs blaring in the background. But for some kids, they work fine.

Deciding on the best time to work

Each child works on a different schedule. Lucky you if your child prefers to finish homework right after school. Perhaps your child likes having evenings free, or finds she works more efficiently while still in a school mode. Or maybe you call the shots. You believe that children should work first and play later.

If a work-first approach is your thing, be alert to whether your child requires a break after long school days. Maybe you have the kind of child who needs to run around and let off steam after hours of concentrating. Or you notice that changing activities for a while helps her focus better when she returns to work. That's okay, too.

But watch out for the procrastinator. You know, when your child tiptoes around the work table, giving you one lame excuse after another why starting homework now is impossible: "The dog needs exercise." "Just five minutes more before this show ends." This child can't organize enough to start anything, let alone homework.

Time for you to assume your role as homework guru. Whichever type of child you have, agree with your child on the best place and time for homework. Then make your child stick to the routine. If your child needs a break after school to unwind, suggest starting work after a snack and trip to the bathroom. Take time to discuss your child's day together, whether it be in person or by telephone if you work outside the home. Allow an hour before starting homework, if a play break or time alone is important to refocusing.

Be honest with your kids about your most alert times to help. If you spend eight-plus hours each day at a paid job, you may not take homework traumas kindly the minute you walk through the door. Or if you're up at 4:00 in the morning washing clothes to get kids ready for school and yourself ready for work, let your night owls know that asking homework questions after nine o'clock can be dangerous.

Given everyone's busy schedules, try not to delay beginning homework for too long. You never know when a difficult fraction problem, writer's block, or an occupied computer will interfere with the best-laid time plans. A late start may extend homework into the night when everyone is the most frazzled and it's past your child's bedtime.

A good way to make sure homework gets done in a timely fashion is to establish a family work time. Decide together on a time with everyone brings their work, whether it be homework or bill paying to the same room at an agreed-upon hour. As you work together with your kids, you remain available to assist with homework, while being able to finish your chores. Gradually, your kids view homework as a fun family activity, rather than a drag. What's more, your kids see you model good work habits, the best encouragement I can think of.

Stocking up on necessary supplies

Part of being a good student involves being prepared to work, even at home. Stock the homework area with a range of supplies, such as paper, pencils, crayons, markers, construction paper, and poster board. That way, you won't need to make surprise runs to the store for each new assignment, and your worker bee won't spend precious time collecting materials each day. I can't impress upon you the difficulty you will have trying to find poster board at midnight for a project due the next day!

Another option is to keep a special homework box filled with materials. Store the box in a designated spot. Removing the box becomes part of the routine that signals work time.

Smart computer tips

Computers provide information, teach skills, and help kids write reports. They also expose your kids to health hazards, such as neck, shoulder, and back strain. To help your child stay healthier while using the computer, pediatricians recommend the following adjustments:

- Align the top of the computer screen with your child's eyes. Suggest that your child sit on a pillow or telephone book to reach the right height.

- Place the screen 18 to 26 inches away from your child's eyes.

- Insert a pillow or rolled-up towel to brace the lower back, if your child's chair doesn't have good support.

- Relieve strain from hanging feet by placing them on a stool, pile of pillows or books, or backpack.

- Arrange the keyboard so that arms bend from the waist when keying.

- Put the mouse level with the keyboard.

- Buy an inexpensive foam mouse pad to support the wrist.

- Remind your child to take regular breaks to stretch and relieve eye strain. Switching activities every 20 minutes breaks the focus on the screen. What you want to avoid is staring at the monitor for hours, which causes strain and dry eye.

Making the Most of Homework

Homework is a good way to become and stay involved in your child's education. You see a snapshot of what the class studies, and you discover some information about your child's academic progress. Does your child doodle drawings of Mickey Mouse or complete papers? How much has he learned? Is the material too difficult, not difficult enough, or not presented well?

The problem is that many schools provide few clear guidelines for parents about homework. Much of your child's after-school classwork may land in your overburdened lap. You may be expected to monitor and help your child, which you're probably happy to do. But too often, the job crosses boundaries into teaching skills, some of which you never learned, in order for your youngster to complete assignments. At some point, you may wonder what and how much parents should do. The following sections explore more about a parent's role in homework.

Knowing how much to be involved

Basically, your job as parent is to keep homework in perspective. Be your usual helpful, supportive, and rational self. Don't overdo, take over, or become so involved that you don't allow your child to make mistakes and learn on her own.

To get your role straight from the start, seize the homework bull by the horns. Talk with your child's teacher about homework at the beginning of the school year. Let the teacher guide your level of homework involvement, if your philosophy jives with the school's.

Homework plans

Ask about the teacher's philosophy for homework, such as:

- ✔ What type of assignments do you give?
- ✔ What do you want students to get out of their homework?
- ✔ How often can my child expect homework?
- ✔ How long should my child spend on homework?

Find out as much as you can about the teacher's expectations. Make sure homework is assigned on a regular basis to build smart work habits. Papers and projects should directly relate to schoolwork, either by practicing a concept or by requiring your brain to explore or discover something.

Watch out for teachers who don't believe in homework. If your child's teacher professes a lack of enthusiasm for assigning homework, you may want to provide after-school activities of your own during the designated homework time.

Homework rules

Find out whether the teacher has specific homework guidelines your child needs to follow. Ask:

- ✔ What happens if my child's homework is late or incomplete?
- ✔ Can he hand in papers late and still get credit?
- ✔ Is he expected to correct homework papers and return them to you?
- ✔ Do you offer feedback to students about homework?

Be alert for teachers who rarely make time to review papers in a timely fashion, if at all. They give your kids the wrong message — that homework doesn't count, and you know better. Discuss your concerns with the teacher.

Homework and parents

The trickiest part of all with homework is knowing what involvement the teacher believes you should have. Be sure to ask:

SMART KID TIP

Understanding brainstorming

Brainstorming is a great way to help direct your child when ideas aren't flowing. Tell your creative thinker to say the first words that pop into his mind about the issue at hand, say life on Mars. Accept all mind meanderings — no offering is too outrageous. Then ask questions to either expand the ideas or come up with alternatives. "What would your day be like on Mars?" "What would sleeping on Mars be like?" "How would a day in school go?" "What would you wear?" With so many options on the table, your smart thinker takes the ideas that seem workable, incorporates the favorites into his project, and shapes them into his own work.

✔ How much do you expect me to be involved with homework?

✔ Do you have a hands-off homework policy? Or do you encourage parent involvement? Should I teach my child whatever he doesn't understand from class?

✔ Do you expect me to review and correct papers before you see them?

Teachers differ in how much they encourage parental involvement. Decide where you stand. Discuss how much you expect to be involved with your offspring. Then stick to the guidelines you establish together. At the very least, you want to be there:

✔ To get your child started, in case questions arise

✔ To check that homework is done

✔ After homework comes back from the teacher, to reinforce the positive and help your child improve what went wrong

Debating the right amount of homework

When your child starts school, expect homework. Nowadays, the fun begins as early as kindergarten. Six-year-olds today spend significantly more time on homework than you did a decade or two ago.

The jury is out about how long your kids should work. Advocates of bigger workloads point to studies showing that the typical elementary school teacher assigns students less than one hour of homework per week. I believe that's way too little to stimulate smart thinkers, unless they're in kindergarten or first grade. Compare that number with studies that report kids watch about 22 hours of television per week. You can understand why parents like you who want smarter kids say, "Bring on the homework!"

Critics remind those who beat drums for more after-school work that your returns on the homework investment diminish with homework overload. They contend that too much homework creates homework monsters. You may have a few at home: kids who feel homework preys on them each night like a stalking tiger. They feel angry and defeated. Your previously agreeable bundles of joy may now fight homework simply because the amount overwhelms them. They feel the burden of unbalanced lives without time for anything else, even family outings with you.

Most homework measures estimate about ten minutes per grade. That doesn't consider personal speed, quality of homework, or whether your child receives worksheets or projects so difficult you need a PhD to understand, let alone help, your child.

If you feel your child receives too much homework, let the school know. Teachers may think that's what you want for your kids to meet higher achievement goals. You may have to start a movement of like-minded parents to protest. In the meantime, read ahead to see what you can do to ward off the homework monster in your student.

Troubleshooting homework problems

Face it. Homework can be as frustrating for you as for your kids. The nightly grumbling. The last-minute trips to buy materials for a science project due tomorrow that your child knew about for a month. You may feel you've taken your turn as a student already, so you adopt a hands-off, hang loose policy, even though my advice recommends otherwise.

But you can't ignore when your child constantly reports hating homework, especially if you have a whiner. Nor can you ignore when your child wants to complete the work but dissolves into tears because the assignment proves too difficult. In either case, every night can turn into a battle over homework. After awhile, your whiz child feels dumb because he can't produce what's expected, and you go to bed discouraged about what to do. You grow angry at being forced into the position of homework police.

Even the smartest students find homework a hassle sometimes. Homework is supposed to be challenging. Your kids learn by exerting the extra effort that certain projects take to make problems and reports work. But when pleasant homework times turn into regular paper-ripping, tear-filled shouting matches, you've descended about as far from homework heaven as you can get. Here's how to help your kids organize, so that you prevent the homework demons from taking over your home life.

- ✔ **Go over assignments with your child.** Ask him to read the directions to you and explain what to do. If directions prove difficult to understand, reword them until the light bulb goes off in his brain and you see some indication of awareness. Even then, you may want to do a sample problem together.

- ✔ **Identify and list assignments with your child.** Estimate how much time each task should take. As he finishes each assignment, tell him to check it off. The list acts as a guide, while checking off completed items reinforces how much he accomplished.

- ✔ **Set a deadline for completing the entire list.** Encourage your child to work within the time frame, which helps build time-management skills. Projects that take too long can be a signal that your child either has difficulty with the material or problems staying focused.

- ✔ **Help your disorganized child develop a system to organize assignments.** Your child may like color-coded folders for each subject, a pocket organizer/calendar that shows when something is due, accordion folders, or notebooks with pockets, separate sections, or tabs.

- ✔ **Help your child find a homework comfort zone.** Remind him of this optimum setting whenever he can't settle down to work. You could say: "Remember when you said standing on your head in the corner of your bedroom helps you concentrate?"

- ✔ **Decide whether different supplies or equipment can help, depending upon what troubles your child about homework — other than doing homework itself, of course.** Think about corrals to block out sights, earplugs or headsets to block sounds, a slanted or larger desk to make writing or drawing easier. Other, more high-tech homework helpers, such as calculators and computers, may help, too, if budgets allow.

- ✔ **Schedule realistic break times to help your child refuel and find the energy and attention span to finish.** Your child may like a timer to indicate breaks. Set the timer again as a signal when to return to homework. A timer relieves you of your policing duties, making homework interactions less emotionally charged.

Ultimately, homework is your child's responsibility, including organizing to begin. You're just planting the seeds for smart work habits.

Sometimes, homework help merely requires your child getting an attitude adjustment, such as the following:

✔ **Explain connections between your child's homework and real life.** Your student, particularly if he's older, may resist homework because he sees little relevance in what he's doing.

✔ **Show just the right amount of interest in your child's schoolwork.** I should explain about showing too much interest. Think about whether your child is angry with you over something you did, your upcoming divorce, your taking his brother for ice cream without him. Too much bubbly enthusiasm about homework, and your child may refuse to complete assignments as a weapon for getting back at you for these or other transgressions you may not have a clue about. Or your cherub may withhold homework information simply because you're so overzealous. No one says kids have to be rational all the time to be smart.

✔ **Help your overloaded child figure out times each day to study.** Be clear about priorities. Homework first. Sports, school groups, and socializing second. But try to be creative and support endeavors that balance your child's life. Perhaps your child can wake up an hour early each day or study during part of lunch.

✔ **Bring in the big guns.** I read that one mom told her daughter that if she didn't complete her homework, she was going to ask the teacher to keep the laggard in for recess. Supposedly, the message got across. Her daughter turned in her work on time ever after. But this could put your child's teacher in a tough spot. I mention this story only to show the lengths some parents will go when they have a true dawdler.

✔ **Create a reward system to connect positive thoughts with homework.** Offer a reward (or a bribe if that's the way you feel after reading Chapter 9) for finishing homework within a predetermined time frame. Say your homework hater likes movies or basketball. Tally points for each day homework is finished independently and in a timely fashion, whatever you deem the problem to remedy. At the end of the week, plan to rent a movie, shoot some baskets together, or play games, whichever reward tweaks your kid's desire enough to collect the points.

Now, about your role during the homework process. Think about the following:

✔ **Check with your child regularly to encourage specific homework efforts.** Honest praise for sticking with something difficult, writing neatly, or completing five math problems goes a long way toward boosting your child's feelings of competence.

✔ **Let your child know you're willing to help, should it be needed.** If you're away from home, check in regularly by telephone. Tell your homework lover that you're available for questions.

✔ **Work together, if your child asks for help.** First, have your child watch how you complete a difficult problem. Talk about each step. Then let your child take the next problem. If the teacher uses a different approach in class, have your child complete whatever is possible and save the unanswered questions for school. Teachers need to know what their students can't understand.

✔ **Get in the habit of asking leading questions, rather than supplying answers when your child seems stumped.** "Why do you think that?" "How do you think that happens?" "What would you do next?" Similar questions help your child think of alternatives to solve the problem, instead of having you provide the answer.

I know I already said this, but this point is important. Even kids who struggle need to know their number one homework goal is to work independently — and they can reach that goal.

✔ **Talk with the teacher, if your child can't manage to bring home or turn in assignments.** Devise a communication plan, perhaps a sign-off note coupled with backpack checks, that keeps you and your child informed about homework and when the assignment is due. Some teachers create Web sites that students and parents can reference for updates. Ask the teacher to report to you regularly, possibly daily at first. Your child may need home-school monitoring as a nudge into acting responsibly.

When to hire a tutor

Tutors aren't only for homework haters and lazy-bones. Consider a tutor:

✔ For your gifted child. You may not want your smarty booted to a higher grade. Tutors can challenge your child's intellect with special projects to keep the glow of learning bright.

✔ For your child who needs special attention. Extra attention isn't just for kids at either extreme — super smart or somewhat slower. Sometimes, a special coach is just what's needed to boost your kid's morale, like a diet coach or personal trainer.

✔ For your child who needs help in one subject but otherwise does fine

✔ For your child who could use help taking notes, outlining, picking out the most important points from a reading passage, and studying for different types of tests, the building blocks of smart schoolwork.

✔ For giving your child an academic edge over classmates.

To make the most of your child's tutor time:

✔ Decide in advance what you want your child to get out of the sessions.

✔ Talk about the nature of the sessions, such as homework help, test-preparation habits, how many sessions, and the cost.

✔ Don't feel locked into one person. Search for the best match for your child by asking your child's teacher or school counselor for recommendations, which could include another teacher, a professional tutoring service, or older student at the local high school or college.

✔ Plan for regular chats about how sessions went. Discuss the tutor with your child's teacher and provide regular updates.

✔ **Suggest that your child invite a study-buddy over.** Keep phone numbers of responsible friends handy for your child. Nothing is quite like a little peer pressure to help your child stick with a job until homework is done. (If you read Chapter 1, you know that that the ability to work with others is important for success.)

Be prepared to rush in if you hear too many giggles. You want studying to be fun, but not enough gets done if your child fools around too much.

✔ **If your best efforts fail, hire someone outside the family to help with homework.** A tutor adds a different perspective while not getting caught up in family battles. Outsiders don't respond the same way to tears, shouts, or tantrums. If your child understands homework but requires someone to provide structure, pay an older child to work alongside yours. The good grades — and family peace — will be worth the cost.

Preparing for Tests

Tests rank in the same categories as pulling teeth, getting your finger smashed in a door, and staying up all night with a vomiting child. They're no fun. Distasteful as they may be, they are a fact of life. Try to help your child embrace tests for their positive qualities.

Tests provide easy (from your perspective) ways to find out whether your child understands classroom material. Because tests cause great anxiety, their approach puts a fire under your darling to pay attention and learn something. Some challenge is a good thing, as I mention in Chapter 1. Combined with other evaluations, tests offer a picture of how smart your student really is.

At times, decisions about your child's future depend upon test results. Find out about the different types of tests your child may face and how best to help him prepare for them.

Getting ready for tests

Hiding, stomachaches, asking you to schedule a doctor's appointment: Your kids will try anything to get out of tests. Yet, tests still don't go away. To help your child, offer solid test-taking techniques to reduce test anxiety and keep practicing them with your child until acing tests becomes second-nature.

No putting it off. Smart kids prepare for tests. Here's how to help your child whiz through tests:

✔ **Keep up with assignments.** Urge your child to read assignments as they are assigned. Trust me on this one. Last-minute cramming for tests may make the grade sometimes. But long-term, short bursts of studying never work. Drum into your child's head not to expect to be able to study everything from the past week or month or more in one evening. He may have questions that need answering. He needs time to build up a store of knowledge.

You can do your part by setting aside time each night to review reading selections together. Verify that your child keeps track of materials, because misplaced pages may have necessary answers to questions. After you confirm that everything is available, make sure your child knows the work. That way, your child feels comfortable with the information, even for a pop quiz.

✔ **Know test particulars.** Despite what your kids say, teachers rarely spring major tests on them. Usually, they give some clues, like saying when the test is and what it covers. Encourage your child to write down these facts for future reference. Talk together about a schedule that budgets enough time to prepare.

✔ **Use sound study tactics.** Teachers often review with students before a test. Encourage your child to stay awake during these times and take notes. Teachers give good information about what's important to them and the test.

Your child should never be lulled into studying only what the teacher says during a review. Tests, especially in higher grades, cover everything that's read and discussed about a subject. Similarly, I know many kids who skip shaded boxes, special features, and long captions in textbooks. Some even read only the summaries at the end of each chapter. Then they're surprised when questions about the material show up on a test.

✔ **Drill your child.** Some kids may balk at this one, but it helps, so keep trying. Walking your child through information in a variety of ways helps the facts sink in. After your child feels comfortable about the material, pick out important concepts together, ask questions, pose problems and possible test scenarios, or listen to oral recitations of spelling words, multiplication facts, or the constitution. Point out weak spots. Suggest that your student study those areas more and offer to go over them again together.

✔ **Prepare your child's body for success.** Send your child to sleep at the regular bed time. A good night's sleep does as much for acing tests as knowing the material. In the morning, make sure your livewire eats a nourishing breakfast. Nothing distracts from performing well like a growling stomach.

Terrific test-taking tips

The big test day comes. Enough facts are stuffed into your child's brain to fill a library. But none of these matters if your child chokes at the sight of the test. Here are some strategy reminders your child may find useful to capitalize on the hours spent studying:

- **Listen to or read directions carefully.** You may be surprised how many kids fail tests because they put the right answer in the wrong spot. Ask questions if you don't understand — you're never dumb to ask smart questions. Besides, other kids probably have the same question. If you're given written directions, underline the tricky parts so that you can easily get back to them later.

- **Jot down facts you may need.** Write important dates, rules, formulas, or names before starting, so that your mind is freer to think and so that you have them handy in case you clutch on a question.

- **Skim the entire test before starting.** You discover what's ahead of you and how to budget your time. Make sure you leave enough time to answer questions that gain the most points.

- **Answer the easiest questions first.** That way, you finish more of the test. Try not to let one question slow you down and distract you from doing your best on the rest of it.

- **Outline ideas for essay questions.** Writing main concepts or an outline before you start gives your answers direction. The idea with essay questions is to write your brains out, putting in as many remotely relevant facts that fit as possible to show your teacher you know the subject. Even if you're wrong in some parts, if you write a coherent essay and prove your point with enough accurate facts, you win points.

- **Give educated guesses.** Some believe that your first response is usually the correct one, if you're unsure of an answer. I can't validate this one, however.

- **Show your work.** Teachers often give points for the right steps needed to complete math problems or science experiments, even if the final answers are off.

- **Check and double-check your answers.** If you remember nothing else, remember to leave time to check your work. This strategy separates you, the smart one, from the rest of the class and gets you points because you've corrected misspellings, grammar errors, and careless calculations. Be sure to check essay answers for sense and

On the day of the test, keep the morning low-key. If you have test anxiety, so will your child. Instead, ship your prepared student to school with a hug, a kiss, and good — but matter-of-fact — wishes for test success.

Looking at different kinds of tests

Every few years, educators get stuck on some issue the way certain birds return to the same nest each year. For better or worse, testing has become

America's latest obsession. To investigate the pros and cons of tests further, read *The Educated Child* (The Free Press) by William Bennett, who's a former U.S. Secretary of Education, so he ought to know. Meanwhile, the following sections give an overview of the tests your child may face.

Classroom tests

Teachers give tests regularly to determine what your child knows. Teachers either prepare the tests themselves or copy them from workbooks, teacher guides, or textbooks. Tests cover specific skills or masses of information.

You probably remember the drills. In the early grades, tests are simpler: spelling words, addition and subtraction problems, and short answers to questions from books the class reads. Later on, teachers add more complicated multiple-choice questions that can be easily scanned by machine for correct answers and essay exams, which can be take-home. Feedback for tests usually comes in the form of letter or number grades.

Try not to get too bent out of shape about test grades. They are part of the learning process, not an end unto themselves.

Standardized tests

Schools, districts, or states give commercially prepared standardized tests to certain grade levels or to everyone on a yearly basis. Your student takes these tests under the same conditions given to other students around the country, including being read the same directions. That's one quality that makes these tests *standardized.* Tests usually conform to a multiple-choice format. For feedback, you receive results expressed in weird assortments of percentiles, *deciles* (which distribute test-takers into ten groups of equal frequency), or *stanines* (another form of statistical distribution that I've never gotten the hang of), as well as regular numbers.

Another characteristic of standardized tests is the way results are assigned consistent levels of achievement. Test-makers give tests to samplings of kids in different grades. They compare scores of the most kids at certain grade levels and determine an average score for a specific grade. I tell you this to emphasize how subjective particular tests are. Your child's score really depends on what type of child the sample testmakers based their criterion.

Many schools use scores from the popular Iowa Test of Basic Skills, Metropolitan Achievement Test, or Stanford 9 to place your child in a given class or as the basis for skipping or holding back your child a grade. SAT (Scholastic Aptitude Test) and ACT (American College Testing) serve similar purposes as entrance exams for college. Some districts tie standardized test results to school funding and to teacher, principal, and superintendent salaries, which encourages teachers to put pressure on your child to succeed at standardized tests.

You need to ask questions if you don't understand the grading or if you find the use of tests inappropriate. Consider asking: What will these tests be used for? What accounts for differences between test scores and my child's classroom performance? Good schools consider more than tests when planning placements. Make sure your child's future is based on more than a single standardized test result.

State assessments

State assessments are the latest craze to hit schools, and they're making everyone crazy: teachers, parents, and, of course, your child. The more at stake from the results, the crazier everyone gets.

Originally, states developed tests of short answers and writing samples to monitor and equalize academic standards among schools within their borders. A noble goal. Results were for evaluating schools, not kids. Then government officials all the way to the U.S. president got into the act. "Close any school with low scores," they said. "Fire any teachers who have kids with low scores." "Let's pay teachers based on how well their charges score."

Suddenly, your child's score on an assessment means much more than it should, as with standardized tests. With the ante upped, schools now strongly urge teachers to essentially teach to the test, instead of teaching a well-rounded curriculum.

I've been in schools where teachers spend weeks of valuable learning time coaching kids for the big day with sample test items. Some districts buy thick books published just to help kids score higher. If that's going on in your district, someone's making big bucks off your school's anxiety. What's worse, your child probably loses valuable learning time.

Similarly, with all the test jitters, you may blow your cool if your child brings home lower scores than on previous tests. The most out-of-whack idea is that states continue to change the tests, which means that you have no way to compare how your child is progressing over two different years, because the tests may not be the same.

Do yourself and your child a favor and chill out about assessments. Put them into perspective. If you truly believe your school provides your child with a poor education, think about switching to a different school, which is discussed in Chapter 16. Otherwise, do what you can to ease your child's test-taking anxiety by following the guidelines throughout this chapter.

Diagnostic tests

A time may come when your child's teacher or principal recommends further testing. Your child then takes one or more individualized diagnostic tests over one or more sessions. Depending upon what the school is looking for, your child sees the school psychologist or a specialized teacher for testing. Diagnostic tests uncover whether your child is gifted or has learning difficulties that require special attention or another learning setting. By law, schools must contact you before any changes, including administering the tests, take place.

Chapter 14

Connecting with School

In This Chapter

▶ Evaluating grades, homework, and report cards

▶ Deciding whether your child is gifted

▶ Consulting with your child's teachers

▶ Staying involved with your child's school

*T*he telephone rings. Your child's teacher starts a chatty conversation at the other end. You hardly pay attention, because the voice strikes terror in your heart. What has your child done? Was the last test or project so bad to warrant a call? Your mind races about how to handle the impending news about your child's academic ability. Cut out all outside activities or put an end to allowance. Seems extreme, but you never know. Sell the dog. Fry the pet fish for dinner. Doesn't agree with the concept of let-the-punishment-fit-the-crime discussed in Chapter 9.

In desperation, you launch into everything your child may have flubbed recently and worry aloud how these failings ruin future aspirations forever. Then the teacher breaks into your harangue. "I just want to talk about the book Junior brought to school."

Admit it. Sometimes, you go overboard about raising a smart kid. You try so hard that any question of total success causes over-the-top reactions. Time to get a grip, not to mention perspective, on this smart stuff. This chapter gives you different strategies for thinking about grades and whether your child is truly gifted. Discussion covers reasonable and constructive alternatives for getting involved with your child's teachers and the school, so that you keep that perspective in check.

Analyzing Grades and Homework

Remember report cards: those wonderful sources of pride or reasons to run away from home, depending upon your past school experiences. Now your child gets a turn with them. My advice to you is to tread lightly this time around. Even if your child aces everything, be sensitive to the fact that your enthusiasm about grades may not be shared by your offspring.

That said, grades are a fact of life, like death and taxes, as the saying goes. For better or worse, grades give the most objective picture of how your child performs during a given time frame.

Grades are not a goal in and of themselves but a jumping-off place to start building toward the next grading period, the next learning milestone.

The good, the bad, and the ugly about grades

Grades and report cards certainly have their pluses and minuses. The good news is that they pinpoint your genius's progress:

- ✔ They offer information — both strengths and weaknesses — about skill levels.

- ✔ They serve as a way for your child's teacher to communicate information to you about how your child stacks up with classmates in mastering certain goals for the grade.

- ✔ They give you clues about what your child needs next: more challenge in this area, extra help in that one.

- ✔ They hold your child accountable for learning, thereby motivating your darling to study.

- ✔ They provide you with strong indications about class, and possibly school and district, expectations.

On the negative side, report cards can be downers for you and your kids. Nothing sends your little loved ones into hiding faster than the sight of you opening a grade sheet or reviewing a test that earned less than spectacular results. Remember that report cards and grades:

- ✔ **Confuse you when you have difficulty interpreting what the teacher means by a grade or comment:** Confusion is a clue that you'd better contact the teacher quickly and ask questions.

- **Differ from school to school and teacher to teacher:** Here again, communicate with the teacher to understand the code used to describe your child.

- **May not be accurate appraisals** because of misguided attempts to either pump up the morale of all the kids in your child's class or make the class or school look better. Neither reason does what it intends. Instead of a morale booster, your child gets the message that mediocrity is acceptable, knowing full well how little effort went into those grades.

  As for the school, the practice of grading high may be an indication of low academic expectations overall. If your kids receive a watered-down curricula, they will be ill-prepared for strenuous academics at the next level, whether at high school or college. Beyond voicing your concern, you may not be able to do anything with the school about these *inflated grades*. But you can spice up your youngster's extracurricular life by adding heavy doses of enriching ingredients, such as those suggested in Chapter 12.

- **Deflate psyches when your child doesn't do well or when she believes recognition should have been higher.** In most cases, kids don't get their grades to spite you. Go easy, because your child probably feels bad enough already without having you beating the ratings to death. Instead, focus on the next step: how to improve. Read on and see the "Nine reasons why kids underachieve" sidebar for ways to proceed tactfully.

Reacting to grades graciously

You want to throw something or send your child to military school at the sight of poor grades. You aren't the first parent to freak out about a report card. But none of these reactions is appropriate, let alone practical.

I truly that believe that everyone has their time, even you and your darling. Try to think of a bad report card as not your child's time to shine now. But know that time will come.

Studies prove that if you react negatively to your child's lower-than-expected grades, your child gets you back later, ruining his academic future in the process. That's because your kids internalize the criticizing, faultfinding, and blaming. Then they spit it back in the form of more poor grades. But if you can be supportive, poor grades get better. Trust me on this one.

Exactly what's a worried parent to do?

✔ **Stay calm.** Take a deep breath. Go for a walk. Anything that detaches emotions from the grades.

✔ **Separate yourself from your child's report card.** Understand that grades do not reflect your parenting skills. Similarly, separate the report card from your child, meaning your child is more than a few grades and test scores.

✔ **Talk with your child about the report.** Be supportive. Understand that your child probably feels bad enough about the report card and about disappointing you.

Be positive. Point out something good about the report card: grades that improved, those that stayed the same despite the difficult time with a subject, grades in subjects that indicate special talent, comments about agreeable behavior. Then discuss the poor grades in a non-threatening way. Ask what your child thinks went wrong and what can be done to improve: study longer, work in the bedroom or dining room instead of the television room, do homework with someone who understands algebra better. Offer to help, so that your child feels you're in this together.

If the report notes behavior problems, talk about why they may be occurring: problems concentrating, boredom with the material; fatigue from lack of sleep. After sorting through the options, set realistic goals for improvement.

Don't expect your C student to bring home all As on the next report card. Better to shoot for Bs or improvement in one or two subjects in the beginning. Unrealistic goals undermine motivation.

✔ **Talk with the teacher.** Ask for clarification of any problems. Gather information from the teacher about work habits, subjects your child finds difficult, and whether your child is in the right work groups or class. Make sure your child is handing in her homework. Plan ways to help and monitor your child together.

✔ **Give your child hope that tests will get easier.** Point out what your child does well on a regular basis. Small successes will build into bigger ones. After your child believes she can succeed in school, grades will start to turn around, too.

Evaluating Your Genius's Smarts

The most popular way educators evaluate smarts is by assessing intelligence. But intelligence is one of the more elusive concepts, even in today's technically advanced world. Read this section to understand the part intelligence plays in identifying gifted children.

Nine reasons why kids underachieve

So your child gets a bad grade or two. No big deal. That happens to the best of students. But downslides that last for weeks or months are cause for concern. Maybe something else is going on. Get into your kid's head. See if any of these reasons are causing underachievement:

✔ **Too much pressure at home:** Strike a delicate balance between too much and too little emphasis on schoolwork. You want your child to feel supported but not hounded. See Chapter 3 for more about providing a balanced life for your youngster.

✔ **Rebound effect:** Is your high-achieving child burned out? Need variety in life? Need to chill out? Check out Chapter 15.

✔ **Misunderstandings between you and your child:** Sometimes, your child's twisted mind conjures up a plan to slack off in school as a great way to get back at you, as mentioned in Chapter 13.

✔ **Squabbles with sibs:** Who can think with hostility breathing down your neck? Time for a family meeting, as discussed in Chapter 11, to sort out sibling issues.

✔ **Too much space:** Kids need time to express themselves. But there's such a thing as too much freedom. Perhaps your slacker is calling out for structure and attention from you. Read more about this in Chapter 3.

✔ **Friend troubles:** What classmates think counts. Check who your child hangs around with. Are these kids part of the anti-school crowd? Or is your child having problems with peers, which interferes with concentration?

✔ **Teacher problems:** Not every student clicks with every teacher. But open warfare between the two shuts kids down. Talk with the teacher to investigate the relationship.

✔ **Too much or too little challenge:** Nothing stifles enthusiasm like work that's too hard or too easy. Talk with the teacher about hidden learning differences that may dampen your child's enthusiasm to comply.

✔ **Physical problems:** Your child can't perform well when eating a poor diet or not getting enough sleep. Evaluate your child's schedule together to set eating and sleep schedules that work.

Dispelling myths about IQ

Intelligence, like the wind in this poem, is difficult to pin down. Many experts have tried. The best they can do is measure your child based on a standardized test and come up with an IQ, or *intelligence quotient*. Your testee takes parts of the test, which are graded individually, and a collective score tells you where your child stands in the brain-power pecking order.

Detractors find IQ wanting. They claim that IQ tests can't measure all that's involved in achievement; therefore, tests are poor judges of future success and, possibly, of giftedness. Naysayers charge that reducing intelligence to a single number poses significant problems. Low scorers feel academically doomed, while high scorers constantly chase moonbeams, many out of their reach. Those in the middle simply give up, convinced they can't compete against the designated smartees.

Because many districts and teachers use test scores for class placement, this can be problematic for your child. I know of a teacher who sat kids in rows based on their test scores. Smart kids in the front; not-so-smart kids in the back. Although this happened long ago, my friend who inhabited a seat in the back remembers this class as the first telltale sign that he was a failure.

The modern anti-IQ crowd promotes the idea that everyone has what they call *multiple intelligence,* a conglomeration of attributes that signify how smart a child is. Everything your offspring does counts, not just the heavy academics or specific skills tested by an IQ test. Your child can excel academically in one or more subjects or be gifted in nonacademic areas, such as music or visual arts.

I personally go with the anti-IQ folks, probably because I like the premise that every child is intelligent and gifted, including yours and mine. This more inclusive definition works for me because I buy into the larger definition of intelligence covered in Chapter 1. I embrace more than standardized test scores. Instead, I wrap social skills, problem solving, analytical thinking, creativity, common street smarts, and a host of other everyday talents into the total intelligence package.

Following this logic, the unrealistic expectation of across-the-board superiority is gone. Your child can shine in reading but still sing off key and not feel like a failure. Your job as a parent is to help your child identify these outstanding pockets of intelligence and encourage their development.

With-it versus gifted

Now for the big question. How do you know whether your child is truly gifted: you know, over-the-top intelligent?

I realize that true giftedness takes the discussion about intelligence to a whole new dimension. Specific achievements in the areas of multiple intelligence definitely lead to success. But this definition of intelligence doesn't get you very far in discovering whether your child qualifies for special gifted status in school.

While I don't want you obsessing about giftedness, I do think you need a realistic frame of reference for what the people in-the-know call "gifted."

Identifying giftedness

Unfortunately, no clear definition exists for giftedness. What makes gifted-ness harder to pinpoint is the fact that gifted students differ as much as those in the general population. Your child's range of talents and levels of across-the-board development may vary from the next child, who may be gifted, too. Do your homework to determine whether your child qualifies for special programs based on the local school district's definition of giftedness.

The one criterion promoted by the National Association for Gifted Children (NAGC), www.nagc.org, identifies "someone who shows, or has the potential for showing, an exceptional level of performance in one or more areas of expression." Pretty vague, huh?

Schools generally look and test for the following combination of gifted ingredients that the U. S. Office of Gifted and Talented recommends:

- ✔ **High scores on standardized intelligence tests:** Can't get away from these tests. If you want a number to look out for giftedness, figure scores above 130. Intelligence tests usually examine general information and skills in using vocabulary, word associations, analytical thinking, memory, and abstract and mathematical reasoning.

- ✔ **Superior aptitude or talent in a specific area:** You or your child's teacher may be able to spot some special talent, or the school psychologist may administer a test, like the Scholastic Aptitude Test (SAT) that's used by college admissions departments, to identify advanced skills.

- ✔ **Leadership ability:** Gifted leaders use their decision-making and problem-solving skills to sway peers into action. You and the teacher may see evidence of this in your child's everyday interactions. Higher-ups at school may choose to find some test instrument to validate those observations.

- ✔ **Creative thinking:** School personnel may not take your word for the amount of creativity your child possesses. They need more to go on than the gigantic amount of questions your child asks or the way he takes apart and fixes computers. So they rely on still other tests. School psychologists look for ways your child puts ideas together, takes risks, and handles new and known information.

- ✔ **Visual and performing arts:** Special talent in the arts is one of the more obvious signs of giftedness. Your child may excel in visual art, music, dance, acting, or creative writing: sculpting preschool, writing music in the primary grades, and being published when in junior high.

Your child may exhibit many of the qualities just listed. But the difference between gifted kids and the rest of the population boils down to frequency and extent. Gifted kids show almost all these signs most of the time.

Here is a checklist of clues that indicate your child's possible giftedness. Check out other signs of giftedness in the light-hearted book, *You Know Your Child Is Gifted When . . . : A Beginner's Guide to Life on the Bright Side* by Judy Galbraith (Free Spirit). Consider whether your child:

- ✔ Grasps sophisticated concepts easily and with great abstract reasoning and problem-solving skills.

- ✔ Seems advanced compared with others of the same age. In school, your child soars ahead of classmates, already knowing the curriculum before information is presented.

- ✔ Shows unusual interest in words, both for reading and speaking. Your child talks early and reads early with an advanced and extensive vocabulary for his age.

- ✔ Experiments to see how devices work, tests boundaries, challenges accepted theories, and solves complicated problems. Your child likes puzzles, mazes, and number and word games.

- ✔ Questions constantly and is always curious, which can try your patience. This kind of child loves learning.

- ✔ Has a memory like an elephant. You can't put anything over on this kid, so don't bother trying.

- ✔ Sticks with chosen activities a long time but has a high activity level. As a baby, this child probably prefers to build block towers rather than take naps. Now his persistence boggles your mind.

- ✔ Shows sensitivity and empathy for others. This child says she "feels your pain" and probably does. She also perceives the world more intensely, reacting strongly to noise, pain, or other sensations.

- ✔ Tends toward perfectionism.

- ✔ Bores easily. A gifted child may be a daydreamer or the child who acts out because school provides too little stimulation.

- ✔ Demonstrates peaks of unusual performance in the arts or an academic subject area.

Programming alternatives for your gifted child

You received the school's confirmation. Your child is gifted. What now? First, run, don't walk, to school for a meeting of everyone's mind. Devise a program together that nurtures your child's abilities. Depending upon what your school district can offer, consider these options:

✔ **Separate gifted (also called *honors* or *talented*) program:** Specially trained teachers devise accelerated and enriching activities to stimulate faster learners.

✔ **Pull-out (or enrichment) program:** Your child goes off with other like-minded kids and a specially-trained teacher for a given period of time each day or each week. Usually, they take part in activities that augment the regular curriculum.

✔ **A classroom with an individualized program:** With the focus on individuality, your child can progress at her own rate but still enjoy spending time with the other kids and exploring advanced activities without seeming like an oddball.

✔ **Placement with a flexible teacher who accepts and plans for uneven development and adjustable groupings:** For example, your child is free to explore with discovery-oriented projects while learning to tie her shoes.

✔ **Ability groups within the class:** The teacher chooses kids who function similarly to work together. Kids who read quickly or compute advanced problems move faster through the material.

✔ **Special schools:** Some districts offer magnet schools that draw gifted kids together under one roof.

✔ **Speeding up the content:** Gifted kids work with students in a higher-grade class for specific subjects. Elementary kids may go to junior high for an hour, or junior high kids may be bused over to the high school. In high school, the program includes accelerated classes for college credit.

✔ **Advancing a grade:** Your talented youngster moves into a higher grade. Weigh this option with your child carefully. Decide how socially mature your child is. Your child may welcome the chance to feel less odd with kids more his academic equal. Or she may miss her friends who provide social and emotional support.

If the school refuses to test your child, go it alone. Ask around at school or your pediatrician's office for a recommended private psychologist. Have your child tested independently. Then come to school armed with recommendations for nurturing your child's talents. If the school can't help because of budgetary or other reasons, arrange your own activities. Hire someone who can help you. Find a private school. If your pocketbook can handle it, your child is worth it.

Staying behind — or not

The news hits you like a bolt of lightening. You know your child struggles to keep up. But the teacher's recommendation to hold your child back still shocks you. The suggestion comes as a blow to you and your child. Time to sort out those feelings — yours and your child's: the anger, the disappointment, and the guilt (always guilt if you were raised like I was).

Ways to satisfy gifted cravings

Gifted kids are like regular kids. They require the same love, discipline, and approval. Show you care about your gifted child's need for extra inspiration by:

✔ Increasing access to enriching places, such as the library, museums, and interesting places around town.

✔ Making books, periodicals, and tapes about topics of interest available.

✔ Locating chess clubs or other special groups that have kids with similar interests.

✔ Attending concerts, plays, and other mind-expanding events.

✔ Arranging to go behind-the-scenes in stores, factories, or other community establishments, so your child can see how products are made and jobs completed.

✔ Taking your child to meetings and conferences organized by any of the gifted organizations mentioned in Chapter 22. Your child won't feel so isolated or different interacting with other kids like her.

Call a meeting for a major family attitude adjustment. Talk about ways to help your child progress. Decide that this wakeup call does not mean failure: It signals a new beginning. Here are some options to plan your attack on the battle to beat grade retention:

✔ **Meet with school personnel, some combination of teacher, principal, and psychologist, to investigate the problem.** Many factors affect poor performance. Check the list of reasons why some kids underachieve in the "Nine reasons why kids underachieve" sidebar. Evaluate whether your child sees and hears well. Suggest tests for hidden signs of learning disability. Discuss study habits. Investigate your child's relationship with the teacher and other problems that could come from the school.

Even gifted kids can have learning disabilities that interfere with producing and attending in school.

✔ **Weigh the idea of retention.** Consider the pros and cons of retention. Each situation is different. Discuss whether your child feels so deflated that staying back will prove disastrous. Or think about retention as a way your child receives the needed academic boost while getting a kick in the pants to work harder.

If you decide your child should repeat a grade, get your child's input, if you can. Some families prefer to stick with the same learning situation because the child feels more comfortable in the setting. For others, the same setting is like a jail sentence for their child. If this is your situation, make sure your child is moved into another setting. Either a different teacher, method of teaching, or another classroom is better than putting your child back into the situation where failure occurred.

After everyone agrees on a course of action, focus on the positives of retention: ease of work and familiar routine. Find tasks your child does well and praise them as the basis for a good school year ahead.

✔ **Discuss alternative solutions.** School systems often offer a variety of alternatives to retention.

- Placement in a multi-grade classroom: With two grades together, the current one and next, your child can learn the missed material while staying with classmates.

- Summer school attendance: The school must agree to retest your child at the end of the summer. If significant improvement occurs, she moves ahead.

- Tutoring assistance: Working with a tutor over the summer could function the same as going to summer school. Here, too, you want the school to agree to retest your child before the next semester.

- Movement to the next grade, with caveats: Caveats include your child going into another class or working with a resource teacher to repeat specific subjects.

✔ **Stay on top of schoolwork.** Now that you have a plan, don't let your child slip into what caused the problem in the first place. Review assignments, check homework, and offer assistance and tons of encouragement daily. Turn a negative into an academic positive.

Communicating with Teachers

Teachers are people, too. They may even be parents, like you are. But just like you, they are busy people who take their jobs seriously. When you want to connect with your child's teacher, plan ahead. Prepare what you want to get out of the communication. And whatever you do, forget about the cute stuff your child said on vacation, how your child sings songs from Don Giovanni and is only 8 years old, or other stories that don't relate to your conversation together but take up teacher time. This section tells you when you should check in with teachers and gives you ideas about what to ask.

Keeping up with everyday business

Staying in touch with teachers on a regular basis is important to raising smart kids. Think of these professionals as partners in the parenting process. After all, teachers probably spend the most time with your kids outside of family members.

Trouble in school alert

Kids give lots of warnings about trouble at school. Your job is to watch out for them and make changes *before* the school suggests that your child repeats a grade. Be ready to help if your child:

✔ Seems depressed, sad, or agitated

✔ Acts out at home or at school

✔ Says she hates school or gets angry when you bring up school subjects

✔ Refuses to show you papers, tests, or homework

✔ Balks at going to school in the morning

✔ Feigns illness or complains of aches, pain, or being exhausted

✔ Never knows when tests or assignments occur and is generally discouraged

✔ Lacks self-confidence

✔ Blows off homework

You're not adversaries, as some literature from parent groups suggests. You want the same goals for your child: to learn and grow at a rate that makes the most of development. Keep a positive attitude and open mind with all your teacher communications:

✔ **Contact your child's teacher early in the school semester to introduce yourself.** Take your child to school the first day, write a note, or call to connect. Ask the teacher the best way to communicate: by e-mail, note by backpack express, or telephone. Tell the teacher you want to know how your child is doing, which will be wonderful of course, so that you can work with the school about anything that changes before situations spiral out of control. No one likes feeling bushwhacked at conference time.

While you're at school, you may introduce yourself to the principal or anyone else who works with your child. You never know when their services and influence will be helpful.

My neighbor offers information about her child to each new teacher. She finds communicating in writing beforehand especially helpful because her son has special learning needs. He is extremely advanced in certain areas but has some learning difficulties in others. She shares quirks her child has and suggestions on how to manage them, should they prove problematic in class.

✔ **Check in with the teacher, but not so frequently that you become a pest, to review how the school year is going.** Don't expect the teacher to initiate unscheduled conversations. Good teachers keep parents informed of the class goings-on. But face it: With grading papers, preparing lesson plans, and the tons of paperwork that school districts require now, talking to you won't be top on their list.

✔ **Share timely stories from home that are pertinent to how your child may do in class.** If the dog dies, the teacher wants to know that your child probably won't be in the best spirits. By the same token, reinforce that you want to know about traumas at school, such as a playground fight or bursting into nervous tears in front of the class while giving an oral report, that may affect behavior at home.

Preparing for the hot seat: Parent-teacher conferences

Oh, Oh. What's the teacher going to say about your child? You're on the hot seat now. If you've been communicating with the teacher on a regular basis, there should be no surprises. But if you haven't, you may feel a lump in the pit of your stomach at the thought of someone evaluating your brilliant little darling — this perfect little being that you and your spouse created.

Try to think of parent-teacher conferences as fact-finding missions, a good way to learn more about your child. Teachers view various aspects of your child. Different rules apply at school. More kids vie for adult approval in class than at home. Teachers see how your kid's idiosyncrasies compare to the next kid's, information you aren't privy to unless you transform into a fly on the classroom wall.

But understand that conferences can be frustrating. Time is short, between 10 and 20 minutes a session (less for high schools). The worst meetings come complete with bells to signal time's up. You feel like you're back in school again, scrambling to finish a test before the school bus comes.

To make the most of your limited teacher time and relieve a little anxiety:

✔ **Arrive prepared.** Come to the conference with questions and concerns for discussion. You want to know about your child's achievement in different subjects (best and worst), work habits, behavior in class and with classmates, and confidence levels. Come prepared with papers, tests, or a recent report card to back up your points and concerns.

✔ **Discuss the impending conference with your student.** Your child may have issues for you to bring up. Kids should be part of the evaluation process, not find out about it only if you hear bad news.

✔ **Arrive on timeand leave when time's up.** Because schedules are tight, latecomers may miss part or all of their session. Understand that teachers have an entire class, many classes in junior high and high school, of student's parents to meet. Besides, being prompt and ending on time graciously shows consideration to the teacher and other parents who come after you.

✔ **Start the meeting by saying something positive.** Sharing pleasantries sets a good tone for working together. Good teachers do this; so should you.

✔ **Request explanations for education-ese — jargon and test results you don't understand.** Just like you tell your kids, you probably aren't the first nor the last to ask the same questions.

✔ **Hear the teacher out, no matter how painful or how much you may agree or disagree.** Again, teachers aren't put on this earth to destroy your family dreams. You are partners on the same team. So:

- Ask what you can do, what the next step is, to move your child forward. Decide together whether you can do activities at home, the teacher can give extra assistance to your child at school, or an outside tutor will be effective. (Check Chapter 13 for information about choosing a tutor.)

- Request another meeting, should you have more to discuss.

After the conference, clue in your child about the conference. Mention the positive stuff first to catch her attention. If you need to deal with problems, let your child know you and the teacher will work together with her to solve them.

The smartest kids get the best education in classes where parents and teachers work together.

Going to School: Participating and Volunteering

Raising smart kids takes involvement, and not just at home. If you want your kids to achieve better grades and stay out of trouble, know what's going on at school. To get the inside story, become involved in school activities.

I know. Your time is precious. Everyone's is nowadays. But involving yourself in your child's school community is time well spent. You find out how the school functions and how your child is being taught. Best of all, your child sees another example that you take school, and education, seriously.

But don't be guilt-tripped into helping with time-consuming events you really have no interest in or can't handle. Let other parents with different time constraints and agendas manage those. Instead, consider volunteer efforts you enjoy and can fit into your schedule. Here are some examples of school activities that may work for you:

- ✔ **Join the school parent-teacher group.** Your school may support the PTA (Parent Teacher Association) or PTO (Parent Teacher Organization), while others sponsor totally independent groups without national or state affiliations. Going to meetings helps you meet other parents and school representatives and share information. If you work during the day and meetings are held during that time, suggest to the principal or group president that alternate meetings be held at night for working parents.

- ✔ **Work on class events.** Teachers often need help with details of parties and special class programs. Offer to make or buy food, decorate, or contact other parents who can complete these tasks. You can call to locate volunteers whenever your schedule allows.

- ✔ **Volunteer to read or tutor in your child's classroom.** Assist the teacher with whatever needs to be done for an hour a week. You really get a bird's-eye view about your child's education then.

- ✔ **Assist in the library, computer lab, or lunchroom.** Go on an occasional field trip. You'll enjoy seeing your child interact in different settings.

- ✔ **Participate on school decision-making committees.** Sometimes, schools or districts need parent input about the direction of the school. Certain committees are required by state or federal law. The most powerful but most time-consuming committee is the school board. That takes tons of commitment in time and energy, but if you like politics and want to affect change, this is the place to be.

- ✔ **Read district newspapers or school letters and reports you receive.** These keep you on top of school news. Nowadays, districts put tons of information about how they operate online, so that you can keep up with school's goals, curricula, and events without leaving the comfort of your home.

- ✔ **Attend school functions and meetings.** Open houses, assemblies, and fairs all have their purposes. Your kids will feel proud that you care enough about the school and your kids to come.

Chapter 15

Developing Smarts for Success Outside of School

* *

In This Chapter

▶ Helping your child cope with relationships

▶ Enabling your kids to handle a greater work and play load

▶ Preparing your child to manage money

* *

*B*eing smart means more than acing tests. Smarts include handling one-self with civility at home and in the community and making and keeping friends. Acting smart incorporates day-to-day details, like managing money.

This chapter acknowledges the growing independence an aging child acquires. With a little luck and emphasis on a few of the following odds and ends, your child can mature into a self-reliant child who makes you proud.

Getting Along with Family and Friends

Here are changes you can expect to occur by the end of eighth grade:

✔ Your child now spends double the time with friends and more of them than when a preschooler. These ever-changing social arrangements come with new rules, which you may have to dance around to maintain order at home.

✔ Your child prefers to spend more time away from family than together. Where's separation anxiety when you want it?

✔ Your child is perfectly capable of taking care of everyday needs independently. Whether you approve of how they are executed remains another matter.

✔ Your child gains an average of 2.5 inches and 7 pounds each year. That comes with doubled muscle mass and more strength than you're used to. You can't just pick up and deposit your child somewhere, should he act evil.

✔ Your child notices body changes in other young people that fall into two categories: his and hers. Play groups separate by gender, which is good because hormones begin to pulsate in junior high.

✔ Your child is now capable of reading, writing, paying attention, and abstract thinking. Prepare for great debates when you won't cough up money or disagree about study habits.

These social and physical alterations contribute to other changes and emotions.

Changing loyalties

During early elementary years, your child chooses friends based on what they can do together. As long as buddies don't fight or tease and can share, most interactions go well. By ages 8 to 10, relationships deepen to include lengthier conversations, loyalty, and helpfulness. These closer bonds are critical for maturation and a sense of identity that bolsters book learning.

From friends, your child learns skills for achieving success in today's school and work world:

✔ How to negotiate and cooperate

✔ How to navigate group norms and rules

✔ How to be responsible to more than oneself; in other words, how to be sociable and caring

✔ How to feel part of another group besides family

Your child will do better in school if he can form healthy friendships.

Branching out brings all the joys and sorrows of trying to get along with people who may not see the world as your child does. Whether your child feels accepted or isolated by friends can affect everything else: grades, self-confidence, and enterprise. Kids who feel accepted feel better about themselves, want to go to school, and enjoy interactions with other students that build on social learning. Conversely, no matter how academically talented your child is, if he hates attending school because he has no friends, you're going to have a difficult time getting him out the door for school each day, and he definitely won't stick his neck out in class to shine.

The tricky part for you is knowing your role in your child's life outside the family. Here are some guidelines:

- ✔ **Let your child know you are always there to listen and help.** Don't keep talking, thinking your wisdom will guide your child, when what your child really needs is your ear for listening. Instead, reinforce that he is capable of working through relationship issues, both good and bad.

- ✔ **Remain the one constant in your child's life as friends come and go,** which they will. Keep rules and follow through consistently no matter how much you hear, "Everyone is going," "Everyone has one," "Everyone . . . (you fill in the blank)."

- ✔ **Shift into counselor/consultant mode, rather than protector.** Ask, listen, and help clarify as needed, instead of telling your child what to do. Suggest alternatives, but don't say, "This is the way we. . . ."

  This may take practice, because you've had years of total control — or you thought you had.

- ✔ **Model positive relationship behaviors,** such as getting along with others, respecting people from different backgrounds, handling sticky situations, and resolving conflict peacefully.

Stay connected with your child. In other words, even though your little darling starts pulling away, make sure you let him know that you love him the same as before, maybe more. Remind your child that relationships are difficult but can be managed.

Eliminating shyness

Nothing seems more painful than learning about your shy flower's failed attempts to interact, whether he tries to get called on in class or searches for playmates at recess. Visions of your youth flash before your eyes. Perhaps the pain you feel is for your own missed opportunities. Or you were so gregarious that you wonder where the shyness comes from and aren't sure how to react.

While you can't change your child's inborn nature, nor should you want to, you can help your child be bolder about making contacts that further his learning by:

- ✔ **Avoiding the view that shyness is a problem rather than a personality trait:** In fact, eliminate the label from your vocabulary altogether because many folks consider shyness a negative, including your child. If you must talk about your child, use words like *cautious, quiet,* or *private,* traits everyone could use more of.

✔ **Accepting that shyness is part of your child's personality:** As long as your child makes eye contact and seems happy with himself and his class participation, he's doing fine. He's probably the kind of child who needs to get to know someone or feel comfortable in large groups before opening up, which is okay.

✔ **Refraining from mentioning this trait to people in front of your child:** Your child exhibits many more qualities than shyness. Focusing on this trait only reinforces it. And never, ever compare your child's lack of gregariousness to anyone else's.

✔ **Encouraging your child to bring a friend home:** Your child may feel more comfortable on his home turf. And a younger child may be less threatening to befriend at first than someone your child's age.

✔ **Building your child's confidence:** Check out some confidence builders in Chapter 1 and read on for more ideas:

- Find something your child loves to do and encourage it. Special talents or skills give your child something to talk to others about with authority.

- Put your child in charge of something, such as feeding the dog or helping grandma shop. Added responsibility makes your child feel important and gives him something other than himself to think about.

- Ratchet up the compliments for social behavior. Praise playing peacefully with another kid, sharing toys, asking questions in school, or bringing out snacks when someone is over.

✔ **Moving slowly with your child:** Try not to thrust him into unplanned social situations or put him on display. That means no spontaneous requests to perform a piano piece at a family gathering, or putting your child on the spot with, "You remember Aunt Susie?" when your child last saw her at age 2. How embarrassing!

✔ **Practicing conversation starters together:** Role-play saying hello and shaking hands for introductions. Review topics your child can bring up, such as a favorite movie, song, or game, to bridge communication gaps. Talk about making eye contact and smiling as ice breakers.

✔ **Modeling hospitable social skills:** Mention that you were considered shy at one time, too, and that you did A, B, and C to overcome your hesitation. Your child will not feel so alone or weird. And he'll see that socializing is safe to do.

✔ **Suggesting that your child say hello to one new person every day, or ask someone a question:** He could ask a teacher or police officer for directions or compliment someone's dress or skills. While he may never be gabby, your child will be thought of as friendly and caring.

Finding ten smart ways to treat friends

Kids like other kids who treat them well. And smart kids know how to treat buddies. Positive social skills translate into successful managerial skills later in life, a smart direction for any career. Be sure your child understands that getting along with others means:

- ✔ **Respecting different people and their beliefs, no matter what ethnicity, religion, or gender:** Kids want friends who are their equals, people who don't try to boss or manipulate them. Smart kids know what it means to be fair and just.

- ✔ **Caring for someone else, empathizing, and wanting to be helpful:** Smart kids know how to get beyond themselves. They want to help others and make their mark on the world.

- ✔ **Resolving differences peacefully through communication, negotiation, or seeking out a mediator:** Smart kids know that conflict interferes with time better spent on learning and having a good time.

- ✔ **Understanding that others have rights and opinions, no matter how much your child agrees or disagrees:** Smart kids accept others, warts and all, because they understand that everyone now lives in a global world.

- ✔ **Following through with the courage of convictions:** Smart kids have strong beliefs and reasons for them.

- ✔ **Accepting responsibility for what he does and says:** Smart kids don't need someone else representing them. They feel confident enough about who they are to stand by their convictions.

- ✔ **Being mannerly:** This one may not kick in until college, but you want to instill polite behavior as soon as your child starts talking. Waiting your turn and saying "please," "excuse me," and "thank you" bodes well at any age. Smart kids learn this mode of operating earlier.

- ✔ **Remembering to tell the truth even in difficult situations:** Cheating and lying definitely do not win friends. Smart kids tell the truth because they think too much of themselves not to.

- ✔ **Sticking up for buddies** — and anyone else, for that matter, especially kids that aren't part of the in crowd — when they are being treated unfairly or mistreated: Smart kids feel powerful enough to buck an unjust crowd.

- ✔ **Having a strong sense of himself and what friends can offer each other:** With this knowledge comes the realization that no one is perfect. Help your child weigh whether a friend with a bothersome trait is worth keeping as a friend given the person's other qualities. Smart kids understand human frailties, even their own.

Beating back bullies

Nothing brings out the tiger in you more than someone bullying your kid. But resist the urge to rush in and save your child. Better to empower your child with smart alternatives, so that the same situation doesn't happen again.

✔ **Get the facts before attempting any action.** Find out your child's role in this unwanted relationship. Is there something your child does to bug the bully? What has your child tried already? What were the results?

✔ **Talk with your child, if you discover that he causes the problem.** Yes, your darling is as capable of threatening others as the next kid. So identify the reason for any undesirable behavior. Impress upon your child that bullying or joining in bullying is wrong. Offer healthy ways to handle aggression and activities to build confidence, so that he won't feel the need to bully anyone else.

✔ **Let your child try to handle the bully alone at first.** Suggest these options:

- Confront the bully and ask why the incidents occur. He may want to square off with, "I think people who hit/chase/call me names must feel awful inside."

- Stay nonchalant. Say something like, "Thanks for telling me," and walk away. Bullies want to get a rise out of their victim and embarrass them. When that doesn't happen, they go elsewhere.

- Inform the bully in a firm voice that this type of behavior must end. Bullies choose kids to bother who they don't think will challenge them. Your child's nemesis may back down when confronted.

- Avoid the bully, if talking doesn't work. Advise your child to steer clear of bathrooms or secluded places where the bully knows he's alone. Recommend that he take alternate routes to school, a job, or the playground.

- Recommend that your child tell an adult at school. Teachers and administrators have the responsibility to provide a safe place to learn. Emphasize that this is not tattling. Your child is actually helping other kids who the bully may hurt.

✔ **Contact the child's parents yourself, should your child's efforts fail.** But understand that parents may be of little help. Chances are a troubled child comes from a troubled family.

✔ **Talk with school personnel.** Go as high as you need, even to the superintendent, to get results. If nothing seems to work or a large group bullies your child, you may want to consider transferring your child to another school.

✔ **Instill in your child the confidence to ward off bullies.** Kids who feel confident are more apt to compromise and negotiate without feeling they are losing face in front of other kids, which is what a bully wants. See Chapter 3 for confidence-building suggestions.

Adding Responsibilities

Chapter 10 mentions some benefits of chores for growing successful kids. Now that your child is older, the benefits multiply: responsibility, building a work ethic and the willingness to pitch in, accountability and dependability, a sense of pride and accomplishment, and a mishmash of other valuable stuff that relates to the definition of being smart (see Chapter 1).

Here are some helpful hints for handling chores at home:

- **Hold a family meeting to divvy up chores.** Look at the "Jobs your child can do" sidebar for ideas. Take interests, time, and skill level into consideration when assigning tasks.

- **Post chores on a chart or calendar, so that everyone knows who does what when.** That way, your child takes ownership by completing them himself without you nagging.

- **Refrain from nagging about chores.** Give one reminder and stop talking before your child tunes you out. Be direct, such as "Please brush the dog before dinner time." If being direct doesn't work, try some creative alternatives to get chores done. Challenge your child to complete the job in so many minutes, or leave notes that read "Wash me!" or "I stink! Put me in the garbage."

  If humor doesn't work, allow consequences of undone chores to encourage compliance. When your child runs out of clothes, he'll remember to do the laundry. If you say he can't go with friends until his bedroom is clean, you bet he'll hustle and clean it. Smart kids make wise choices about priorities.

- **Alternate jobs whenever possible.** No one likes to do the same chore every day. Besides, you want your child to gain a range of skills for independence.

- **Complete chores alongside your child.** Hold a family chore day. Work seems more fun when it's done with others. Play music, sing, and dance around. Afterward, do something special together, such as eating out, going to a movie, or playing a game together.

  No one says chores have to be serious.

- **Bring on the praise.** Acknowledge a job well done, or acknowledge that the job was done at all.

Never redo your child's assignments. First, that's your child's responsibility. Second, nothing defeats the ego more than someone redoing something you just spent time and energy completing. If your child does a slipshod job, be specific about what you want improved. Reinforce that his job is to always do his best and not only in school. But if you want something done a certain meticulous way and you will accept no other, do it yourself.

Jobs your child can do

Middle-school kids can handle myriad jobs around the house without your being accused of causing a Cinderella complex:

- Baking treats
- Bathing the dog
- Dusting the house
- Emptying the clothes dryer
- Feeding pets
- Folding and putting clothes away
- Grocery shopping (helping at the store and putting items away)
- Ironing clothes
- Loading and unloading the dishwasher
- Mowing the lawn
- Planting flowers and grass
- Polishing shoes
- Polishing silverware
- Preparing meals
- Running simple errands
- Sorting recycling items
- Taking out garbage
- Tidying their bedroom
- Walking the dog
- Washing clothes
- Washing dishes
- Washing/dust mopping floors
- Watching the baby
- Watering house plants

Participating in Extra Activities

Like younger kids, middle-graders learn through play. They like board games, sports, hobbies, and their collections. Only now, your child spends more time playing in larger groups, such as on sports teams and in academic clubs, that set their own rules. Play in middle years serves as a barometer of responsibilities and social interactions that lie ahead. Following this logic, the more experience with extracurricular activities to practice and fine-tune this quest, the better off your child will be. Or will he?

Getting out and about: Valuable or troublesome?

A smart education goes beyond academics. Experiences gained outside the classroom during middle years provide:

- ✔ Skills and capabilities that last a lifetime
- ✔ Social skills
- ✔ Wider interests
- ✔ Creative outlets

Trouble with activities comes when either too many fill your child's day, or his heart isn't in them. Then your child becomes over-scheduled and stressed out — you know, with a bad case of the *overs*, which kids can get at any age. Watch for signs of stress and over-commitment with any of these changes in your child's behavior:

- ✔ Becomes anxious, especially before leaving for the activity
- ✔ Cries easily
- ✔ Downturn in grades
- ✔ Eating problems
- ✔ Feigns illness
- ✔ Fights more with siblings and friends
- ✔ Frequent and unclear emotional outbursts
- ✔ Frustrates easily
- ✔ Loss of confidence
- ✔ Refuses to budge out the door, the clearest sign I know
- ✔ Sleep difficulties
- ✔ Unusually tired, even after waking

When you crusade for your child to participate in yet another activity, consider this thought: If you constantly push to enrich and boost skills, you may be sending your child the message that he isn't good enough the way he is. And that's not cool — for your child's self-confidence or for family harmony.

Creating creativity from boredom

One major benefit of doing nothing is the creation of something. In other words, creativity comes from being bored. That's when your child looks around, scavenges materials to play with, and invents something new to do with them.

Stress busters

Kids, even smart ones, get stressed out in the same way that adults do. Why not give kids ideas for how to reduce stress, too? Start practicing alternatives when your child is young. That way, the skills become automatic, should the need arise. Choose from these alternatives to help your child bring mind and body back into balance when anxiety builds:

- **Reduce the load, if over-scheduling is the problem.** Ask your child what three activities he likes best or what he'd like to change most about his schedule. You may be surprised about the answer. You think you are making your child happy by schlepping him from activity to activity. But I predict he says he'd rather have more family and hanging-out time than more activities.

- **Add yoga.** Even kindergartners are learning the art of breathing and muscle control to reduce stress. I know yoga requires yet another class for your child, but the skills yoga offers may last a lifetime.

- **Breathe deeply,** possibly paired with counting to ten.

- **Switch activities for a while.** Sometimes a break provides enough respite to go back and tackle difficult projects.

- **Listen to soothing music.** Read in Chapter 5 how music calms the evils.

- **Think about something pleasurable and calming.** Examples include playing at the beach, a favorite stuffed toy, and listening to leaves rustle. Ask your child to visualize these settings, which refocuses energy and anxiety.

- **Talk to a sympathetic ear about what's going on.** Discuss the idea of stress-busters and to whom your child can turn for consolation.

- **Participate in physical activity, such as running, jumping, bicycling, or walking around the block.** Kids who sit or concentrate a long time or have activity issues anyway can relieve tension with a period of sustained activity.

- **Help your child learn to say "no" before enrolling in something he doesn't want to do or begins to feel overwhelmed.** That means you have to listen to your child's decision. You want to raise someone who feels confident enough to say "no" in more serious situations. So you have to pay attention when your child says, "No more activities," or "I don't want to continue ice skating (piano lessons, French lessons, whatever)."

- **Calm your hyper-parenting beast.** No parenting law dictates that your child has to be involved in every activity, club, or team sport that exists in your community. Be a little selective here: Make time together your family's most important activity.

 The more you plan entertainment for your child, the more entitled he feels to be entertained and the less likely he'll be able to entertain himself. Beyond stimulating creativity, which is discussed in Chapter 1, I'm talking about an important life skill here.

Plan to stimulate your child's creativity by:

✔ Making sure you arrange time for your child to be bored. Steel yourself for this one, especially if your child is used to a packed schedule of stimulating activities. Plan to not interact with your child or invite friends to play. Tell your bored buddy this is his time alone to figure out what to do.

✔ Choosing creative toys and materials, as suggested in Chapter 7, to keep around the house.

✔ Unplugging all media for a given amount of time.

✔ Refusing to cave and be sucked into play or allowing television, no matter how much you get nagged with "I'm so-o-o bored."

✔ Reinforcing the message that, "Certainly such a bright child like you can think of something to do."

Dealing with competition

Competition is a fact of life. Your child competes for grades. He competes in sports, for a place on student council, and for your attention. For many kids, competing fuels motivation. But competition isn't all about winning, at least it shouldn't be.

Don't get me wrong. I'm not against winning. Winning feels good. I enjoy a good win once in a while, and I'm sure you do, too. But don't you also feel warm and fuzzy from knowing you do the best you can, whether you win or not? Don't you find joy in performing better this time than you did the last? These are the messages you need to send your child.

The problem with focusing on winning is:

✔ Your child feels pressured to always be tops.

✔ Your child feels like a failure if he doesn't win, although he's put a lot of effort into an activity and has had successes. The next time around, he figures, "Why bother if I can't win?" Then he puts in less effort, if any at all.

✔ Your child loses interest whenever competition enters the picture.

✔ Your child fears winning because of the expectation that he must win all the time, which he knows is unrealistic.

✔ Your child misses the message that something can be good for him, fun for him, or just plain smart for him to continue. He loses sight of how enjoyable the process and socialization can be.

Your child needs to feel strong and confident to face competition.

How do you instill a healthy outlook about competition? Whether you're talking about sports or grades or running for office in school:

✔ **Reinforce the job done, not the end result.** Rather than saying, "Who won?" or "What grade did you get?" ask, "How did you do?" or "What was the best/easiest part of the game/test for you?" or "Are you pleased with how well you did?" Achievement should bring its own rewards.

✔ **Cultivate in your child the ability to lose without feeling like a failure.** Help your child understand that he wins and loses every day. Acknowledge when he feels badly by saying, "Losing does feel awful, but. . . ." Then help him move on. Point out his unique strengths. Urge your child to keep trying because working at something feels good inside.

Encourage your child to write in a gratitude journal. Figuring out what to enter each day helps any Negative Ned focus on the positive.

✔ **Restrain yourself from being dramatic at competitions.** Bite your tongue. Put tape over your mouth. Stay home during competitive events, if that's what it takes. Keep yourself from getting so caught up in the game or activity that you pressure your child and spoil the fun of participating.

This isn't your event. It belongs to your child. If you're too involved, back off.

✔ **Praise something other than the win or top grade.** Choose something about your child and how he participates to reward. "You warm the bench with patience and a smile." "You keep your composure when. . . ." "You scored ten points higher on this test than the last." Kids who give their all always win.

Guarding girl brain power

As kids sneak up on adolescence, something strange happens. Girls and boys notice they are girls and boys. So does everyone around them.

I know life is supposed to be different for females now. But you and your child's teachers may still treat the genders differently, in terms of both education fairness. You may inadvertently sell your daughter short when emphasizing how smart, assertive, and capable she is. Make sure your daughter receives a gender-neutral education at home and at school:

✔ **Never give into stereotypes.** From babyhood, dress your daughter in clothes that allow her to play and climb freely. Shower her with bold primary colors. Eliminate the frilly bedroom decorations, unless they are specifically requested. Instead, choose wallpaper, accoutrements, and wall hangings that display action and strength. And when doling out household chores, please don't only assign your daughter the cooking and your son taking out the garbage.

Get beyond gender-specific clothes, items, and jobs. Let your daughter's natural inclinations guide choices.

✔ **Find nonsexist toys and games that build curiosity and encourage learning adventures.** Check out toy guidelines in Chapter 7 that work for both genders. Build things and play sports and mind games together. Roughhouse with your daughter the same way you would with your son.

✔ **Review your child's books for gender stereotypes.** Watch out for stories that assign male characters the action and female characters the jobs of watching and cheering. Try to equalize the number of books with male and female protagonists.

✔ **Monitor your child's classroom.** Make sure the teacher calls on girls as much as boys. Ask if jobs are divided by gender or the teacher rotates who does what. Check whether school programs give equal value to female role models and their accomplishments.

When studying Native Americans at our local school, the teacher directed the girls to make papooses and boys bows and arrows. Give me a break!

✔ **Send the message that your daughter can do anything she chooses.** Let her know that no door should be closed only because she is female.

✔ **Encourage your daughter to speak out in class and ask questions.** Reinforce that she never has to hide her brains to please anyone.

✔ **Discuss gender stereotypes in media together.** Ask your daughter what she thinks is a stereotype. Point out, for example, reed-thin models wearing sexy, scant clothes. Share how most girls and women can never look like this.Champion your daughter's pride in her looks, body, and most of all her brain power.

Your high expectations override the traditional messages she receives from everywhere else, like on television, in movies and video games, and in print materials.

✔ **Assume your daughter has an interest in and can perform well in math, science, and technology.** All kids are naturally curious about these subjects. Girls score fine in these areas until they receive negative messages about what they can accomplish. Don't let your daughter become a statistic of the self-fulfilling prophesy that says girls can't succeed in science or technology. (The myth was probably started by some boys who wanted to look better in their class ratings.)

✔ **Expose your daughter to math and science opportunities outside school.** Involve her in figuring the shopping budget. Show her what's under the car hood or how to flip circuit breakers in the basement. Make learning practical and fun.

✔ **Champion your daughter's sport's efforts.** Studies prove that girls who play sports are stronger and healthier in body and mind. They feel better about themselves, stay in school longer, and are less likely to abuse drugs or get pregnant. As adults, more women CEOs have played and still play some organized sport. That's because playing a sport gives them confidence to take risks, compete, and be a team player.

✔ **Arrange for your daughter to meet female mentors who are scientists, sportscasters, and computer jocks.** Let her know she can be any of these or any other choices. Help her learn how to pursue nontraditional careers, if these are her interests.

✔ **Start a mother-daughter mentoring program.** A good time is during your daughter's middle or junior high school years when stereotypes and discomfort about a maturing body really kick in. The group can hold discussions, read and discuss nonsexist books, meet women in various fields, or take field trips to unconventional work environments for women, such as an engineering firm, scuba diving company, court room, or fire station. Check the resources in Chapter 22 for organizations that can assist you.

Appreciating the Value of Money

You know your child is successful when he understands dollars and cents. Smart kids know how to manage money. Sound attitudes about money cover budgeting, saving, and spending wisely. To fulfill your duties as the parent of a smart kid, help your child learn money management basics.

Sharing the economics of running a family

Relate money matters to your child's everyday experiences. This reality-based form of education causes infinitely less eye-rolling when imparting your wisdom about money and safe ways to handle it:

✔ **Start talking about money early.** Get in the habit of explaining personal experiences, mistakes, and how you handled them according to your child's ability to understand. Kids as young as 3 can learn to identify coins and numbers on dollar bills. Reinforce the idea of trading or exchanging money for goods. Show your older child when you handle money, either by writing checks, giving real money, or charging.

Knock-out summer activities

Smart kids like to stretch their brains outside school but welcome the change of pace summer brings. To make the most of time away from formal instruction, brainstorm with your child about experiencing some of these alternatives:

- **Camp:** Consider general day camp, overnight camp, and camps that emphasize special interests, such as foreign language, sports, or the arts. Camps go for the entire summer or for weeks, weekends, or certain days, leaving time for other activities — or nothing.

  Don't let college be the first time your child leaves home alone. First-timers are at greater risk of having adjustment problems and dropping out because they miss the family nest.

- **Camp counselor trainee program:** Investigate camps that provide counselor training for your over-age-12 child. Your child receives leadership training, a different view of camp life, and a possible paying job in a couple years.

- **Summer school:** Many school districts or community centers offer individual classes that are usually less demanding than regular schoolwork. But they provide opportunities to explore something new or practice and investigate current interests further.

- **Recreation programs:** Rather than a full day of camp, your child may prefer picking up some lessons, such as pottery or golf, at the local park district or community center.

- **Programs run by special interest groups:** Check online or at the library to locate a group or association (find these in the *Encyclopedia of Associations*) with programs to satisfy your child's wildest desires,

such as to study more about butterflies, botany, or a certain sport.

- **Research project:** Identify a subject your child is crazy about or has always wanted to investigate. Then let him lose in libraries, museums, bookstores, and online. He may enjoy writing a paper or drawing pictures or maps to go with the information he collects.

- **Volunteering:** Smart kids are caring kids. Why not encourage your child to do good deeds for someone else during the summer? Your child can pull weeds for an older adult, walk someone's dog, or read to blind residents in a nursing home.

  Charity begins at home. Your child can clean out his closet to donate unwanted clothes and toys, help you with house and yard work, and do odd jobs at your place of employment.

- **Self-initiated businesses:** Encourage your child to test his business skills, alias math, organization, and persistence, by selling his used clothes and toys or refining his lemonade stand to include bottled water and snacks. Put the stand along a bicycle trail, at a bus stop, or near a kid's sporting event for more traffic.

- **Community projects:** Encourage your child to organize friends to start a project to better the community, such as weed-pulling in parks or walking dogs for shut-ins. High-achieving kids like to solve problems and improve conditions while sharpening leadership skills.

- **Establish summertime goals:** Suggest that your child write down activities he doesn't have time for during the school year. Think of learning a new skill, such as riding a bicycle, or reading a stack of books for fun. Make the list detailed. That way, when your child says "I'm bored," you can direct him

✔ **Allow your child to handle money as he ages.**

- Practice money transactions by playing store at home.

- Give your child coins to get treats, healthy ones, of course, from a vending machine.

- Encourage savings in a piggy bank, special container, or real bank account after a certain amount is saved. Open a separate account for your child with a separate passbook, so that he figures out how to handle bank transactions and can watch the money grow. Consider requiring your child to save a portion of gifts or allowance to ensure financial growth.

  Keep the bank book in a safe place where you can monitor its use. You don't want a dog-eared, page-ripped-out version, and you don't want to lose proof of savings.

- Send your child to the store. Write down one or two items on a note at first, and place the note and money in a wallet, pouch, or envelope to keep the receipt and change together. With practice, your child can choose items, stand in line to pay, and count change independently. If travel to a store isn't practical where you live, take your child to the store but let him handle the transaction.

✔ **Talk through the mental evaluation process you usually go through silently before purchasing something.** Casually mention these deliberations to your child on trips to the mall or supermarket. Discuss what's a fair price for a good or service. Ask your child's opinion about whether the product has good value for the quality and cost.

✔ **Reinforce the idea that planning ahead avoids impulse buying, the purchase of unnecessary stuff.** But realize that planning ahead is not a strong trait among most kids. You want to plant a few seeds for later, such as the idea of making lists of what you intend to purchase before hitting the stores.

Impress upon your young spending machine that money is usually for what you need, not for everything you want. Expect this distinction to elude your child as it does most kids until he's spending his own hard-earned cash.

✔ **Decide how much you want your child to participate in family financial-planning discussions.** You may feel that your child benefits from hearing where the money goes and how spending choices are made. Your child may like contributing to vacation, decorating, or repair plans.

Be careful that your child doesn't hear so many gory details that he feels guilty about causing any change in the family finances, such as by asking for milk money or telling you he's sick.

✔ **Respond to questions about how much money you make by confirming that your child will always be cared for and safe.** Should your child sneak into your bank book or overhear news about financial assets, remind him that the family's bank account is family business. In other words, family money matters cannot be the next topic for show-and-tell.

✔ **Tell your child something costs too much instead of saying you can't afford it.** The slight difference in emphasis may keep your child from worrying that your family's next home will be a homeless shelter.

✔ **Consider buying your older child a couple shares of stock in a company he recognizes.** Point out the company code in the newspaper and follow the stock's ups and downs together.

Giving allowance: Art or science?

The best way to learn about money is to have some to manage. That's where allowance comes into the picture. As someone who received allowance as a child and who gives it as a parent, I wholeheartedly advocate presenting your child with a regular allowance as soon as he can understand that money buys goods and services.

If you don't agree, add up the money handouts you've given your child lately. Include the unnecessary purchases your child had to have. Would you feel better forking over one sum regularly and knowing you're in control of the situation?

Allowance is not free money. As part of the family income and expenses, it should come with rules and responsibilities. Think about these allowance considerations:

✔ **Set amounts according to what your child realistically needs.** Decide what he must pay on his own. Look at Table 15-1 for ideas. Then add a small amount more for recreation, saving, or maybe buying you presents.

If you can't estimate, keep track of what your child spends during the first couple weeks of school. Then add up costs and necessary purchases and decide on a workable allowance together.

Review the amount at the beginning of each school year when your child's expenses change. Increase the amount as your child matures and handles more responsibility. The flip side of greater independence is that it usually means your child goes to more places that cost money.

You may want to find out the going rate for allowance in your area. One child having too much money can be just as problematic as having too little. Different folks recommend different amounts. I've read anything from $1 for every year of age to a weekly allowance based on half a child's age. The exact amount boils down to your family's comfort level and your child's business expenses outside the home.

Never measure your child's allowance based on what you received as a child. Times change.

Table 15-1	Expenses Your Child May Have
The Early Years	*Preteen/Teenage Years*
School lunches	School lunches
Milk	Bus fare
Bus fare	Fuel for family car
Toys	Media (CDs, videos)
Snacks	Snacks
Gifts	Gifts
Books and magazines	Books and magazines
Clothes	Clothes
Lessons/activities (music, sports)	Lessons/activities (tutors, entertainment)
Collectables	Cell phone

✔ **Define your rules for allowance.** Make sure everyone understands the same parameters and expectations. Be clear with your child if you expect the money to go for savings, pay for school lunch, or function as a donation to charity. Set limits upfront about how much junk food or the type of video games he can buy. No one likes surprises: They're not fair.

✔ **Deliver allowances on time and consistently.** Your child can't practice managing money if payments are sporadic. Pay younger kids at least once a week. Older kids can receive money weekly or wait until the breadwinner gets paid.

Make sure your child knows that after the money goes, he waits until the next allowance for more. Restrain yourself from feeling sorry for your kid. Don't give in to pleas, tears, or threats that your blackmailer will become a street beggar unless more money is forthcoming. Dealing with running out of money is the way your child learns the lively art of budgeting.

✔ **Remember these three no-nos:**

- **Never deny allowance as punishment.** You don't want you or your child connecting money with love. This plays poorly on a smart kid's psyche.

- **Never offer extra allowance for achieving more, such as getting higher grades.** If you do that, the money, rather than the accomplishment, becomes the payoff. Smart kids achieve because of an inner desire to perform well. But you can celebrate in other ways, like going out together or making a favorite recipe.

- **Never link allowance to everyday chores.** Household chores, such as cleaning the bedroom or helping with dinner, are responsibilities of living in a family, something smart kids understand. They are expected and required.

✔ **Offer an allowance without strings attached (except for those discussed in the original allowance agreement).** The money belongs to your child to manage or mismanage as he pleases. What better ways to learn budgeting than to pay too much for a CD, find a cheaper one at another store, and have no money left to join buddies at a movie theater?

Plan ahead what you will do when your child saves hard-earned money for something you don't think he should have. This gets tricky because the money is his to do with as he wishes, and you want to encourage saving for special items. But this is *your* house with your rules about what you deem an unhealthy intrusion.

Over the years, many studies have shown that high achievers glean their primary satisfaction from performing well, rather than from getting tons of money. But try explaining that to the child who craves the latest fad toy or your preteen who wants the newest style jeans.

You have your work cut out for you. Budgeting is not reinforced in this buy-buy, credit-card society. But understanding money management in elementary grades builds a foundation for remaining smartly solvent as a teen and adult.

Chapter 16

Deciding to Switch Learning Situations

*Y*our brain claims class is a bore. The teacher's a pain. Homework's a giant nuisance. You listen to your child with a guarded ear. After all, every student has a bad day — or two. You assume the grumbling is mostly for your benefit. And you're probably right.

But when you see your child constantly unhappy, frustrated, or angry at having to go to school, you may need to step in and review the situation. Time to turn into a squeaky wheel or at least a thorn in the school district's backside. Your child's education, and possibly her future, may be at stake.

This chapter takes you into school to evaluate what's going on in your child's classroom. You weigh when and how to investigate changes.

Reviewing Your Child's ABCs

The education landscape displays a range of quality in schools. Many do a great job of educating kids. Many more get by without inflicting much damage. But some are terrible. Your job is to ensure that your child winds up in the best possible situation, which isn't an easy task.

Don't assume a good reputation guarantees a top education. The reality is that good and bad teachers and excellent and poorly run schools exist everywhere.

Staying connected to your child's education is key to determining which type of school your child attends. No matter what anyone tells you, you don't need a professional education degree to know whether your child is learning. Here are some ways to evaluate your child's school day:

- ✔ **Request the school's course of study for each grade.** What does the curriculum emphasize? Does the program seem realistic yet demanding? Does every subject students take have a plan, goals to achieve, and a means of evaluating when goals are met?

  Check with your child's teacher at the beginning of the semester. Find out what the class expects to cover. Does this coincide with the school's curriculum?

  As the semester unfolds, allow a little leeway here. The teacher may decide that the class needs more time on one area, or students may learn so quickly that the class can zoom ahead with additional material or another topic. Good teachers need the freedom to use their judgment and accommodate the curriculum to meet students' needs. That's what they're trained to do. You have a right to question, but respect teacher's judgment, too.

- ✔ **See where students at your school stand on state and national tests.** Many states require schools to send out report cards that show how many kids perform well on which type of tests.

  As with individual student evaluations, test scores shouldn't be the only criteria for evaluating a school. Some states change their tests so frequently that scores are meaningless. But testing gives indications about strong and weak spots in relation to other schools in the community and across the country. If your school consistently falls at the bottom of most measurements, find out why and join ranks with the school to plan for improvement.

- ✔ **Visit your child's classes.** I don't mean barging into classes or embarrassing your child by intruding on lessons. But an occasional appointment to observe the teacher and your child in action gives you important information about how the teacher fosters learning, holds kid's attention, and disciplines. You also find out what classroom expectations are and how well your child responds to those expectations. Notice the student work on display, which tells you what's important to the teacher.

  Try to get a sense of how important standardized tests are. I've been in schools with so much emphasis on test results that teachers lose valuable teaching time because they spend so much time preparing students for the test. Scarce school funds go into buying test preparation books, and curriculum gets short shrift compared with test items. Recent studies discredit the value of this country's increased preoccupation with standardized testing. Speak up if this is your district's philosophy.

✔ **Review textbooks and other student materials.** Look for teachers who rely on worksheets to do their jobs and read texts to make sure they don't dumb-down the material. Texts and worksheets should supplement curriculum, not drive it.

✔ **Talk with other parents and educators.** Find out if their experiences coincide with yours to get an indication of whether your child or the school needs extra attention. Check with the next level school, such as junior high or high school. Investigate whether teachers find students from your child's school prepared. Ask what you can do to supplement your child's learning.

✔ **Check out other schools.** Investigate which schools have good reputations and visit them. Look at student work on display, find out what teachers expect of students, and see how students respond. Visiting other schools gives you better perspective into how your school measures up.

✔ **Ask your child what's going on.** Discuss how your child feels work and class are going. Find out whether the work is too difficult or too easy. Ask why. Does the teacher move too slowly or too fast? Are topics a repeat of the previous year's curriculum or new material? Question whether assignments seem worthwhile in terms of learning new skills or reinforcing current ones, or whether they're busywork. See whether the teacher keeps control of the class.

When your student and teacher don't click

You may encounter a situation in which your child and her teacher seem at odds with each other. Consider these options:

✔ **Stay objective.** Listen to your child's side. Don't automatically take the teacher's side because the teacher is boss. Sometimes, burned-out teachers pick on specific kids who cause them more work or irritate them for whatever reason. Get specifics of what your child does and the teacher's responses to make sure the problem is justified. By the same token, don't assume the teacher is the entire problem, either.

✔ **Discuss alternatives.** Ask your child what can be done to change the situation. Talk about ways your child can make interactions better, especially if your child is the

problem. If nothing seems plausible, ask your child what she would like you to do, if anything. Sometimes, lending a supportive ear is enough to relieve a tense situation.

✔ **Arrange for a teacher conference.** Flip to Chapter 14 for suggestions about how to prepare. At the meeting, explain the problem as you understand it. Be courteous, but determined. Bring in schoolwork to back up academic problems that haven't been addressed. Write down examples of problematic situations that your child mentions. Ask what you can do together to remedy the situation. With luck, the teacher will be reasonable, not defensive, and you both can define a workable plan.

(continued)

(continued)

Watch out for a teacher who blames the student or isn't willing to acknowledge a problem. Chances are, this professional doesn't have the student's best interest at heart.

✔ **Meet with someone higher up, such as the principal, if the teacher won't budge.** Bring your case in writing, including proof that you've tried to go through proper channels with your child and the teacher.

Expect the principal to support the teacher. Effective bosses work to improve their staff without condemnation. But also expect the principal to intervene on your child's behalf, if warranted. Your child's education depends upon change.

✔ **Suggest alternatives.** If the principal won't intervene, find out whether a social worker, counselor, itinerate teacher, or aide can support your child and supervise her relationship with the teacher. If this proves unworkable, you may have to ask that your child be transferred to another class.

You may get resistance, depending upon restrictions of class size, number of other classes at the same grade, school finances, or lack of interest in rocking the boat. One alternative in a departmentalized grade involves your child going to the library or somewhere else to study the subject during that specific class time. Whatever you suggest, be persistent but civil.

✔ **Go to the top, if the principal refuses to intervene.** Talk with the district superintendent or a school board member. You may hear that your child's placement is a local school issue. Even so, suggest a call from someone at the district level. Hearing from higher-ups may shake up the school enough to get action on your child's behalf.

✔ **Organize other parents in your child's class.** Strength comes in numbers. If your child truly has a terrible teacher, and other families are complaining, too, get together. Present a united front for change.

Ever since we moved into our neighborhood, neighbor kids talked about how awful one teacher was. One year, parents decided to do something about it. They organized, got their facts straight, and approached the principal. While the principal couldn't get rid of the teacher because of tenure rules, he did arrange to give her support in the form of training, relief from some responsibilities, and increased supervision to make sure students received what they needed throughout the year.

✔ **Look for another school, should your child receive no relief or if the situation worsens.** You can always get a tutor to plug information gaps. But restoring confidence

Choosing Another School

A lot of schools don't handle unique learning styles very well. Anyone who needs alternative educational approaches, including a student who excels, is made to feel like a failure. Part of the problem is that some teachers aren't trained to identify special needs, such as giftedness, learning disabilities, or emotional/behavioral problems. Too many haven't a clue what to do with any child who thinks outside the box of educational tools, even if the unusual behavior is because the child is extra bright.

If you've done your homework, attempted the school communication overtures mentioned in Chapter 14, and truly believe your child's current learning situation can't meet her needs, consider an alternative.

Embarking on a new school treasure hunt

The decision to choose another school depends upon your child's progress and your family's educational orientation. Think about:

- ✔ **Type of environment your child needs:** Less or more demanding? Smaller class size? Same-gender classroom?

- ✔ **Emphasis on particular subjects:** Broader curriculum? Targeted curriculum, for example in the arts or sciences?

- ✔ **Philosophies and methods that help your child blossom:** Some kids need military-type structure to function, while others thrive in more creative, independent-study arenas.

- ✔ **Family finances:** Moving to another district, transportation to a school outside your district, or private school tuition can be costly. Weigh the impact on your family's finances when choosing a different educational arrangement for your child.

Deciding on public versus nonpublic school

Evaluate whether to push for a new setting in another public school, in a private school, or at home.

Private schools tend to have smaller classes. Many give teachers freer reign to be more creative with curriculum. But they follow the same standards as public schools. Often, this means similar grading systems, emphasis on testing, and structured curriculum. All this comes for tons more money that you pay out of pocket.

Even if your state allows *vouchers,* with which money follows your child whether to public or private school, the sum covers only a small portion of fees for nonpublic education. Seriously investigate voucher program's claims to equalize education opportunities, because currently, it doesn't.

Weighing your options

To help you make a decision about switching schools, prepare to do some legwork. Visit different schools to see how they operate. Talk with other parents who send their children to your possibilities. The current government philosophy of education encourages parents to explore options other than traditional public school. But nonpublic doesn't always mean better.

Investigate each option and ask the staff the following questions:

- ✔ What is the typical class size and teacher-pupil ratio?

- ✔ How are children placed in classes and groups? Does the school favor homogeneous or mixed-skill groupings?

- ✔ How much money is spent on each child? This is particularly important with for-profit enterprises that may market themselves as offering something better but may, in fact, offer less to students.

- ✔ What is the philosophy of education? Does it jive with your family's?

- ✔ What will your child learn this year? Which textbooks are used? Is there a healthy mix of core subjects, computer technology, the arts, and physical education?

- ✔ How does the school/teacher handle discipline problems? What type of behavior constitutes misbehavior?

- ✔ How does the school evaluate student strengths and weaknesses? What is the testing policy? How are grades handled?

- ✔ What are teacher qualifications? Some private schools hire less qualified and less experienced staff because they are cheaper, and your state may allow the practice. Of course, many public school districts lean toward newer, less experienced teachers to save money, also.

I'm not saying inexperience equals bad teaching. But schools should have a mix of teaching experience to provide both innovation and mentoring. Schools with high turnover of teachers fresh out of college may affect teaching quality.

- ✔ Do children look happy and engaged in classes?

- ✔ Is the facility taken care of? Stopped-up drains and holey walls may be an indication the entire school suffers from low self-esteem. That's not a good place for a smarter education for your child.

- ✔ How is parent involvement encouraged? Ask what you can do to help your child learn.

Surviving New-School Blues

After you decide to change your child's school, think ahead about easing the transition.

I still remember my encounter with the great unknown called Clinton School in first grade. I got lost in the halls the first day. My cheeks still redden as I recall the embarrassment of constant stares from other kids because I was the interloper, the new kid. The worst was not being able to find the bathroom.

Moving to a new neighborhood hurts at any age. But the older your child, the greater amounts of grumbling you'll hear. That's because older kids leave behind a stronger peer network, their own little society. Therefore, your child may view breaking into a new group as difficult and overwhelming.

Review these survival tips for easing your child's transition into a new learning situation:

- ✔ **Prepare your child, so that she feels more confident.** Talk about reasons for the move and differences between the old and new school. Discuss your child's feelings throughout the adjustment process. Share how you understand any concerns, maybe ones you've experienced in your day.

    Stay positive and reassuring about the move. Reassure your child that fears will lessen as she gets acclimated. Cross your fingers and hope that this happens quickly.

- ✔ **Contact the school ahead of time.** Ask to speak to a counselor or someone who can look out for your child. Identify a teacher, counselor, or social worker who can evaluate your child's adjustment and stay in contact with you.

- ✔ **Request a peer helper to accompany your child to key places, like the lunchroom, for the first few days.** Is anything worse as a child than eating by yourself in a sea of strange faces?

- ✔ **Visit the school with your child before moving, if possible.** Take a tour. See the classroom, bathroom, and other important locations. Try to meet the teacher or teachers who will educate your child.

- ✔ **Establish a school routine that includes before- and after-school activities, homework, and bedtime.** Consistent routines build confidence when everything else changes.

- ✔ **Keep outside activities to a minimum at the beginning.** When your child feels confident about what seems manageable, encourage her to join extracurricular groups, such as choir, band, or sports' teams. They provide common interests that may spur school friendships.

- ✔ **Seek outside professional assistance if your child continues to acclimate poorly.** But give the new situation time and a couple rounds of lower grades before panicking. If performance stays down in the tubes, act quickly.

Schooling at Home: The Cozy Alternative

Home schooling involves teaching your child at home with no other formal teachers: Just you and whatever experiences you provide for your child.

Visiting the pros and cons of home schooling

You may consider home schooling because:

- ✔ You find public school lacking in quality curriculum and educators.
- ✔ Your family values differ from what you perceive goes on in school.
- ✔ You want to limit exposure to neighborhood elements.
- ✔ You're scared to let your darling out of your sight.
- ✔ You are sure you can do a better job personalizing what and how your child learns.

You may dislike home schooling because:

- ✔ You believe public school provides the broadest curriculum with more opportunities for extracurricular activities.
- ✔ You aren't comfortable with the role of full-time teacher. After all, home schooling can be demanding. You have to like the research, gathering of books and teaching materials, and constant home-as-school mode of living. Home schooling is not for the faint of heart nor for every parent, and that's okay.
- ✔ You're scared to let your darling out of your sight and know this may prove destructive to your child's growing independence.
- ✔ You know that children need both peer socialization and authority figures that school offers.

Taking the home-schooling plunge

Think you're taking the easy way out with home schooling? Guess again. Depending upon where you live, you may encounter rules that cover curriculum and reporting, evaluating, and testing your child at home.

Seven indicators of a quality school

Look for these traits of a quality school:

✔ **Clear academic guidelines:** The school has a vision of what children learn in each grade. Subjects covered in one grade augment those in the next.

✔ **High expectations:** Everyone from the principal to janitors requires high academic and behavior standards and refuses to accept less.

✔ **Dynamic leadership:** Strong principals set the tone for how teachers operate and students learn. They create a learning atmosphere that supports teachers and high student achievement.

✔ **A safe and healthy environment for learning:** No child can learn in threatening or unsafe surroundings. That includes a school atmosphere where teachers are able to control the class, hallways are safe, and traveling to and from school doesn't make your child feel vulnerable. A safe environment is the least a school should provide.

✔ **Motivating and enthusiastic teaching staff:** Teachers can make or break a school year for students. Look for teachers who like what they do, like kids, and seem knowledgeable about the subjects they teach.

Teachers receive a lot of pressure and blame nowadays. Many systems smother them with paperwork and take their valuable teaching time for standardized-test preparation. So be kind and don't expect miracles. How many truly great teachers do you remember? Just make sure your child's teacher isn't harmful to your child and her enthusiasm for learning.

✔ **Student accountability:** Schools that hold their students accountable for learning evaluate progress based on specific realistic guidelines. You and your child receive unbiased feedback based on performance in class participation, homework, and exams.

✔ **Community involvement:** Good schools create a sense of welcome for students, their families, and the community. Parents are encouraged to assist in their child's education and to connect with teachers.

The good news is that many folks have followed the home-school route before you:

1. **Get yourself some thorough books to get started.**

   The following books tell you what you need to do and how to begin your home-school journey:

   - *The Homeschooling Handbook: From Preschool to High School* by Mary Griffith (Prima Publishing): This overview contains lesson plans, activities, and information about state laws affecting home schoolers.

- *Homeschooling: The Early Year: Your Complete Guide to Successfully Homeschooling the 3–8-Year-Old Child* or the newer *The Ultimate Guide to Homeschool Ideas* by Linda Dodson (both from Prima Publishing): Both are excellent resources for starting and continuing home schooling.

- *The Homeschooling Almanac 2002–2003: How to Start, What to Do, Where to Go, Who to Call* by Mary Leppert (Prima Publishing): This book has it all — contacts, Web sites, product listings, and anything else you need to begin home schooling.

2. **Investigate home-schooling state laws.**

   Contact your local school district or state office of public instruction for the most up-to-date requirements.

3. **Connect with other home schoolers for recommendations, support, and opportunities to network and arrange for joint educational outings.**

   Here are some places to begin:

   - National Homeschool Association, P.O. Box 157290, Cincinnati, OH 45214, 513-772-9580. This group has a newsletter and contacts.

   - Homeschool Foundation, P. O. Box 1152, Parcellville, VA 20134, 540-309-8999, www.hslda.org. This advocacy organization also covers news and issues for home schoolers.

4. **Combine your resources and materials into a curriculum and enjoy teaching your child at home.**

Part IV
The Know-It-All Years: Middle School and High

The 5th Wave   By Rich Tennant

"How can you not feel confident? You're wearing Versace sunglasses, a Tommy Hilfiger sweater, and you graduated from the Albert Einstein private school with a Stephen Hawking science medal. Now go out there and just be yourself!"

In this part . . .

Well, parent: You're not in Kansas anymore. You're entering the often-turbulent teen years, a time when you're convinced that all signs of smartness disappear. Your kids are testing their boundaries. Meanwhile, they seem to be pushing you away, but they need you more than ever.

What's a parent to do to keep your smart kid on track? This part suggests ways to appreciate the ups and downs of teenage years, understand what you're up against and how to handle sticky teen situations, look at life for your grown child after high school, and enjoy every one of these years (because you'll soon have to let go). Enjoy the ride.

Chapter 17

Working with the Teenage Psyche

* *

In This Chapter

▶ Raising a smart older kid

▶ Understanding why smart teens act the way they do

▶ Adjusting to a new version of smarts

* *

*R*emember the toddler years, that rambunctious divide between baby-hood and childhood? Well, your family is about to (or has already begun to) bridge another uproarious developmental gap. This time, your child is crossing over the maturational bridge between childhood and adulthood. This stage is called adolescence, or the teenage years, and is the focus of this chapter.

Be forewarned. As teens mature, they act differently and assume different roles in the family and community. This chapter investigates how teens internalize the smart modeling and values experienced during their youth and turn them upside down as they practice life. Welcome to the teenage years of raising a success story!

Admitting That You Have a Different Species in the House

Your child is still as smart as when he was young. But these days, you may not always be able to tell. I'm not one of those folks who buys into the idea of the "terrible twos" or "troublesome teens." Yet I must admit to feeling twinges of fear at the thought of raising a smart teen. Teens seem so worldly nowadays on their own, and not always from the most positive resources and experiences.

I say "tumultuous" because the quest for separation from you that begins during the preteen years may show itself as full-scale revolt by high school. On the other hand, your child may not ever be rebellious. Or your teen may lurch into independence later or earlier than your neighbor's kid. Be assured, though, that the quest for finding himself as separate from you will come. This section helps you understand why your smart child may decide to do some dumb stuff now and then.

If you can hang a little looser, choose your battles, and keep up the great parenting job you began long ago, your tumultuous teen may come through these years with his smarts intact.

Understanding preteen behavior

Preteens start itching for greater independence. Because independence is not theirs for the asking yet, they experiment within their limited boundaries. Sometimes, experimentation takes the form of petty theft, pranks, teasing, sneaking out of the house, and other behaviors that test your response. what they do can be pretty scary.

Why so much experimentation? Because kids this age are grappling with defining who they are while trying to fit in: two important motivations for separating from you.

Bodies change in outwardly obvious ways. Cliques form, which can be agony for those outside the group. Insiders pick on outsiders as a way to bolster their own forming psyches. Ask any teen. Remember back to the preteen years yourself. These are tough times, socially and emotionally.

If you stick to the household rules and their consequences unwaveringly, keep lines of communication open, and act fairly, you'll sail through this stage quicker than you can say, "Oh my goodness, a teenager lives in this house!"

Knowing your teenager

By the teenage years, your child turns into another type of animal altogether. Your teen pushes you away even farther as he draws you nearer. He wants to become his own person yet still seeks your approval. And then car keys, late-night outings, and expanding financial needs enter the picture. In trying to wade into adult waters, your teen may:

 ✔ Test the child rules that have kept your family balanced for years. Your older child is trying to come up with a smart system of behaviors and philosophies that work for him.

✔ Feel a strong need to separate from you. In fact, the more stringent you are, the more your teen rebels. He figures the only way to attain independence is to reject you and everything you hold dear.

Teens also respect individuality and being different, which is weird considering most dress like clones. Prepare for your child to find expression of this individuality in different behavior, music, hairstyle, dress, and possibly a tattoo or pierce or two. All this trouble arrives in because he now finds the family routine stifling. You may think he's thrown all his marbles out the window. He hasn't. He's just rebelling.

✔ Criticizes, avoids, or otherwise views you as the source of his embarrassment and roadblock to living life. You are the parent of a teen. Therefore, you know nothing short of Neanderthal wisdom, if any wisdom at all. Smart kids outgrow this attitude with time.

✔ Exhibits wild mood swings. He suddenly balks at a request you've made many times before, gives you a bear hug thirty minutes later, or storms out of the house with little provocation. Turbulence is from teen hormones, and boys as well as girls have high and low cyclical swings. Don't worry. Moods don't affect brain power. It just seems like they do.

✔ Looks to friends for what's cool. After all, your talk, dress, and value system are so retro (or whatever the term for old fashioned is today).

✔ Spends an inordinate amount of time communicating with friends, the known and unknown. Besides e-mail and cell phones, teens use instant messaging (IM to your savvy teen) to fill their off-school time. In fact, multitasking is in, meaning your teen may watch television, send and receive e-mails, talk on the phone, and IM, all while convincing you he's studying.

✔ Finds greater need for space and privacy, which oddly enough gets expressed in large amounts of time spent communicating with peers electronically. Expect to hear a lot of "Leave me alone" or see a closed bedroom door.

While you want to take your teen seriously, try not to take teen antics too personally.

Keeping in mind that the hormones make them do it

Whatever gripes you have with this stage, these transgressions aren't all your teen's fault. Adolescent hormones hit some kids like gangbusters and affect bodies, emotions, and actions.

✔ **General changes:**

- Puberty extends over three to four years. Although age of onset varies, girls usually undergo puberty earlier than boys.

- Body clock shifts to a later setting.

- Bones and muscles mature to almost adult size. But coordination and strength decreases for a time because bones are growing faster than muscles.

- Sex-linked hormones cause related body changes, even dreaded acne.

- Brain growth continues through adolescence, which is why interference from mind-altering substances (drugs) can short-circuit wiring so easily.

✔ **Female changes:**

- Puberty, the body's route to being able to reproduce, begins between ages 8 and 13.

- Menstrual cycle starts during puberty. This is a terrifying sign that your daughter is ready to conceive and carry a baby, which she's really not. The hormone estrogen causes periods when ovaries release eggs into fallopian tubes. Thus begins a monthly cycle that runs 400 times over the course of her lifetime.

- Skeleton grows in a specific order, unlike unruly male bodies. First, hands and feet expand. Then forearms and shins. Finally, upper arms and thighs. After menstruation begins, leg bones usually stop growing, but hip bones widen and the spine continues to elongate until the body achieves adult height.

- Womanly curves appear. Breasts develop.

- Hair sprouts under arms and in the pubic area.

✔ **Male changes:**

- Puberty begins between ages 10 and 14.

- Testicles produce greater amounts of the hormone testosterone. The sex-relate hormone changes the size and texture of the testicles, otherwise called your son's *manhood*. By age 15, this anxiety-producing pair of glands has increased 400 percent and can produce 1,000 sperm per second. With all this testosterone pulsating in a small space, no wonder males can't control their penile erections at this age!

- Shoulders widen. Jaw and nose bones grow faster than the rest of the face, winding up with the chiseled jaw of a man.

- Voice deepens.

- Hair develops under arms, on the face, neck, and chest, and in the pubic area.

Talking teen talk

Your teen may talk differently than the rest of your family. The jargon can be quirky, the opposite of what you think the words mean, irreverent, or all of the above. According to my expert teen sources, your adolescent says these terms because he doesn't want to talk like you. But don't take it personally. Instead, acquaint yourself with words and phrases so that you aren't totally left out of conversations.

Although terms change month by month and according to what's hot in the media, here is a sampling of 20 popular phrases you can expect to hear:

Your term	Your teens version	Your term	Your teens version
Old fashioned	Old school; retro	That's bad	That bites
What's new?	What's shakin'? What's the haps? 'Sup?	Serious	Heavy
		Okay	Cool
Great	Cool; sweet; awesome; that rocks; off the hook	Leave quickly	Jet; split
Good	Sweet	Information	The 411
Really good	Kickin'; slammin'	House/room	Pad; crib
Hello	What's up?; yo; hey	Friends	Peeps; homies; dudes
Goodbye	Later	Good-looking guy/girl	Hot; cute; fine; hottie
Relax	Chill		
Over-reacting	Freakin' out; flipped out	Brainy person	Nerd; geek
Unjustified	Harsh	Parents	'Rents; folks

Remembering Parenting Skills That Should Never Change

Want to still have some influence in keeping your teen on a smart track? Work hard to remember when you were that age. How did you like to be treated? What made you feel like pushing harder and achieving your best?

Here are some simple ways to help you help your teen live and work smarter:

✔ **Respect your child's opinions and choices.** You don't always have to agree with your teen and much of the time, you may wonder which planet he's from. But saying "I respect what you say" goes a long way toward building relationship bridges with adolescents. When you get his attention, you can make inroads into keeping him focused on achieving his best.

✔ **Offer explanations when you disagree.** You're not in the dark ages of your parent's youth when folks emphasized "Because I said so" and expected rules to be followed blindly. Teens today are savvy, articulate, and brazen. If you want respect, you need to show a little yourself for his brain power. If you must lay down a law for your child's health and safety, offer an explanation of why that makes sense. Your child deserves as much.

✔ **Listen to your teen.** How many times have you heard, "You don't listen to me!" or "You really don't get it!"? Your teen just wants to be heard, acknowledged, and understood. Listen to his dreams no matter how unrealistic. You had dreams once, too.

Your course of action is really quite simple. First, make yourself available. Then listen to what's important to your child, no matter how painful a topic. Listening, reflecting back what you've heard, and reacting to news in a nonjudgmental way keeps your child confiding in you, which gives you a leg-up on remaining a strong influence in his young life. (For more detailed guidelines about active listening, see Chapter 7.) In return, he listens to you and stays focused, sort of.

✔ **Trust your teen.** Trusting is like expecting high achievement. If you believe your child is trustworthy, he will live up to those expectations — well, most of the time.

If your teen offers some way-out explanation for something that defies credibility, you have a right and obligation to investigate further, especially with unsafe behavior. But if the facts prove your child's case, be ready and willing to apologize.

✔ **Ask your child's opinion.** Your child claims to want more say in household matters, but his behavior sends the opposite message that he isn't interested. Look beyond the negative behavior, surly responses, and closed doors and keep asking your child for ideas, alternatives, and opinions to show that you respect his judgment and actions. The more your child feels connected with you, your family, and what goes on at home, the less he'll be enticed by dangerous temptations from friends.

Reinstate regular family meetings, as discussed in Chapter 2, if you've let them slide for awhile. Offer your teen a regular say in making decisions and family rules because he's more likely to follow rules if he owns them. If your teen refuses to attend sessions, coax him to join the group by telling him he has to abide by decisions made without him. Let your teen know you value his input and truly believe he's smart.

✔ **Read in Chapter 2 about different ways to say positive statements and lots of "I love you."** Everyone needs to receive positive messages as often as possible, and so does your teen. I don't mean to plant a wet smooch on his cheek in front of friends. But your child needs to know that you care as much and believe he's as capable as always, even though he's changing and may do some dumb stuff now and then.

✔ **Model wholesome behavior.** Teens throw your do-as-I-say-and-not-as-I-do actions back in your face. If you want a teen who doesn't drink and drive, swear, do drugs, or fill his body with tattoos, don't engage in these behaviors yourself. But if you want a teen who picks up a book now and then, works hard, and acts responsibly, show him how these activities are done.

✔ **Play fair.** Don't expect your teen to finish a ton of household chores knowing he has a debate to prepare for and a load of studying. Hire a babysitter for your younger child when your teen has a big dance on the same night you want to go out. Fairness counts big-time with teens, even if you think it's one-sided in your teen's favor.

Let punishments fit the crimes. Grounding your teen for every infraction only makes him angry at you. If the problem is with the car, come up with a fair, car-related consequence to misbehavior. If completing math homework is the problem, get a math tutor instead of taking away allowance. Smart kids require even smarter parents to keep them in line.

✔ **Choose your battles.** Lots of teen behavior can be irritating. But are all your teen's irritating actions worth fighting over and ruining the relationship you've worked so hard to build? As long as your child acts in safe and healthy ways and performs well in school, hang lose and understand that teens like to express themselves. Reinforce the smart decisions he makes and remember that:

- Your teen exhibits wonderful qualities beyond green-striped hair, belching, and outrageous dress. Strange haircuts grow back, and styles change with the season and peer group. As for belching, this talent eventually loses it power and will die a slow death, after you stop reacting to it.

- Earrings can eventually be put back in the jewelry box. As for tattoos, remind your child that tattoos last for 80 years or are painful to erase, and see if that makes an impression on him before the deed is done.

- Messy rooms don't hurt anyone unless items on the floor crawl by themselves.

- Dishes in the sink and forgotten chores aren't the sum-total of your child's best qualities.

Check out the Web site at www.parentingteens.com and the book *Positive Discipline for Teenagers* by Jane Nelsen (Prima Publishing) for more ideas about raising smart teens.

Adjusting to high school

On the plus side, moving into high school may shake up cliques and widen opportunities for new friends and activities. On the negative side, a larger building with more kids and classes to keep track of can be scary. Suggest that your child consider these tips for making high school easier:

✔ **Visit the new school before classes start.** Suggest that your teen locate each class on the schedule and plot routes to reduce chances of getting lost in crowded hallways.

✔ **Call current friends before school starts to determine who has the same lunch period.** Plan a place to meet. If no one has your child's lunch break, suggest that he try to connect with someone in the food line or scan the lunchroom for a friendly face and ask to join that person. Eating alone is no fun.

✔ **Arrange for transportation.** Review how buses/bicycle route/car ride/foot power work before the first day of school. Take practice bus trips together, if necessary.

✔ **Decide what to wear the night before the first day of school.** You don't want your teen to miss a ride when he's already anxious because nothing looks right. And no matter how shallow this sounds, your child will feel more confident wearing clothes that raise his comfort level.

✔ **Come prepared.** Make sure your teen brings his class schedule and writing materials.

This isn't junior high where every teacher knows about where every student goes. And many teachers start lecturing the first day of school and expect students to get right to work.

✔ **Get involved from the beginning in at least one school activity that seems remotely interesting.** Joining something of interest connects your teen to school in a positive way and gives him common interests and topics to talk about with at least a few other kids. He can always drop or add activities as interests change.

✔ **Join a sport team.** Sports build any number of skills. But getting rejected from a team can be rough, especially if you're new to high school. As an alternative, encourage your child to ask whether the school offers any no-cut teams, such as cross country, or intramural teams that play each other for fun.

✔ **Smile and seem open to meeting other people.** If your child walks with his head down, shoulders slumped, and a grumpy facial expression, no one will ever approach him. You may offer to role play a few introductory interactions at home.

✔ **Remember that everyone in the grade is new to the school and probably has the same reservations as he does.** Keep drumming this point home. Teens think they invented whatever they're going through.

✔ **Stay connected and supportive.** Let your child know you care about his life. Ask about what's going on. Attend school and outside activities that your child supports. Be truly interested, not fake, about your concern.

An unwritten law dictates that your child's activities happen during snow and rain storms and are also timed to coincide with your important work deadlines. But make sure someone represents the family. Horror stories of uncalled rain-soaked games make great family lore. Better than that, your teen remembers that you are willing to go the extra mile to encourage his successes.

✔ **Reinforce that schoolwork comes first.** Let your teen know that activities are great and friends make life fun, but school remains the number one job. Emphasize that high school is the time when grades really count toward future plans, whatever they may involve.

✔ **Refrain from lecturing.** Long dissertations usually result in a fight or in your teen spacing out. Lectures lead to nowhere unless the listener wants to hear what's being said. To avoid battles, ask permission to impart your adult wisdom. Then get to the point and be brief. You don't have much time to keep a teen's attention.

If your request to give advice is turned down, back off. Your teen has a lifetime to learn. Now doesn't have to be the only occasion. And don't be offended with your teen's attitude that he knows it all anyway. That's a teen thing.

✔ **Shower your teen with unconditional love.** As your child grows older, you may find yourself liking fewer things about your child. Similarly, your child may act less approachable and lovable. But even so, send the message loud and clear that no matter what he does, with whom he hangs out, or into how much trouble he gets, he's still your kid, you love him, and you will weather any storms together.

Kids who feel secure have higher self-esteem. And higher self-esteem means your teen makes wiser choices in school and when confronted with peer pressure.

✔ **Show you're on your teen's side.** When he makes mistakes, which are inevitable, refrain from "I told you so" or negative comments. Such comments are neither helpful nor necessary. Your teen feels bad enough from natural consequences of his actions. If you respond to your teen as if what he does is awful or dumb, which it may be, he'll look for ways to get into trouble and live up to your interpretations (see Chapter 18).

Chapter 18

Eliminating Brain Drains

* *

In This Chapter

▶ Dealing with problematic school issues

▶ Troubleshooting when your teen does not-so-smart stuff

▶ Understanding teen angst

▶ Helping your teen know herself

* *

Media tries to scare you with oversexed images of turbulent teens. But most smart kids rarely generate problems. In fact, Yale University documents that smart kids who hang around other smart kids are less likely to engage in risky behaviors, such as smoking, drug and alcohol use, and unsafe sex.

Still, adolescence may not be an easy time for anyone — not you or your teen. For everyday gripes, like room cleaning or pitching in with chores, check Chapters 2 and 3 for suggestions. Thornier issues, however, may take more in-depth planning. This chapter gives you some options — just in case — should your teen decide to experiment with risky or unpleasant behavior.

Skipping School-Skipping

Your child may have different reasons for not attending class. For some, you'll have to be merciful and trust that your child meant no lasting harm, no matter how bizarre the excuse. Show your displeasure with a slap on the wrist, but generally give her a break and move on.

For other reasons, you may find you have more serious problems on your hands. When you get a call that your teen has missed school:

   ✔ **Stay calm.** Take a few deep breaths or give yourself a timeout, if you're too angry to approach your teen rationally.

✔ **Talk with your teen.** You want to discover why she skipped school. Was it to avoid certain classes or specific people? Was it for fun and the thrill of escape? Or are drugs or drinking involved?

Never talk to your teen in front of friends. Find a private place to talk where both of you can relate without losing your cool. If she's too angry and defensive about being caught to talk, suggest a later time to meet when she's calmer.

✔ **Admit that you know your teen's skipped school when you talk.** Give her a chance to explain. If an explanation never comes, tell her you'll find out anyway, so she may as well tell you what caused her to leave school and what she did during school hours.

✔ **Administer consequences depending upon what you hear:**

- If your child has school problems, offer to arrange an appointment with the appropriate teacher, counselor, or principal who can help. Suggest a tutor if schoolwork seems difficult. Read Chapters 13 and 14 for ideas about monitoring schoolwork and finding a tutor.

- If your child has an emotional problem that can't be resolved by talking with you, insist that she meet with a school or private social service professional.

Make sure your child goes right back to school. Most kids who are allowed to stay home to clear their heads find returning to class more difficult.

- If your child just wanted some fun, check out her story with other teen's parents, someone at the places she visited, and the school. For a one-time adventure, restrict some privilege that fits the situation, such as taking away the car use if she drove.

- If your child has dabbled in drugs or alcohol for the first time, explain your displeasure, restrict access to the other kids she was with while skipping school, and administer a reasonable punishment, such as coming right home after school for a few weeks. If you think the problem runs deeper, involve a social service professional before it becomes more serious.

Reversing Slipping Grades

Give your teen a break. Not every test or paper or semester grade needs to be tops. But if you see a dramatic and consistent slide in grades, you may want to investigate.

✔ **Be a support for your teen.** Don't overreact. In fact, try not to react at all. If your teen receives a bad grade, chances are she feels bad enough already.

Instead, try to talk about what's going on. Ask your teen whether underlying reasons are interfering with her ability to concentrate on schoolwork. Is she working too many house outside of school, is she involved in too many activities, or is she having emotional problems? Ask what she thinks will help remedy the situation. Follow her lead and develop a contract or plan to monitor progress.

✔ **Be realistic about your kid's abilities.** You want to set high standards. But maybe Calculus isn't her thing. Accept that grades in this course this semester may be down. Praise her effort and hard work in a class that's difficult for her. Some colleges prefer a B in Calculus to an A in a lower-level math class.

No one is good at everything, but everyone can be good at trying.

✔ **Be aware that you can do only so much.** At some point you may want to remove yourself from the situation. If your teen sloughs off schoolwork but is perfectly able to perform well, tell her your relationship is worth more than grades. Explain that you want her to get better grades, or at least pass every subject, because you know she's intelligent enough. Clarify that you know she'll do better after she discovers what she wants to shoot for study-wise or career-wise. Then step back, bite your tongue about anything related to school, and follow through with your plan.

Your teen may come around quickly after you stop nagging or pressuring her to perform. Or she may not take time to think before the consequences of her poor schoolwork become apparent, which means putting up with low grades for awhile. Whatever she decides, it will be her choice and one she's motivated to make.

Backing off from micromanaging schoolwork lets your teen know her importance to you comes from more than good grades.

Ending Substance Abuse

I won't scare you with statistics about how prevalent teen drug use is. Instead, I offer suggestions about how to prevent substance problems or handle abuses, should they begin.

Preventing substance abuse

Studies show that the best way to prevent drug use is to monitor your teen's behavior. Kids with involved parents who set rules fend off pressures to mix with a risky crowd.

No matter what your teen says, you have a right and responsibility to know where she goes and with whom. You also have a responsibility to offset bombardment of offensive media. To balance your desire to supervise your teen's behavior and your child's growing need for privacy and independence, see whether these alternatives strike a balance:

- **Impose media guidelines that filter drug-infested influences.** (Read suggestions in Chapter 12.) Understand that while your teen has access to many sources beyond your control, she needs to understand your position about what she sees.

- **Explain in plain language how you feel about addictive substances.** Without being a parental pain, express how worried and upset you'll be if your child uses them. Establish no-drug, no-smoking rules in your home, and let your teen know that every friend of hers is welcome, just not with drugs, alcohol, or cigarettes.

  Don't lecture. Give facts, especially about how addictive certain drugs can be and how mind-altering drugs also reduce brain power. Quote docs who say growing teen brains are more susceptible to addiction and more prone to permanent damage. You can find more information from the National Institute on Drug Abuse at www.nida.nih.gov.

  Scare tactics about what may happen in the future could have little impact on your teen's behavior. But many teens respond to talk of how smelly and unattractive smoking is, or how alcohol and drugs lead to bad breath, yellow teeth, early wrinkles, and impaired physical and mental performance.

  If you can't get through to your teen by talking, find objective reading material and slip it under the door for bedtime reading. Make sure information covers alcohol, tobacco, marijuana, cocaine in various forms, and inhalants, such as gasoline, glue, paint thinner, and aerosol can fumes, and how addictive each can be.

  What your teen doesn't know can be harmful to her.

- **Institute a calling policy that makes sense, so that you know where your child is.** Few kids call everywhere they go, especially in neighborhoods where kids meander from house to house before landing. But say you want to hear from your child by a certain hour, and you expect the truth about her whereabouts. Some parents set a curfew and expect their teen to walk through the door at the appointed hour or call if they're running late.

✔ **Call a proposed sleepover or party house to confirm adult supervision.** In fact, stay in contact with other parents to find out the scoop on whether "Everybody's going," or "Jeremy's parents let him," is true.

✔ **Stay alert to warning signs of a medical or substance-abuse problem.** Look for blood-shot eyes, chronic cough, change in eating habits, weight loss or gain, excessive fatigue, slipping grades, negative attitude changes, a switch to friends who seem unsavory, and a general uncaring demeanor. These may be signs your teen travels a more dangerous road than you want to admit. At the very least, let a doctor examine your teen for other health issues, including depression, anxiety, or the infection mononucleosis (which may arise from lack of sleep).

✔ **Talk regularly with your teen, and not just about logistics.** Hold discussions about her feelings, interests, and how life's going. Chat over a meal together. Share during regular family meetings. Reinforce the good decisions your child has made lately to ward off the bad ones. Kids with positive self-esteem care enough about themselves to make smart choices.

Kids experiment with risky substances for lots of reasons: curiosity, rebellion, appearances, role models, and pressure from friends. Make sure your behavior, supervision, and love override these dangerous influences.

Beating back the addiction monster

Jump into high gear when you discover your teen has been drinking or experimenting with drugs.

✔ **Time for another heart-to-heart discussion.** This time, mention relatives with chemical dependency problems and the fact that addiction runs in families. Mention how you love your teen and always will, even though you differ about your attitudes about addictive substances. Say how worried you are without condemning, name-calling, or tempers flaring. Then give her a hug. Reaffirm that you will always be there when she decides to help herself stop abusing these substances.

✔ **Remind your teen about the no-drug or alcohol rule at home.** Make sure that, at the first sign of discomfort, you don't take medicines or swig a few beers yourself.

✔ **Get help outside the family, if your teen can't stop abusing drugs.** Encourage your teen to join support groups, like Al-Anon, Alcoholic's Anonymous, or another individual or group therapy program.

The best programs target young people instead of offering standard adult fare. They require involvement of family members and allow teens to continue school work. If you aren't part of the program, join a group yourself. Substance abuse affects the entire family.

After her son landed in the hospital with alcohol poisoning, one parent woke up to the seriousness of her son's addiction. She worried about the safety of her son and those around him. But he wouldn't agree to treatment. She mustered her courage and contacted the court system. She pleaded with the judge to order her son to undergo substance abuse evaluation. The judge agreed with her concerns. Within a few hours, police picked up her teen from school and drove him to a local hospital. From there, he entered a drug treatment center.

✔ **Don't deny that the abuse exists, trivialize the problem, or make excuses for your child.** The worst approach you can take is to "save" your teen by covering up the truth. Addiction can be powerful. Your family needs help. Your teen's life depends upon her getting treatment.

Taming the Hostile Teen Beast

Your adolescent's crabbiness and emotional roller coaster rides are one thing. Teens are supposed to be obnoxious now and then. But regular explosions of hostility or physical force require your immediate and strong action. You can regain control of your kid's inappropriate behavior by doing the following:

✔ **Set rules about which behaviors you will accept and which inappropriate behaviors bring consequences.** Read Chapter 3 for suggestions about creating a structured positive discipline plan that includes documenting when outbursts occur, what triggers them, and how you respond.

✔ **Tell your teen calmly when she is out of control.** Don't try to reason with her during an outburst. Say you will talk with her after she settles down, and then follow through with that approach. When you talk, try to identify what triggered the outburst: friend problems, drugs, not enough sleep, or school stresses. Discuss appropriate alternatives to losing control when feeling angry or frustrated, such as writing in a journal, drawing your aggression, running or other physical activity, or talking with someone.

✔ **Identify the destruction.** Ask your teen to explain what happened and what she thinks you should do about it. Make sure your child takes responsibility for cleaning up, fixing, and paying to replace what has been ruined.

✔ **Analyze whether you're afraid of or embarrassed by your teen's outbursts.** You may be giving in to your teen to avoid confrontation. Giving in neither acknowledges your teen's feelings nor teaches her how to cope with them without being disrespectful or destructive. Worse yet, you're reinforcing negative behavior on both sides: You show less respect for yourself by accepting inappropriateness, and your teen learns that blowups bring results. Your teen depends on you for boundaries. Who's the adult here?

Saying "no" to your teen is okay. Your teen has a short-term memory, even if you don't.

✔ **Seek outside assistance when your teen scares or hurts anyone in the family.** Some alternatives include:

- Enrolling your teen in a conflict resolution class. Schools, community recreation and healthcare organizations, and colleges sometimes offer classes. Ask the school psychologist, counselor, or social worker for ideas.

- Identifying another adult your teen can confide in, should you be unable to talk. You want someone you both trust who will listen to your teen without taking sides.

- Seeking trained therapists to determine what causes your child's behavior and how you and your teen can handle it better. Treatment may involve individual or group counseling or family therapy. Severe abusive or self-abusive behavior may require inpatient treatment at a mental health facility.

Find someone to talk with yourself. Confiding in a friend, family, or therapist eases the isolation and guilt you may feel from going through these challenging times.

Separating Your Teen from the Anti-Education Crowd

You've done a good job grounding your child with attitudes about high achievement and safe behavior. But you're not sure she can hold her own with the intense peer pressure she faces, such as:

✔ Long-time buddies who turn into highly manipulative trouble

✔ Pot and beer parties

✔ Older siblings who buy alcohol, cigarettes, and pot for younger teens

✔ Fake IDs

✔ Parents who purchase mind-bending substances for their kids and their friends — saying "I'd rather have them drinking/smoking inside the house than out" doesn't cut it

High school is a teen testing ground and parent nail-biter. All teens come in contact with and know how to get addictive substances. Praise her often for keeping her cool in the face of horrendous peer pressure.

If you've done a good job with your child at an earlier age, trust that she'll muster the good values she's learned. Research confirms that your teen's relationship with you or any adult is much greater an influence than with peers. Eventually, she'll move away from potentially dangerous kids and situations.

Waiting for the turnaround is easier said than done, however. In the meantime:

✔ **Investigate that gut feeling that your child's buddies really mean trouble before you hyperventilate.** Not every multiply pierced, skimpily dressed child takes drugs. Ask school personnel to alert you about whether your concerns are well-founded: They can't impart personal information from therapy sessions or school files, but they can share who they view as an unhealthy mix of kids. They see lots of teens every day and may be able to evaluate your teen, her friends, and problem behavior better than you can.

✔ **Keep lines of communication open.** Try to find out what makes these kids seem so attractive. Maybe your child is looking for something that's lacking at home.

Talk honestly with your teen about your concerns that certain friends may be bad influences. Use role playing, family meetings, and casual discussions to bolster your child's skills for handling potentially difficult situations before they occur. Make sure your teen can read responses of others and know when danger lurks. Let your teen know you're available at any time to pick her up from anywhere she feels uncomfortable.

Tell your teen she can always use you as an excuse whenever manipulative buddies won't take "no" for an answer or she wants to save face with peers. Suggest alternatives to participating in something objectionable by saying something like, "My mom wants me to go shopping with her this afternoon," "I promised my dad I'd . . . this evening," or "My folks say I have to stay in and study."

✔ **Know the enemy.** Welcome all your child's friends into the home, whether you approve or disapprove of them. Let your teen bask in the knowledge that you want her and her friends to feel comfortable there. When teens bring their friends home, you get to know them as your child does. You also get to monitor activities, from a distance, of course, and support your child, should sticky situations arise. With time and lack of tension, your child will probably grow weary of the relationship on her own.

✓ **Reinforce regular rules and what happens should they be broken, especially with the objectionable buddy.** You may try grounding or making the telephone or computer off limits, if an offense warrants. Especially, forbid talking to the buddy while grounded. Rebellious teens don't like to hang with supervised kids and may dump your child as a friend.

Forbidding the troublesome relationship totally never works. If you dictate a no-contact rule, you may see the following results:

✓ Your teen will push you away, feeling that you're more out of touch with her feelings and what teens are like today than she originally thought.

✓ The friend becomes more attractive to your teen as a vehicle to gain independence by opposing you.

✓ Your teen becomes protective of the offending friend in the face of your fault-finding assaults, even if she agrees with you.

✓ She'll merely stop telling you when she's around this person.

You may get away with keeping your younger adolescent away from certain people. But battles with your older teen could escalate to the point where she chooses to leave home rather than abide by excessive restrictions.

Dealing with Failed Relationships

No one likes rejection. But teen splits with a friend can be catastrophic and can have negative effects on schoolwork. Although you may have to do a lot of patient listening to discover why your teen is acting extra belligerent or sad, after you retrieve this information, show your concern by:

✓ **Acknowledging the loss:** Try to get your teen to open up with the feelings involved in her grieving process. Refrain from bad-mouthing the other person or trivializing the relationship by saying, "there will be others." Your teen hurts and wants to be understood.

✓ **Listening to what happened without judging:** Avoid taking sides. This is your child's relationship, and she has to deal with the consequences.

But you can help her sort out her feelings and what she'd like to do to make the situation better.

✔ **Encouraging your teen to talk with the friend to resolve any problem, if she hasn't already:** Reassure her that friends often disagree. But true friends talk about their differences and reconcile them. Whatever the outcome, give her a pat on the back for having the courage to try mending the relationship.

✔ **Asking your teen how she suggests getting over a breakup, romantic or otherwise:** What has she done to lift her spirits in the past: music, sports, contacting other friends? Remind her to use the support network that has been there for her before.

Reinforce that your teen should never abandon friends and activities for a romance. Teenagers who stay engaged with a variety of activities and friends find romantic breakups less traumatic.

✔ **Talking about your heartbreaks:** Share how you survived. Build on your teen's problem-solving skills.

✔ **Understanding that losing a good friend takes time to overcome:** Go a little easier on your teen for awhile.

Holding Off Raging Hormones

Your baby, the one with the raging hormones, is growing up. Not only that, her body tingles at the sight of the opposite sex. Now doesn't that make a parent light-headed with fear?

Many teens become sexually active as early as junior high. The good news is that most teens *believe* in waiting until marriage for intercourse. The bad news is that most don't wait.

Educating

You may be waiting for the "right time" to talk about the birds and bees, but your teen won't wait to explore sexual activity. Don't risk your teen's life by not preparing her for reality. Although teens by nature view themselves as invincible, all teens need information about:

✔ **How male and female bodies work:** Research shows that teen pregnancy goes down when kids have the facts about sex. Schools vary in how well they explain human anatomy and the reproductive system to students, so the job falls in your lap. If you absolutely cannot bring your-self to broach sensitive topics about biology, find a doctor you both trust. Your teen should get regular checkups, anyway. Good docs want teens informed about their bodies and how they work, and that includes sex and its repercussions, smoking, eating right, and pierces.

✔ **AIDS, what the disease is, how it's contracted, and how to prevent it:** Sure, abstinence is the best prevention, but your teen may not agree. So make sure she knows that unprotected sex is dangerous and that con-doms save lives.

If you think your teen is sexually active but won't discuss it with you, keep a store of condoms in the vanity or wherever you store toiletries. The supply reinforces using condoms for safe sex and provides easy access for kids who may feel embarrassed or not have money to buy condoms.

✔ **Sexually transmitted diseases (STDs), what they are, and how they are transmitted:** Again, a storehouse of condoms helps make the point for safe sex.

Imparting wisdom

This gets tricky because your teen probably won't want to hear what you have to say. But if you can be brief, refrain from lecturing, and ask for opin-ions, you may get somewhere.

✔ **Discuss your views about premarital sex.** You and your teen may dis-agree, but hearing her out without judging may give you some common ground. Open discussions comfort your teen with the knowledge that you are approachable should concerns arise. Who knows? With time and good communication, you may ultimately win her over to your way of thinking. But don't count on it.

✔ **Talk about relationships.** You teach everything else. Why not teach the ins and outs of dating. Mention some of your relationships and how you handled sex. Ask what qualities your teen looks for in a mate. Talk about the caring and responsibility that comes with a sexual relationship. Ask whether your teen feels pressure to become sexually active before she's ready. Tell her you support her decisions but want her to consider readi-ness and ramifications before embarking on intercourse.

✔ **Explain alternatives to sexual intercourse, such as kissing, exploring a partner's body with hands, and masturbation.** If these don't work, sug-gest cold showers or add saltpeter to your food the way the Army used to do.

A good book with ideas for handling these and other sticky situations with teens is *You're Grounded Till You're Thirty!* by Judy Craig (William Morrow). I don't agree with everything the book says, but many of the options make sense. And you need all the alternatives you can find to turn around a wayward teen.

Chapter 19

Thinking Beyond High School

In This Chapter

▶ Discovering today's activities that help tomorrow's choices

▶ Exploring options for after high school

▶ Applying to colleges

▶ Knowing when to let go

*Y*our child will do something meaningful after high school. (Keep this as your mantra!) The question is, what?

This chapter explores your teen's investigation into smart decisions about the future, whether they include work or college.

Transforming Interests into Career Options

Advanced placement (AP) classes, which are considered college level, and honors courses are great, as are high college entrance exam scores. But competitive universities and potential employers today look for more than test scores when evaluating incoming students. They want well-rounded kids who can someday contribute to their communities beyond earning a paycheck, and that means they look for kids who have participated in activities outside of school.

The extracurricular activities your teen chooses may also lead to a major in college or a career choice.

How does your jeans-wearing dude get varied experiences? One is from the extracurricular activities offered at schools: band, choir, drama, sports, and so on. After that, they can learn from any number of sources, covered in the following sections.

Taking classes outside school

You've really done something right if your child loves learning so much he pursues summer school or classes outside of school. The reasons for extra schooling vary. Perhaps your teen's school doesn't offer what he wants to learn, such as watercolor, photography, or specialized sport's training, in the regular high school curriculum. Or he views regular school stifling but gladly enrolls in classes that tickle his fancy in a more relaxed setting.

Your teen can find extra classes at:

- Local community, recreation, and religious centers
- High school adult education programs
- Museums, zoos, botanical gardens
- Libraries
- Youth groups
- Fitness centers
- Theater workshops
- Community bands, choirs, and dance troupes
- Community colleges: Some states, such as Minnesota, pay for seniors to take courses at local advanced institutions. Contact your local college's advanced high school admissions or post-secondary education departments for more information.
- Online, aka *distance learning:* Many colleges and universities now offer what used to be called correspondence courses or independent study that were offered via snail mail. Online classes take the form of chat rooms, while meetings with professors happen by e-mail. To find out more, check out *College Degrees by Mail & Internet* by John Baer (Ten Speed Press).

Some eager-beavers want to jumpstart college so badly that they take too many extra courses, leading to overload. Getting post-secondary experience and racking up advanced hours that ultimately save you money is commendable, but not at the expense of your teen's health.

Volunteering for fun and experience

Suggest that your teen volunteer — that is, perform a regular task or job without monetary payoff. Through volunteer work, your teen discovers that job satisfaction comes from more than money.

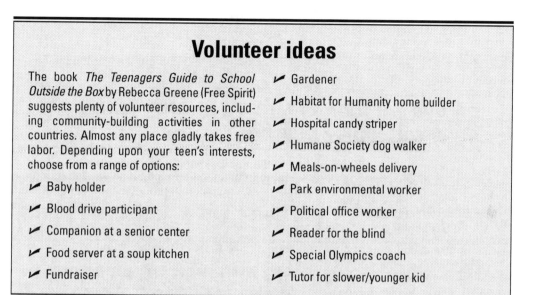

Volunteer ideas

The book *The Teenagers Guide to School Outside the Box* by Rebecca Greene (Free Spirit) suggests plenty of volunteer resources, including community-building activities in other countries. Almost any place gladly takes free labor. Depending upon your teen's interests, choose from a range of options:

- ✔ Baby holder
- ✔ Blood drive participant
- ✔ Companion at a senior center
- ✔ Food server at a soup kitchen
- ✔ Fundraiser

- ✔ Gardener
- ✔ Habitat for Humanity home builder
- ✔ Hospital candy striper
- ✔ Humane Society dog walker
- ✔ Meals-on-wheels delivery
- ✔ Park environmental worker
- ✔ Political office worker
- ✔ Reader for the blind
- ✔ Special Olympics coach
- ✔ Tutor for slower/younger kid

You may think that volunteering is a tough sell with teens. But volunteering fulfills an often unspoken craving that teens often feel for performing good deeds for others, learning new skills, meeting different kinds of people, contacting adults who perform jobs he wants to explore, and keeping busy in a worthwhile way.

A good reason for your teen not to volunteer is to do so just because it looks good on a college application. You'd be surprised how many anxious college-bound teens volunteer for short spurts of time just for that reason. To me, this avenue seems dishonest, and your teen never experiences the positive aspects of the job.

Help your teen find voluntary assignments that:

- ✔ **Are enjoyable enough for repeat returns.** Your teen needs to understand that any job gets boring at times. Start off with one that has enough basic appeal to hold interest for a long while, because money won't be the incentive for showing up.

- ✔ **Make a difference.** Because your teen gives his time, he wants to know that the experience improves some place or someone's life.

- ✔ **Come with training and support.** Your teen shouldn't be expected to jump into a new work situation without some guidance.

Urge your teen to record his volunteer experiences in a log or journal. He'll treasure the memories later, and he can use the information for resumes, job interviews, and college applications.

Considering a mentor, an internship, or an apprenticeship

Your teen may find a positive relationship with a caring adult the most motivating reason of all to find direction. Where else can you discover what the world has to offer but from someone you trust and who trusts you?

Mentoring

Your teen may benefit from a relationship with someone who provides a listening ear outside the family or a career mentor who guides interests into future career possibilities. This could be someone your teen meets regularly, shadows on the job, or contacts on an as-need basis. Your teen can find interested adults through school, family contacts, or the local Big Brothers Big Sisters of America or YMCAs and YWCAs. Online adult mentors can be arranged through the Virtual Volunteering Project, www.serviceleader.org/vv.

Internships

Internships match your teen's interests with an employer who agrees to provide on-the-job experience. A variety of organizations and companies offer internships. Some pay, while others do not. Either way, the experience and contacts prove invaluable, even if your teen decides this type of work isn't for him. This is his time to experiment, and internships allow for exploration under safe conditions. Some schools coordinate internships, or your teen may have to find his own situation. Two good resources are *Peterson's Internships 2003* (Peterson Publishing) and *The Internship Bible* by Mark Oldman (Princeton Review).

Apprenticeships

Apprenticeships provide more serious training in a given field, such as a printing or electrical work. The concept offers kids who aren't continuing their education a chance at a profession. But college-bound kids benefit from apprenticeships, too. Check with your teen's counselor, the Department of Labor Office of Apprenticeship Training, Employer and Labor Services (OATELS) at www.doleta.gov/atels_bat or *Ferguson's Guide to Apprenticeship Programs* (Ferguson Press) for apprenticeship information.

If your teen's school doesn't already have one, ask the powers that be to institute a senior project. With this program, burned-out students in their last semester replace regular classes with community experience. Students who apply for the program identify what they want to accomplish, rather than goof off. They can work in a school, hospital, or office, prepare a videotape, or finish a sculpture — whatever productively strikes their fancy. Afterward, the energized participants prepare an enthusiastic final fair displaying what they've accomplished. What a positive and productive exit from high school!

Working outside of school

To work or not to work? That's the question for you and your teen. Many factors influence permitting your offspring to bring home the bacon: financial need, effect on schoolwork, and type of job and hours involved. Every child and family is different. Check out the pros and cons of teenage work efforts in Table 19-1.

Table 19-1	**Pros and Cons of Teen Jobs**
Pros	*Cons*
Feels good not to hit up parents for money	Takes time away from studies
Teaches responsibility	Replaces after-school activities
Teaches teen to follow directions	Reduces family time
Limits unproductive/television time	Decreases sleep and eating time
Teaches time management skills	Limits leisure time
Gets your kid out of the house	Reduces your control over money

Traveling: Fun and study abroad

Experience has always been the best teacher. So pry your teen from the neighborhood cocoon, if you can afford travel. Should your teen balk at vacation with the family, send him alone in a supervised program of course. Teens can take classes overseas, live with families as part of a foreign exchange program, or join a group, such as Volunteers for Peace, which helps folks in less developed countries, or Habitat for Humanity, which builds homes for people unable to afford them. Some high schools, religious projects, and not-for-profit organizations sponsor similar trips and programs.

Deciding whether your teen should work

Unless your family is starving, the most important variable in your teen's work decision should be school. If good grades come easily, slipping in a few work hours a week probably won't change that. But if better grades take tons of studying on your kid's part, you may feel he can't spare the time.

If you have a shaky student, consider whether he can handle work and schoolwork. Some kids improve grades because they learn to manage time better with a greater workload. The idea of work and earning money becomes a bonus for keeping up grades. With other kids, work turns out to be their academic downfall.

Make a deal with your teen to evaluate together after a certain amount of time, say a month or after the next grading period, how the job is working out. If grades drop, say "no" to a job for now.

Finding the right job

Smart job hunting includes organization and persistence. Before your teen begins the big job search, ask whether he wants to brainstorm. Throw out different types of work options, suggestions for establishments that employ this kind of labor, and ideas about people to contact.

Then let your teen loose to investigate. Remind him to ask anyone he knows for leads. Use your networks to find your child work, if he gives you permission. Think about stores, offices, nonprofit groups, camps, and recreation and community centers near you. Or your teen may want to distribute leaflets throughout the neighborhood that advertise baby-sitting, pet-sitting, lawn work, or odds jobs for neighbors.

Have your teen use the telephone book and pound the pavement to discover prospective employers who seem like a good match.

Approaching Dreaded Interviews

No one enjoys getting sized up. But that's the purpose of interviews, whether for jobs or college. Someone other than friends, family, and teachers want to get to know your child and evaluate whether he's a good match for what they offer.

Interviews are part of life and growing up, and smart kids know how to handle them.

To reduce interview anxiety:

- **Remind your teen to be on time for the interview.** Latecomers start off wrong by creating more anxiety for themselves and by messing up their interviewer's schedule, which sends an irresponsible message.

- **Teach your teen how to communicate with other adults.** If you want your adolescent to get ahead, which is the point of your reading this book, tell him to shake the "duhs," "likes," "yahs," and "ya knows" in conversations with older folks. He must be able to speak up for himself without sounding like his mouth is full of cotton, and he has to make sure he doesn't have a giant chip on his shoulder just because the other person happens to be an authority figure. Role play and give him other good advice to:

  - Greet the interviewer in a friendly manner, preferably with a strong handshake.

  - Seem upbeat and enthusiastic about the school or job, even if he's not sure he wants it.

  - Look the interviewer in the eye when talking. Read the good listening and communication skills sections in Chapters 7 and 8.

  - Ask questions to find out more about the situation and to show interest. Impress upon your tight-lipped teen that questions show interest and intelligence, not the opposite.

  - Leave the interview knowing the next step in the search process and saying "thank you."

- **Prepare your teen to look his best for the interview.** Valid or not, the first five face-to-face minutes determine an interviewer's opinion of the interviewee. Remind your I-gotta-be-me teen that looking strange doesn't cut it in the business world. He doesn't need to look like a fashion plate, either.

To make a good impression, your teen needs to be clean, neat, shaven, and odor-free with combed hair and clothes that cover erogenous zones. As for pierces and tattoos, the reality is that they are more common now. For certain positions, such as salesperson at an upscale store or law office assistant, clean cut still wins the job.

Deciding on College — or Not

I know you wonder what I mean here. After all, you bought this book to raise a smart kid. And doesn't smart mean college-bound? Usually, but not always.

Sometimes, the smartest move for your teen may be to:

✔ **Postpone college until your teen is emotionally and psychologically ready.** If your kid's heart isn't in school and studying, why waste energy and money?

If your teen doesn't go to college, make he gets a job and pays something toward room and board. Not going to college doesn't mean playtime. A job gives your child perspective, responsibility, and an education in the real world and in how important a degree is to succeed. Kids who take time off from school usually return as better, more committed students.

✔ **Enroll in trade school or an apprenticeship.** Maybe your teen has his heart set on being a chef or working with his hands, like in carpentry. You may be able to squeeze a liberal arts degree out of him, but that would be your choice, not his. Then he'd still have to train in his chosen field.

Another option for someone committed to a nonacademic career is college in a related area that augments skills needed on the job. Land-grant universities offer courses in food service for the future chef, vocational education for the handyperson, and business degrees for anyone who thinks about owning a business some day.

Hunting for the right college

For the college-bound, choosing a college can be a long and difficult haul, especially if your child hasn't a clue what to study or where to go, and that's a common occurrence. But if you get nothing else from this section, I want you to understand that a school exists for every type of student. It may not be your child's first choice, but a match is out there.

Basically, the right college is the one that:

✔ Has the major your teen wants or a liberal arts substitute that allows varied academic grazing and dabbling in lots of subjects before honing into one area

✔ Fits your teen's requirements for size and atmosphere

✔ Sends an acceptance letter

Checking in with college counselors

High schools hire different folks to help kids with problems that crop up and to advise them about post-high-school plans. Larger schools in more fiscally sound districts have social workers, guidance counselors, psychologists, truant officers, and college counselors. Smaller or less wealthy districts may have one person who performs all these jobs.

Start the college search by meeting as a family with your teen's school counselor during the junior year. The college counselor's job is to help kids match their talents, interests, and family budget with what colleges want. Discuss requirements and listen to suggestions for possible colleges. Let your teen talk first and carry on most of the discussion, unless he's the sullen type or doesn't see any reason to begin the hunt so early (which is another common occurrence). Even then, hold back. Your child needs to take ownership of the process.

Encourage your student to get to know the counselor *before* college planning or a crisis arises with a simple introduction and hello or anything that gives this professional an idea what your child is like. That way, if your teen needs someone other than you to talk to, needs guidance for some misdeed, or requires a recommendation for college or a job, he has a professional who knows him enough to be helpful.

If your teen's school counselor isn't connecting with your child, suggest that your child see someone else. If that's impossible, your teen can still use the college materials the school keeps on file, such as pamphlets and online programs. Every college has a Web site, too, that they're helpful only if your teen knows a few places to begin. Individual searches take some time and energy on your teen's part.

Two good sources published annually that help you compare colleges are the university issues of *U.S. News & World Report,* which ranks colleges by several factors such as class selection and teaching staff, and the *Fiske Guide to Colleges* (Sourcebooks, Inc.), which covers particulars, such as social life and dorm rooms.

Deciding to be undecided

You may be blessed with a teen who has wanted to be a doctor or pianist or deep sea diver almost from birth. But most kids haven't a clue. That's okay. This is the time in their lives to expand horizons and investigate alternatives. Still, your teen's indecision can be painful to watch when everyone except the dog constantly asks, "What do you want to study in college?"

Help your teen with a little sole searching to get direction. Encourage him to honestly evaluate his strong qualities and interests. Help him identify classes and activities that he likes. Why does he like them? Has he consistently done well in certain subjects since elementary school? What skills does he use to succeed on teams or in activities he finds pleasurable? Is there a common thread among what he's identifying?

Kids often don't take time to consider what goes into what they do. They just do. But being president of the class, drummer in the band, or debater on the team takes specific qualities. Suggest listing these qualities in writing. Seeing the list builds self-awareness and builds confidence. The list also provides a foundation for the college applications that often ask about these qualities.

If a direction doesn't become evident, consider a liberal arts program that allows for all sorts of experimentation. If indecision still seems unsettling to your teen, advise him to meet with a career counselor at college and peruse the Department of Labor's *Occupational Outlook Handbook* and *Dictionary of Occupational Titles* at the library for information about job prospects.

Attending college recruitment events

Most high schools either hold college recruitment fairs or know of regional presentations where one or more colleges send representatives. Dance up and down until your teen agrees to attend these events. They are a chance to find out about different schools without leaving town. Even if your teen isn't interested in the specific college, he gets some perspective about the range of opportunities different institutions offer. At the very least, he hears which schools classmates are considering, which may build a little enthusiasm for the process.

Knowing what to look for

Several factors play into making a decision about which college to attend.

Location

Realtors have a saying that real estate is about three factors: "Location, location, location." Same with choosing colleges. First, decide whether your teen prefers to study at home or live away. Going to college at home saves money, but living away has the benefit of allowing more freedom.

Second, figure out where the best place would be. Think of the city mouse and country mouse from the famous children's story. A few pristine, ivy-covered buildings may look the way colleges are supposed to look. But if the only extracurricular activities turn out to be hiking through corn fields (as is the case at some rural colleges) or boozing in dorm rooms, your city mouse may feel bored and lonely. Similarly, city and big state campuses may overwhelm and scare your country mouse, who lacks street smarts developed by those raised in metropolitan areas.

Does this mean never take your fish out of his size waters? Definitely not. But investigate places with eyes wide open. After a decision has been made, plan ahead ways to circumvent or handle difficult adjustments.

Size

Your teen may have definite ideas about what size school he can handle. Check Table 19-2 for the benefits of small and large colleges.

Table 19-2	Benefits of College Sizes
Small Colleges	*Large Colleges*
Smaller class sizes	More programs offered
More personalized instruction	Greater variety of classes
More homogeneous population	Increased number of extra activities
Know most folks	More diverse population

Cost

College tuition rises faster than you can read this section. If cost is a factor in your teen's next academic destination, be honest and upfront about what your family can afford, but don't necessarily rule out your teen's favorite choice. Instead, start early to investigate workable financial arrangements:

✔ **Select less costly alternatives.** For example, in-state universities cost less than out-of-state, and public schools generally charge less than private.

Factor in living and transportation expenses, too. Weigh what they mean for your student. Schools that are a plane ride away may limit visits home more than those a few hours in a train, car, or bus. And some schools lack residence halls, which means apartment expenses that may cost more or less than school housing depending upon the city.

✔ **Explore scholarships from your teen's high school, community organizations, and at prospective colleges.** Not all scholarships depend upon top grades. Sometimes, high school departments, such as theater or band, give one-time grants to talented graduates. Individual college departments, such as education and business, offer scholarships separate from general university grants to entice solid students. Get ideas for scholarships at www.collegescholarships.com.

Ask at your place of employment whether they sponsor scholarships for children of employees. Push your child to check with the school counselor for a list of places that offer money to college-bound students and to find out how to apply for scholarships at college options.

✔ **Take AP courses in junior and senior years of high school.** At the end of the course, your child can take an advance placement exam. If he passes, the course counts toward a college degree. Get enough of these, and your smart teen can graduate college a semester or two early, thereby saving some bucks.

These classes tend to be for the most persistent kids who don't mind extra work.

✔ **Decide about college loans and who will pay back the debt.** Ask your teen to seriously consider the tradeoff of going to a more expensive school and graduating owing thousands of dollars.

✔ **Question colleges about work-study programs when you visit.** Some colleges let students as young as sophomores work as residence hall assistants, which means after the freshman year, your teen can live room-and board-free.

Visiting campuses

Visit as many campuses as your time and checkbook allow. Sometimes, dream schools *sound* better than they *feel.* Go once as a family. After your teen hones in on some strong possibilities, try to arrange another visit for him alone to determine whether the school culture appears a good fit.

If long trips to target schools prove impossible, visit nearby campuses to get a handle on the differences that size and general location make.

When you visit a college campus:

✔ **Call the college recruitment or admissions** office a couple weeks ahead of when you intend to come for an appointment. Representatives can schedule your family for appointments with people who can best answer your teen's questions.

✔ **Try to visit during the week** to see the campus in full activity.

✔ **Allow at least a half day** to tour the grounds, hear any promotional presentation, and talk with people in admissions and your teen's area of interest. Find out what services and extracurricular activities, teams, and organizations are available to students. Discuss cost, scholarships, and the length of degree programs.

✔ **Take the organized tour** before wandering around on your own. Tour guides, who may be students who talk your teen's language, show you a residence hall, library, academic buildings, and the student union, the prime gathering place. They answer questions and lend personality to the campus visit.

✔ **Discuss questions to ask** before your visit. You may want to arrange who asks what, so that your teen doesn't get embarrassed or upset at your enthusiasm.

✔ **Spend additional time** on campus for a bit of fun. Eat at the union or a dorm cafeteria to taste the food. Go to a campus event. Talk with other students about what they like or dislike about the school.

✔ **Recommend that your teen write thoughts about each school** *right after* the visit. Label and organize free materials in a safe place for retrieval later. After a few presentations and tours, information begins to run together in everyone's mind.

Elicit your teen's response *before* commenting on the school. You don't want to taint his thinking about the place. Because he has to spend four years somewhere, this needs to be his decision, within reason and the family budget, of course. Your teen is applying to college, not you.

Easing the application process

Prod your teen to begin the application process early, even if application deadlines are months away. He has to allow time for:

✔ **Taking college boards:** Your teen should take the PSAT in his sophomore year. This pretend version of the SAT, the entrance exam that counts on transcripts, gives your student an idea of his test-taking skills. If you agree that this test doesn't make your child shine, allow enough time, and money, for repeating the test. Another option is for your teen to take ACTs instead, which most colleges accept, or find a tutor or prep class. Many kids take both exams, because each one measures slightly different competencies, and schools require different ones. Your teen can pick up test preparation classes either at school, if they offer them, or through private individuals and services. Also check out *The SAT For Dummies* and *The ACT For Dummies,* both by Suzee Vlk (Wiley Publishing, Inc.).

✔ **Wading through the materials he's collected to limit alternatives and making sure he has applications for final choices:** Advise your teen to apply to a *reach college* (one that may be a stretch to get into), a couple mid-range schools, and at least one safety school. A *safety school* is one your child knows he can attend. Some counselors recommend a safety college near home, in case an unplanned event changes the ability to leave town.

✔ **Filling out applications and applying for scholarships and financial aid:** Many schools require essays. These take time to do well and check out *College Admission Essays For Dummies* by Geraldine Woods (Wiley Publishing, Inc.). Unfortunately, each college's essay asks for different information, so your teen has to create new stories about himself for each one. The good news is the idea of writing an essay may limit the number of schools where he applies, if he finds writing distasteful. (Colleges charge fees just for applying, so limiting the number is a good thing!)

Suggest that your teen make several copies of each blank application. That way, inevitable mistakes won't result in delays getting new forms. Copy the finished application, as well. Some information may be usable on another form.

Reinforce double checking that the correct form goes in the envelope to the proper school.

✔ **Gathering references, if requested:** Your teen may need to find employers, adult friends, or teachers willing to vouch for his character and brain power. Parents and siblings don't count. These folks may be busy people, and you don't want to rush someone who is doing you a favor, so encourage your teen to give references *one month* to write sparkling recommendations.

✔ **Submitting the applications for your school to mail:** Kids think that when the applications are completed, the process is finished. But your teen's high school school needs at least a couple weeks to process the application and enclose transcripts. Colleges and universities are strict about how forms are filled out and that deadlines are met.

Many colleges and universities are offering early-acceptance programs. This means if your teen gets the application in by a certain earlier-than-normal date and he agrees to go to the school if accepted, he can receive an acceptance or rejection early in the process. Early application programs are good for students who know where they want to go and which career paths they want to follow. Receiving confirmation early lifts the stress of waiting for months to hear. Some college early-admittance programs are loosening their requirement that a student must follow through and not apply elsewhere.

Helping your teen stay sane during trying times

Go easy on your teen as response time approaches. Even if your child doesn't seem traumatized by the process, understand that he's hearing everyone else's anxiety at lunch, after school, and on the weekend. From the time he sends off the application until the acceptance or rejection letter returns, all he hears from family and friends is, "Have you heard yet?" "Do you know where you are going to school?" The coolest teen eventually feels the heat.

Never steam, view against a window or light box, or otherwise open your teen's college letters. Mail is private.

Celebrate with each acceptance. But don't make a big deal of rejection. Acknowledge that your teen may be feeling down because of a negative response and let it go. No one likes to be rejected, even if the letter comes from the third or fourth choice. And no one likes to be reminded of the rejection.

Keep reminding your child that a college exists for everyone.

Packing bags and helping your darling prepare for college

Accept that college isn't like when you were there. Kids take microwaves, computers, freezers, televisions, and other comforts of home. Decide whether you agree with all these options. Some schools have appliances in the room or offer a rental program. Either choice is preferable to schlepping a refrigerator up four flights of stairs. Even if elevators exist, count on their not working on move-in day.

For an idea of other accoutrements to take, get a list from your local mega linen and hardware store. These folks see dollar signs in first-year students. Some colleges provide lists to new students, as well.

Letting Go: The Hardest Part about Being a Smart Parent

Smart parents know when the main part of their job is done. But seeing your baby leave home without you is never easy. You've invested a lot of time and effort in increasing his brain cells and shaping a caring human being. Independence is part of that package.

Luckily, your offspring helps the separation process along. By the end of your teen's senior year:

- ✔ He's probably rarely home, which gives you some idea of life without him.

- ✔ He's probably gotten a tad surly. This is a sign of *his* anxiety about leaving home and his friends. His behavior toward you enables the letting-go process to progress, because you welcome the break. Don't feel guilty about these feelings!

Launching your child at college or work doesn't change that he's still your child. But letting go does mean accepting that you and your teen have a different relationship now. The physical distance between you two forces you to connect as adults who respect each other's freedom and decisions. See some examples in Table 19-3. Even though you live apart, you remain a family. Enjoy your maturing young adult. Your job isn't over yet. Your child will still be home for breaks and summers and maybe again after college, but that's another book.

Table 19-3	What You Are Allowed and Not Allowed to Do
What You Are Allowed to Do	**What You Are Not Allowed to Do**
Write and e-mail	Expect return mail
Send food	Nag about eating wholesome foods
Visit	Arrive unannounced
Send money, as agreed	Send too much money
Be a good listener	Compare your experiences
Tell him you love him and know he's doing his best	Guilt-trip him about being gone with how much you miss and need him
Trust your teen: You've done a great job	Tell your kid how to run his life

SMART KID TIP

Helpful hints for college

Send your teen off to college with these words of wisdom collected from other college-bound teens:

✓ **Everyone else is in the same boat.** The kids on your floor, the kids in class: You're all new.

✓ **Keep an open mind about the people you will meet.** If you come from a homogeneous neighborhood, you may have preconceived notions about other ethnic groups. College is a great place to end stereotypes and find out about others.

✓ **Keep your door open the first week at school.** That way, other kids know you're open to visitors.

✓ **Bake more cookies than you can eat in a week to take with you.** Offer them to your dorm neighbors. What better way to say "Hi, who are you?" than with food?

✓ **Never schedule early morning classes if you don't usually rise until noon.** You'll sleep through class.

✓ **Buy used books whenever possible, which may mean getting books as soon as you know your schedule.** College texts are expensive. Cheaper ones go quickly.

✓ **Make time each day to organize yourself.** Decide which homework and what other commitments need your attention. You're on your own now.

✓ **Try new things: a sport, study habit, hobby, work for a cause.** You decide on your own direction now.

✓ **Keep your priorities straight.** If your choice is to study for finals or party until 4 a.m., be responsible.

✓ **Check in with the 'rents now and then.** They love you, are proud of you, and want to hear from you.

Part V
The Part of Tens

In this part . . .

Time to tie up a few loose ends and get some bonus information that's a lot of fun and takes minimal time to read.

In this part, you get tantalizing information, like the ten qualities that contribute most to raising smart kids, ten reading suggestions for your growing kids, and ten resources that you may never have known existed for guiding your little wizards.

All of the information in this part is presented with humor, good wishes, and above all, respect for your awesome job. So read on. Savor a few tidbits. But most importantly, enjoy raising your smart kid.

Chapter 20

Ten Family Characteristics That Nurture Smart Kids

* *

In This Chapter

▶ Building family unity as a foundation for smarts

▶ Cherishing independence that fosters achievement

* *

*H*ow do you become a smart family? Eliminate the *I* versus *you* attitude in your home, and you're on your way to raising higher-achieving kids with whom other people want to work and play. You won't be perfect at this smart family routine. No family is. Even the best intentions slip now and then, which is perfectly normal. Just strive toward making these ten qualities of smart families your goal.

Willing to Go the Extra Mile for Each Other

Make your family motto *family first*. Ensure that each person knows the important role they play in the family and understands that this role some-times involves pitching in and making sacrifices to strengthen family life. Let cooperation, compassion, and kindness be your watchwords. In healthy fami-lies, members expect to give up time, energy, and lots of other luxuries for each other, even though they may grumble about it.

Smart kids need to feel confident that family members are there for each other, should the need arise.

Reinforce that this major juggling act has a positive side. Clue-in everyone that they will get back much more than they give. And be prepared to reap the rewards of a more confident, higher-achieving child. That's what the strength of family brings.

Respecting Each Other

Don't be put off by all the togetherness. Sticking close as a family doesn't negate the importance of respecting individuality. Every child has the ability to be smart. By respecting her ideas and interests, you allow your child's natural abilities to surface.

Respect is one of those behaviors kids master partly by observation. If you listen without judging and act courteously and politely toward all kinds and ages of people, chances are, your child will gets the message that others deserve respect. The message may not sink in immediately, but eventually, considerate and mannerly behavior rubs off.

Delighting in Each Other

Smart families like yours enjoy each other. You thrill at experiencing enriching adventures together. You build a school-at-home curriculum that encourages fun and learning, so your child grows intellectually. You read, listen to music, and play indoor and outdoor games together, creating a rich intellectual heritage as part of regular family activities. Or you spend downtime together doing absolutely nothing. Yet, you allow everyone their own interests and activities and rejoice at hearing what family members experience when apart.

Cherish family time and the stabilizing connectedness it brings.

Communicating with Each Other

Building a smart family relies on your being able to understand each other's feelings, which isn't always an easy process. As much as humanly possible given each family member's qualities, let every family member know that he or she is understood, and that his or her feelings and thoughts count.

- Share family beliefs at mealtimes.
- Discuss problems and gripes during family meetings.
- Take time to listen and rephrase what someone says to show you understand and help you clarify if you don't.
- Know that it's never too late to open lines of communication.

Say, write, or do something positive for each family member every day. Pep talks keep everyone going in a smart direction.

Growing from Each Other and from Mistakes

Growing from each other runs both ways: for you to counsel your kids and for you to learn from them.

Sharing your wisdom with your kids

Sometimes, the best course of action is to let situations happen. Try to develop an attitude that no matter what or how painful the outcome, the situation is a learning experience, a place to begin again.

When teeth-gnashing, tear-producing, or otherwise scary situations occur (and they frequently do in my household), I try to ask, "What's the worst that can happen here?" If you and your offspring can handle the answer, you can handle anything.

Learning from your kids

Never be so proud and into a rigid I-have-to-know-it-all-because-I'm-the-parent role that you can't learn from your kids. This entire parenting trek is a give-and-take learning experience. If you don't realize the wonderful possibilities of seeing the world from your child's vantage point, you're missing a lot.

Let your child see you make mistakes. Mistakes humanize you — rather than demean you — in your child's eyes. And let your child see how you take responsibility and handle your mistakes.

Valuing Effort, Not Product

Set high family standards. But don't tie your child's self-worth to fulfilling expectations that may or may not be realistic. Kids judge themselves by how others value them. So let your child know through actions and words what's really important:

✔ Celebrate individual accomplishments, no matter how imperfect.

✔ Praise the way family members tackle jobs, instead of praising end-products.

✔ Emphasize your child's character, goodness, and effort.

From this encouraging cocoon, your child gains the inner strength to tackle new endeavors. She also learns that being smart means more than test results and winning competitions and games.

Being smart is about feeling good about yourself for doing the best you can.

Solving Problems Together

Smart families involve everyone in decisions about routines and choices. As a parent, you shape family discussions but aren't an authoritarian "Because I say so!" type. Take cues from every family member, even little people.

As your child matures, arrange for greater responsibility and more independence. But stay on top of what your child is doing at home and at school. Smart families catch problems before they develop into something bigger, no matter what age a child reaches.

Ultimately, you're the parent. As such, you make the final decisions. Show your child you care by setting reasonable limits that include her participation.

Creating an Environment that Values Learning

Smart families continue to learn together. Everyone becomes involved in the child's learning, which then encourages more learning. Freedom to initiate activities and goals exists within a safe and stable framework that:

✔ Limits media

✔ Encourages reading

✔ Allows free play only after homework is done

Reacting Well to Successes and Failures

Smart families accept that they are human. Near-perfection may be a goal, but you all understand that nobody can be perfect, nor should you be.

Encourage family members to accept success humbly and failure with grace. Be an apologizing family. Advocate that everyone, including yourself, sprinkle, "I'm sorry," "Do you need a hug," or "I need a hug," liberally into words and actions.

Nothing gets you through difficult times better than a sense of humor.

Showing and Saying, "I Love You"

The one common denominator of families that raise smart kids is their unconditional love for each other. Any family, no matter what background the family comes from, can produce successful kids if your heart guides your parenting philosophy.

You can read books, talk with experts, and commit their gems to memory. But if your heart tells you something different than the know-it-alls, go with your gut.

Raising a smart kid is no different than raising any child. First and foremost, it takes a loving family that encourages warm, positive feelings to emanate through words and actions. Smiles, a loving touch, a kind word: Loving each other to bits is the most important ingredient for raising a smarter, more successful child.

Chapter 21

Ten Popular Reads from Preschool to Teen Years

Did you know that almost 10,000 kid's book are published each year? No wonder book selection can get overwhelming. This chapter helps you sort through interesting age-appropriate books and magazines to entice your youngster into reading. (You find more than ten popular reads here, so the "Ten" in this chapter's title isn't exactly accurate!)

Playing with Non-Boring Board Books

Young babies need books they can sink their teeth into, literally. So publishers oblige them with books made of plastic, cloth, and heavy-duty cardboard.

Most *plastic books* won't win any awards, but they withstand drooling, bath water, and stuffing into diaper bags. But *board books* are another story. Many are quite entertaining. Sink your teeth into some of these:

✔ Any books with photos of babies. One baby per page is more than enough for the 0–12-month set. Babies love looking at likenesses of people their own size.

✔ *One Fish, Two Fish, Red Fish, Blue Fish* by Dr. Seuss. Check out other Dr. Seuss books to grow on. They have bold, primary-color pictures and simple words. Dr. Seuss books rhyme, which trains the ear for language and are plain fun for adults to read.

Books about books

Pour through the age-related lists in this chapter. Ask your child for interests and ideas. If you still want options for your child that other pros consider great reads, investigate these sources. Of the tons around, I think these books and e-mail sites are reputable bets:

Books:

✔ *Choosing Books for Children* by Betsy Hearne (University of Illinois Press) Hearne presents an easy-to-read book from a kid's-book-loving librarian perspective.

✔ *The New Read-Aloud Handbook* by Jim Trelease (Penguin) Trelease beats the drum for reading aloud and offers his favorites to parents from the perspective of an author, journalist, and parent.

✔ *The Educated Child* by William Bennett (Free Press) Bennett pounds away from an educator's/politician's perspective at what he thinks are books that create kids who are educated and well-rounded, solid citizens.

✔ *MegaSkills: Building Children's Achievement for the Information Age* by Dorothy Rich (Houghton Mifflin) This book covers specific skills for raising educated kids followed by activities. But the best section lists books by the underlying quality they portray, such as responsibility or leadership.

Sources:

✔ **American Library Association:** Posts 700 different book lists, including an Internet guide for teens called Teen Hoopla, and award lists such as the Newbery, Caldecott (picture book), and Coretta Scott King (African-American–related). www.ala.org.

✔ **International Reading Association:** Professional association of reading teachers, but you and your child can benefit from their wisdom. They produce a list of children's choices, the best kind. www.reading.org.

✔ **Parent's Choice:** Nonprofit consumer organization comprised of parents, artists, librarians, and kids who recommend books, magazines, media, and toys. www.parents-choice.org.

✔ *Playtime* by DK Publishing. The company publishes several books with vivid, realistic, and simple pictures and single words, including *First Word* books that include this title. These are great for growing vocabularies. Ask your child to, "Point to the . . . ," and say what the picture contains.

✔ *Spot* books by Eric Hill. These charming books about a black and white pup have been baby favorites for decades. Some are flip-tab, which involve your baby as he improves dexterity and becomes ready for objects to disappear and reappear.

✔ *The Very Hungry Caterpillar* or any book by Eric Carle. Carle's books display simple and cute storylines enhanced by brightly colored pages of everyday creatures.

- *Max* books by Rosemary Wells. Here are baby books you won't get tired of because of their humor. Max and his sister Ruby have one- or two-word interactions on each brightly-colored page. They share everyday experiences that you and your baby grumble about — well, at least you do.

- *Blue Bedtime* by Tara Maratea and *Goodnight Moon* by Margaret Wise Brown. These are classic, simple sleepy-time favorites.

- Nursery rhyme collections. They're short, sometimes weird, and in rhyme, which babies love to hear.

Reading-Aloud Books

So many great toddler/preschool books. So little time. Here are some of my family's favorites. They include a few classics and a few titles worth exploring, depending upon your child's interests.

Remember to include a mix of fiction and nonfiction in your read-aloud selections.

- *The Carrot Seed* by Ruth Krauss (HarperTrophy): A great example of believing in oneself and the value of perseverance, and in only 101 words.

- *The Rainbow Fish* by Marcus Pfister (North-South Books): Eye-catching pictures.

- *A Frog Inside My Hat* by Fay Robinson (Bridgewater): Poetry collection.

- *Market Day* by Lois Ehlert (Harcourt): Nonfiction in bright colors.

- *The Tale of Peter Rabbit* by Beatrix Potter (F. Warne): Classic that touches the heart of every naughty child.

- *The Snowy Day* by Ezra Keats (Viking): Classic day in the snow with all its wonders.

- *Corduroy* by Don Freeman (Viking): Another classic story, this one about a stuffed bear.

- *Bein' with You This Way* by W. Nikola-Lisa (Lee & Low): Rhythmic romp about kids at play in the city and how they get along.

- *Stranger in the Woods* by Carl Sams (Carl Sams Photography): Nonfiction about the environment.

- *Mama Provi and the Pot of Rice* by Sylvia Rosa-Casanova (Atheneum): Simple multicultural theme written in repetition, which kids love.

- *Good Night Richard Rabbit* by Robert Kraus (Simon & Schuster): You'll notice a resemblance to nighttime delaying tactics that you experience in this bedtime story.

- *Where the Wild Things Are* by Maurice Sendak (HarperTrophy): A child handles punishment for being naughty with gusto and through imagination.

- *Strega Nona* by Tomie dePaola (Putnam): A grandma story lovingly told through the eyes of an artist grandson.

- *Get to Work Trucks* by Don Carter (Roaring Brook Press).

- *The Poky Little Puppy* by Janette Lowrey (Golden Press): A classic both with naughty behavior from a pup that kids relate to and repetitive lines that kids can predict.

- *Don't Need Friends* by Carolyn Crimi (Doubleday): A possum and rat find the value of friendship in this snappily written story.

- *The Little Puppy* by Judy Dunn (Random House): Nonfiction with great photos of a dog's life. Check out other animal photography books by this author.

- *The Wild Baby* adapted by Jack Prelutsky (Greenwillow): Great mischievous romp in rhyme.

- *The Runaway Bunny* by Margaret Wise Brown (HarperTrophy): Heartwarming story about a child rabbit challenging the love of his mother.

- *Flying Bats* by Fay Robinson (Scholastic): Nonfiction in rhyme.

- *Underwear* by Mary Monsell (Albert Whitman): Animals who like different kinds of underwear and cause many giggles for listeners and readers.

- *Trains* by Seymour Simon (HarperCollins): Nonfiction for train lovers.

- *Memory Cupboard* by Charlotte Herman (Albert Whitman): Thoughtful story about the value of family and remembering.

- *Green Eggs and Ham* by Dr. Seuss (Random House): Classic Dr. Seuss.

- *If I Found a Wistful Unicorn: A Gift of Love* by Ann Ashford (Peachtree): Classic touchy-feely story with a hidden unicorn in each picture, and this was before *Where's Waldo*. This loving message tugs at heartstrings of any age reader.

Watch out for books and magazines based on TV characters or books written by celebrities. Some may be good. But a successful actor, singer, or politician isn't necessarily a readable children's book author.

Engaging Primary-Graders with Books

Kids this age like to read two genres in particular: humor and suspense. Blend the two, and you really have a winner. Here are a few alternatives for the ages 5–8 crowd, from classics to not-so-classic but fun. The list offers books for brand-new readers and those who are more experienced and independent:

- *Alexander and the Terrible, Horrible, No Good, Very Bad Day* by Judith Viorst (Atheneum): Nearly anyone can relate to this one.

- *Alexander Who Used to Be Rich Last Sunday* by Judith Viorst (Atheneum)

- *Miss Nelson Is Missing* by Harry Allard (Houghton)

- *One Grain of Rice: A Mathematical Folktale* by Demi (Scholastic)

- *Lilly's Purple Plastic Purse* by Kevin Henkes (Greenwillow)

- *Flossie and the Fox* by Patricia McKissack (Dial): An African American tale.

- *Tar Beach* by Faith Ringgold (Knopf)

- *The Velveteen Rabbit* by Margery Williams (Doubleday)

- *Lon Po Po: A Red Riding Hood Story from China* by Ed Young (Philomel): Chinese folk tale.

- *Why Mosquitoes Buzz in People's Ears: A West African Tale* by Verna Aardema (Dial): West African folk tale.

- *Great Snakes!, Many Spiders!,* and *Fantastic Frogs* by Fay Robinson (Scholastic): All nonfiction in rhyme.

- *From Seed to Plant* by Gail Gibbons (Holiday House)

- *Easy Answers to First Science Questions about Oceans* by Querida Pearce (Lowell House)

- *Humphrey the Lost Whale: A True Story* by Wendy Tokuda (Scott Foresman): Fictionalized account of true story.

- *Tooth Tales from around the World* by Marlene Targ Brill (yours truly — okay, I'm a shameless promoter, but I really like this story published by Charlesbridge): The only nonfiction history of the tooth fairy.

- *Seven Brave Women* by Betsy Hearne (Greenwillow): Gently woven stories of different generations of women from one family.

- *Petcetera: The Pet Riddle Book* by Meyer Seltzer (Albert Whitman)

- *Paper Bag Princess* by Robert Munsch (Annick Press)

- *The Polar Express* by Chris Van Allsburg (Houghton)

- *The Day Jimmy's Boa Ate the Wash* by Trinka Hakes Noble (Penguin)

- *Nate the Great* series by Marjorie Sharmat (Young Yearling)

- *The Berenstain Bears* series by Stan and Jan Berenstain (Random House)

- *Terrible Things: An Allegory of the Holocaust* by Eve Bunting (the Jewish Publication): Gentle story about what happens when people don't speak up about their beliefs.

- *Owl Moon* by Jane Yolen (Philomel): Beautifully written tale.

- *Magic School Bus* series by Joanna Cole (Random House): Fictionalized nonfiction — an involving way to learn science.

Looking into Longer Easy Readers and Short Chapter Books

Kids know they're growing up and becoming good readers when they can read chapters books. Never mind that some chapter books are easier than the picture books they've been reading. I'm talking about a rite of passage. Scroll down the following list of favorite *easy readers* (stories with controlled language) and short chapter books:

- *Frog and Toad* series by Arnold Lobel (Harper): Fun for early readers.

- *Ramona the Pest* by Beverly Cleary (Camelot)

- *Allen Jay and the Underground Railroad* by Marlene Targ Brill (Carolrhoda): Fictionalized true story from the 1850s.

- *Kate Shelley and the Midnight Express* by Margaret Wetterer (Carolrhoda): Fictionalized true story.

- *Margaret Knight: Girl Inventor* by Marlene Targ Brill (Millbrook Press): Fictionalized true story of a girl who invented a device for a loom that saved lives during the 1850s.

- *Where Did Your Family Come From? A Book about Immigrants* by Gilda Berger (Ideals): Nonfiction about ancestry.

- *Getting To Know the World's Greatest Artists* series by Mike Venezia (Children's Press): Inviting biographies of famous artists.

- *Mr. Pin: The Chocolate Files* by Mary Monsell (Minstrel Pocket Book): A fun introduction to mysteries: The star detective in this story is an opera- and chocolate-loving penguin.

- *Millie Cooper, Take a Chance* by Charlotte Herman (Puffin)

- *The Light in the Attic* and *Where the Sidewalk Ends* by Shel Silverstein (HarperCollins): These fun poetry collections tickle a child's funny bone.

- *The New Kid on the Block* by Jack Prelutsky (Greenwillow): Another fun kid's poetry book.

- *The Butter Battle Book* and *The Lorax* by Dr. Seuss (Random House): With these books, Dr. Seuss ventures into more adult topics in a kid-like way. This time, he explores war, peace, and the environment.

- *George and Martha: The Complete Stories of Two Best Friends* by James Marshall (Houghton)

- *Math Curse* by Jon Scieska (Viking): This is math with an unusual twist.

- *A Drop of Water* by Walter Wick (Scholastic): Beautiful photography goes with 15 easy science experiments.

- *Amelia Bedelia* by Peggy Parish (Harper): Stories about the antics of a zany house helper, complete with quirky plays on the English language.

- *Ned Feldman, Space Pirate* by Daniel Pinkwater (Macmillan): Fast-paced goofy adventures of Ned with Captain Lumpy Lugo from planet Jivebone.

- *Amber Brown Is Not a Crayon* by Paula Danziger (Putnam): Light-hearted story about third-grade issues.

- *Ramona* and *Henry Huggins* books by Beverly Cleary (Morrow)

- *Step-Into-Reading* and *I-Can-Read* series: Both series offer a variety of topics targeted to specific grade levels.

Knowing about classics in primary grades

Teachers make assumptions about their student's general knowledge. Much of it comes from what kids read. Try to expose your smart kid to these ten classic tales:

- The Ugly Duckling, originally by Hans Christian Andersen

- Paul Bunyan and his ox Babe

- Anansi the spider, the main character of several trickster folk tales

- Goldilocks and the three bears

- Cinderella and her mean stepsisters

- Winnie-the-Pooh and Christopher Robin, A. A. Milne (the original stories rather than modern adaptations, are best)

- Three Billy Goat's Gruff and mischievous trolls

- Gingerbread boy who ran away from people

- Three little pigs, especially the one who works hard

- Dorothy, Toto, and the Wizard of Oz

See what your child, not you, prefers first. Then shower him with other books and magazines in a similar genre. But slyly leave other attractive choices lying around the house, say under the pillow, in the bathroom, or on top of the remote. You may find a convert to another type of book.

Appealing to Middle-Graders through Books

You probably can still influence your middle-grade reader by suggesting good books. So suggest some of these titles for your 9- to 12-year-old, if the teacher hasn't already done so.

- *The Chocolate Touch* by Patrick Catling (Laurelleaf)

- *Little Louis and the Jazz Band* by Angela Shelf Medearis (Lodestar Books): Biography of musician Louis Armstrong in clear text.

- *Superfudge* by Judy Blume (Dutton)

- *Matilda* by Roald Dahl (Puffin): Kids feel for smart Matilda and her dealings with her abusive not smart family.

- *Charlotte's Web* by E.B. White (HarperTrophy): My daughter liked this one so much she plowed through the couple hundred pages in second grade.

- *True Story of the Three Little Pigs* by Jon Scieska (Dutton): Fractured fairy tales prove to be good reads that fit middle-grader's sense of irony and humor.

- *Harlem* by Walter Dean Myers (Scholastic): Poems that feature New York's African American history.

- *The Twins, the Pirates, and the Battle of New Orleans* by Harriette Gillem Robinet (Aladdin Library): Action-packed historical fiction.

- *Diary of a Drummer Boy* by Marlene Targ Brill (Millbrook Press): Civil War historical fiction in easy-to-read diary format.

- *The View from Saturday* by E. L. Konigsburg (Pearson)

- *Harriet the Spy* by Louise Fitzhugh (Yearling)

- *I'm Going to Pet a Worm Today* by Constance Levy (McElderry): Poetry collection about nature.

- *The Devil's Arithmetic* by Jane Yolen (Puffin Books): Time travel book that illuminates the power of history in modern life.

✔ *Holes* by Louis Sachar (Yearling): This part-mystery, part-humor book about a bad boy who digs holes for punishment is a must for reluctant readers. I haven't heard a child of any age who doesn't relate to this main character's plight and the clever, dry humor.

✔ *Bud, Not Buddy* by Christopher Paul Curtis (Yearling): Great character development of a boy searching for his musician dad.

Jumping into Jr. High (Ages 12–15) with Books

You are now entering the zone publishers affectionately call *young adult*. (Not that your child is anywhere near being an adult yet.) Young adult books can be much like middle-grade readers, only a little more grown-up, or they can creep into edgier, sophisticated topics more suitable for real young adults — those in high school. Here are some suggestions to keep your young adult reader occupied and away from Stephen King horror and sexier stuff that causes preteen giggles.

✔ *The Pigman and Me* by Paul Zindel (HarperCollins): Novel about a chaotic childhood guided by a wise old Italian.

✔ *Freedom's Children* by Ellen Levine (Avon): Stories of young civil rights activists during the 1960s.

✔ *Tuck Everlasting* by Natalie Babbitt (Farrar Straus & Giroux): Part fantasy, part science fiction, all interesting story.

✔ *Lyddie* by Katherine Paterson (Puffin): Historical fiction about the trials of being female and working in a company textile mill town.

✔ *The Tribes of Redwall Series* by Brian Jacques (Philomel): This series is for fantasy lovers and makes for exciting reading.

✔ *Chicago Fire* by Jim Murphy (Scholastic): Well-written nonfiction about the fire that leveled much of Chicago.

✔ *Girls: A History of Growing Up Female in America* by Penny Colman (Scholastic): Lots of details you don't usually see in history books.

✔ *The Giver* by Lois Lowry (Scholastic): Novel with valuable lesson about appreciating what someone already has.

✔ *Hatchet* by Gary Paulsen (Pocket Books): Adventure story of survival in Canadian wilderness. Paulsen is king of drama and suspense stories.

- *The Outsiders* by S.E. Hinton (Viking): Often credited as the first contemporary-problem novel, this story tackles teen gang warfare.

- *Anne Frank: The Diary of a Young Girl* by Anne Frank (Doubleday): Poignant personal view of living in hiding until Nazi discovery during the Holocaust.

- *Wright Brothers: How They Invented the Airplane* by Russell Friedman (Clarion): Friedman writes interesting, well-documented, and award-winning nonfiction and biographies worth a read at any age.

- *Slam!* By Walter Dean Myers (Scholastic): Realistic story of a 17-year-old black basketball star moving to a mostly white magnet school. Good for reluctant readers and sport's fans.

- *Surviving Hitler: A Boy in the Nazi Death Camps* by Andrea Warren (HarperCollins): Inspiring story about the strength of human spirit to overcome terrible adversity during the Holocaust.

- *Destiny* by Vicki Grove (Putnam): Teen's life turns upside down as she struggles with poverty and difficult family situation.

- *Speaking of Journals* ed. by Paula Graham (Boyds Mills Press): Well-known children's book author discuss diaries.

- *The Little Prince* by Antoine De Saint-Exupery (Houghton Mifflin): Touching and sensitive, this one's a classic.

Knowing Classics that High School Expects

Before your well-read child reaches high school, make sure his brain memory bank includes a passing knowledge of:

- Robin Hood
- The headless horsemen from *The Legend of Sleepy Hollow*
- Peter Pan and Tinkerbell
- *Alice in Wonderland* and the Cheshire cat
- The four sisters from *Little Women* by Louisa May Alcott
- *Sarah, Plain and Tall* by Patricia MacLachlan
- *The Lion, the Witch, and the Wardrobe* by C. S. Lewis
- *The Secret Garden* by Frances Hodgson Burnett
- *Wind and the Willows* by Kenneth Grahame
- Greek and Roman gods and goddesses

Turning on High Schoolers to Reading

Welcome to the teenage reading years. Your child has entered the great in-between of reading matter. Not quite adult. Yet, not a kid anymore.

Publishers target teens with edgier contemporary books, hoping to keep them from going adult full-time. But many teachers assign classic adult fare for class. They know that colleges consider experience with well-known adult authors a given.

At this point, you shouldn't care what your child reads as long as the publication is legal and your teen is reading. Short of nailing your kid's feet to the floor, you can't force him to read anymore. But here are suggestions that contain a mix of crossover young adult/adult titles, just in case you have a say:

- *Shakespeare's Scribe* by Gary Blackwood (Dutton): Wonderfully written historical fiction for lovers of Shakespeare's time.

- *Queen's Own Fool: A Novel of Mary Queen of Scots* by Jane Yolen (Philomel Books): Exciting historical fiction during swashbuckling times.

- *American Women: Their Lives in Their Own Words* by Doreen Rappaport (Thomas Y. Crowell): Famous women and their words put into historical perspective.

- *There are No Children Here* by Alex Kotlowitz (Doubleday): Glimpse into the lives of two teens struggling in the inner-city.

- *I Can Hear the Morning Dove* by James Bennett (Scholastic): Thought-provoking story of teens in a mental institution.

- *A Year Down Under* by Richard Peck (Dial): Semi-autographical book about growing up in a small Midwestern town.

- *The Joy Luck Club* by Amy Tan (Vintage): Reconciling generations split by old ways from China and new ones from the United States.

- *The Freedom Writer's Diary: How a Teacher and 150 Teens Used Writing to Change Themselves and the World Around Them* edited by Erin Gruwell (Bantam): Inspired by diaries of Anne Frank and Bosnian Zlata Filipovic, a sophomore high school class from Long Beach, California embark on life-altering, thought-provoking writing journey.

- *Ordinary People* by Judith Guest (Penguin)

- *Beloved* by Toni Morrison (Penguin)

- *Turn of the Screw* by Henry James (Dover)

- *One Flew Over the Cuckoo's Nest* by Ken Kesey (New American Library)

✔ *Amistad* by Alex Pate (Penguin): Based on a true story of how in 1839 mutiny erupted on a Spanish slave ship and future president John Quincy Adam's defense of an illegally enslaved man.

✔ *The House on Mango Street* by Sandra Cisneros (Vintage Books): Short stories about life in a low-income Hispanic Chicago neighborhood.

Choosing Magazines to Read

Some kids don't read books for a variety of reasons. Perhaps your genius:

✔ Can't sit still long enough

✔ Doesn't like novels

✔ Equates longer books with schoolwork, which is definitely *not* a leisure-time draw

✔ Leads too busy a life (no time left to read)

✔ Is so sleep-deprived that he falls asleep at the sight of the printed word

✔ Believes only losers or nerds read books for fun

What's a reader-loving parent to do? Chill out. Reading comes in many forms, and not all are books. Try some of the following magazines for starters. Check out others that cater to specific interests on the Internet or with your local librarian, or flip to Chapter 11 for more reading suggestions.

✔ Cricket/Cobblestone Magazine Group publishes a variety of quality magazines for baby through teen ages. Some of my favorites include: *Ladybug* (preschool–grade 1), *Cricket* (grade 4+), topical *Faces* (grade 4+, world cultures and geography), *Odyssey* (grade 4+, science adventure), and *Dig* (grade 4+, archeology). 800-821-0115, www.cobblestonepub.com.

✔ *Highlights for Children,* ages 2–8, more traditional but calmer periodical that focuses on reading and prereading skills through a mix of fiction, nonfiction, and simple activities. Highlights for Children, Inc., 800-603-0591, www.highlights.com.

✔ *Dolphin Log* (ages 9–12) interesting exploration of under water mysteries. The Cousteau Society, 800-441-4395, www.cousteausociety.org.

✔ *Merlyn's Pen: Fiction, Essay, and Poems by American's Teens* (ages 11–18), literature written by aspiring writers. Merlyn's Pen, Inc., 800-247-2027, www.merlynspen.com.

- ✔ *National Geographic World* (ages 8–14), exploration of geography, cultures, and science by leading photographic and adult magazine publisher. National Geographic Society, 800-647-5463, www.national geographic.com.

- ✔ *New Moon: The Magazine for Girls and Their Dreams* (ages 8–14), written and edited for thoughtful girls. Not the usual girlie pop stuff. New Moon Publishing, 800-381-4743, www.newmoon.org.

- ✔ *Sports Illustrated for Kids* (ages 8–14), for sport's enthusiasts who like sports-related photos, cards, and posters with stats and biographies. Time, Inc. 800-992-00196, www.sikids.com.

- ✔ *Biography Today* series (ages 10–12), for those who like to people watch folks from different professions and walks of life. Omnigraphics, 800-234-1340, www.omnigraphics.com.

Knowing classics that colleges expect

By now, your child is expected to know more than any one referral list can handle. But don't worry if these haven't been part of your lives yet. You and your offspring still have years to go. Here is a general idea of what others may expect your child to have read:

- ✔ *Romeo and Juliet* and one or two other titles by William Shakespeare

- ✔ *Catcher in the Rye* by J. D. Salinger (Little Brown): What better classic covers teen angst?

- ✔ *David Copperfield* (Penguin) or other titles by Charles Dickens

- ✔ *Mark Twain: Four Complete Novels: Adventures of Tom Sawyer; Adventures of Huck Finn; The Prince and the Pauper; A Connecticut Yankee in King Arthur's Court* by Mark Twain (Grammercy): Fun, easy reads with offbeat wit and humor.

- ✔ *Animal Farm* by George Orwell (Signet): This story is what happens when a farm is taken over by idealistic overworked animals.

- ✔ *Lord of the Flies* by William Golden (Putnam): Classic tale that boys tend to love.

- ✔ *Of Mice and Men* by John Steinbeck (Penguin): Poignant relationship between two farm workers.

- ✔ *To Kill a Mockingbird* by Harper Lee (HarperCollins): Told through the voice of a preteen girl; hits hard on civil rights, inequality, and the importance of telling the truth.

- ✔ *Fahrenheit 451* by Ray Bradbury (Ballantine Books): Classic science fiction about censorship.

- ✔ *Kidnapped* by Robert Louis Stevenson (Scholastic): Originally published as adult fiction, this tale pits a young man against his nasty uncle.

Chapter 22

Ten Resources That Bolster Parent Confidence

* *

In This Chapter

▶ Locating publications and Web sites that reinforce what a great parent you are

▶ Finding organizations to help with parenting issues

* *

*Y*ou probably feel that you won't be a good parent unless you exhaust every available resource. But that could take years and loads of time you probably don't have. If you *must* scour the world for parenting wisdom, let me help your search by suggesting some favorite resources in this chapter.

Finding Out More about Pregnancy

To learn more about the ins and outs of pregnancy, read *What to Expect When You're Expecting* by Heidi Murkoff (Workman Publishing, 2002). The comprehensive overview prepares you for most of the pregnancy experience as much as you can be prepared for an uncontrollable ballooning belly. But take some of the material with a grain of salt, as with any publication.

If you're still convinced that you want to connect with your bellybutton in an organized and achievement-oriented manner (flip to Chapter 5), read *Prenatal Classroom: A Parent's Guide for Teaching Your Baby in the Womb* by Rene Vande Carr and Marc Lehrer (Humanics Learning).

Be cautious, though. The author uses suspect research. And his followers cajole you into talking, singing, visualizing, breathing heavily, and reading to your belly. They also try to sell you products on the Internet to go with this routine. New-parent anxiety is big business folks!

Reading Your Way through Parenthood

You thought raising a smart kid was rough. Try sifting through the tons of books written about the subject. So many overlapping titles exist that I've limited the general parenting jewels for you.

- *How to Parent* **by Fitzhugh Dodson (New American Library):** This book is worth any difficulty you may have in locating a copy. The book, along with its sisters *How to Discipline with Love: from Crib to Adult, How to Single Parent, How to Father,* and *How to Grandparent,* has been reissued several times because it's so practical, readable, and reassuring.

- *The Successful Child* **by William Sears and Martha Sears (Little, Brown & Company):** Besides an easy-going writing style, this doctor, nurse, and parent pair of eight present a common-sense approach to raising success stories. Their mildly preachy bonding/attachment philosophy, which you may or may not agree with, pervades the text.

- *The Educated Child: A Parent's Guide from Preschool through Eighth Grade* **by William Bennett, Chester Finn, and John Cribb (The Free Press):** Bennett is big on moral development and a quality, back-to-basics approach to educating your child. The book details what the school should be teaching your child, what you can do to monitor schooling, and what you can do to boost education at home. His political agenda leans toward school vouchers and privatizing public education, which I find destructive to public school systems, but his education principles are sound and his suggestions are useful.

- *Your Growing Child — From Babyhood through Adolescence* **by Penelope Leach (Random House):** This book covers the A–Z's of raising smart kids. You discover what's within a normal range at each age and what to do with your child, health-wise and behavior-wise.

- *Positive Discipline A to Z* **by Jane Nelsen (Prima Publishing):** This author, writing alone or with others, has published several books about what she terms *positive discipline.* Each book is simply written with a common sense philosophy and lots of real-life examples that touch on almost any situation. The book covers the broadest areas for raising any age offspring. If you buy one book related to managing behavior, make this one your choice.

Don't let any guidebook make you feel guilty for not buying into or being able to follow through with what they suggest, such as Sears theory of attachment that recommends you carry your infant in a sling all day. Trust your judgment and incorporate ideas that work for you, your child, and your family.

Locating a Parenting Magazine

Many magazines have so many advertisements you can barely find the articles. That is, if the magazine lasts at all. One periodical, however, called *Parenting Magazine,* has been a mainstay for decades. Articles target kids from birth to about 12 years. Regular columns provide some structure and continuity within colorful busy pages. The Parenting Group publishes this magazine, along with *Baby Talk* and *Family Life.* You can read more about all three publications at www.parenting.com.

Surfing for the Perfect Parenting Web Sites

This is a bad heading for this section: No such *perfect* Web site exists. That's because anyone can add his or her two cents on the Internet whenever they want. Online authors need no credentials, and no one oversees their facts and opinions.

Weigh material you find online carefully. Look to see who manages the site. Evaluate whether the person or group seems like a credible source or whether the site pushes a certain agenda.

I like the following sites for information, although I find their advertising and cluttered designs annoying.

Behaving like a kid

Have questions about behavior, either how to change certain behaviors or how to prevent them? Check out author and educator Jane Nelsen's www.positivediscipline.com. With only a couple clicks, you get quick answers to questions without traveling to a library or store for her book. But if you find yourself copying so many articles that you waste reams of paper and run out of room to stash them, you may to decide to buy the book, instead (see the preceding section of this chapter).

Hooking into parent-education topics

Family Education Network, under the auspices of the Pearson Publishing group, runs a Web site for parents, kids (www.FunBrain.com and www.factmonster.com for homework help), and teachers that presents reference materials and connections to other fun and educational places. The site at `www.familyeducation.com` even features an online support chat room for home schoolers.

Watch out, though. Lots of advertising appears as subliminal and not-so-subliminal messages.

Disney can't let any area for children go underserved. The Web site at `www.family.go.com` is filled with ideas, fun activities, and advice articles that make sense. Because Disney products are geared toward younger kids, most of the information is for the baby through early school age. But many articles apply to older kids, too.

The radio show *The Parent Report* hosts the Web site at `www.theparentreport.com` to impart wisdom about many of the topics aired on the show. Articles offer a range of suggestions for raising smarter newborns through teens that are written by professionals in different fields.

Kid Source Online comes from a group of parents who want to share health and education information and resources to raise higher-achieving kids. The Web site at `www.kidsource.com` has forum discussions, including one about gifted children, and links to lots of other organizations and news sources.

You don't have to buy *Parenting Magazine* to get articles. Just go to `www.parenting.com` to find answers to questions about your baby from birth to 12 years old. Not all subjects are covered, but the site contains a store-house of articles from The Parenting Group's magazines.

Raising a ruckus about school

At some point, you may be interested in effecting change in your school district. You're not alone. Many groups have been formed for that very purpose, and you can learn from them. Here are four places to begin:

Alliance for Parental Involvement in Education (ALLPIE) is a nonprofit membership organization that offers a newsletter *(Options in Learning)*, annual conferences and workshops, and education resource links that encourage parent involvement in public and private schools. Contact the group at P.O. Box 59, East Chatham, NY 12060; 518-392-6900; or `www.allpie@taconic.net`.

The Council for Basic Education publishes a magazine that promotes strong curriculum. The group connects with the National Clearinghouse for Comprehensive School Reform to provide up-to-date school reform data and leadership vehicles for school change. Contact the group at 1319 F Street, NW, Suite 900, Washington, DC 20004; 202-347-4171; or `www.c-b-e.org`.

If your local school doesn't already have a parent group, you can organize a PTA (Parent Teacher Association) by contacting www.pta.org or a PTO (Parent Teacher Organization) by keying www.ptotoday.org. Each national group sponsors local groups and offers parent tips for getting involved in schools. The National PTA is the older, more established group. More recently, they have been challenged by the PTO, which subscribes to reduced national dues, less emphasis on parent fundraising, and more emphasis on arranging family-oriented activities at school.

Keeping Kids Healthy and Safe

Health and safety take on different meanings as your child ages. You want your toddler free of colds and your teen free of mind- and body-wrecking substances and diseases. The resources in this section may help in your quest to keep your child germ-free and intact, at least as much as is humanly possible.

Knowing when to call the doctor

An easy-to-follow comprehensive source for healthcare guidelines is *Your Child's Health: The Parent's Guide to Symptoms, Emergencies, Common Illnesses, Behavior, and School Problems* by Barton Schmitt (Bantam). Parents I've talked with give this book points for identifying symptoms and illnesses, indicating when to call the doc, and simplifying the process with it's A-B-C instructions. But, as with other far-reaching medical tomes I investigated, this one falls short on general parenting philosophy, so take that information lightly.

To connect with humans for information, contact the American Academy of Pediatrics, 141 Northwest Point Road, Elk Grove Village, IL 60009; 800-433-9016; www.aap.org.

Childproofing for baby's sake

In case crawling on your hands and knees to get a baby's-eye view doesn't work for you, identify the areas to childproof in your home by contacting www.cpsc.gov/cpscpub/grand/12steps. Call the U.S. Consumer Product Safety Commission behind this Web site at 1-800-638-2772 for a free pamphlet called *Childproofing Your Home,* or look at www.theparentclub.com for additional baby's room safety tips.

Deciding whether to vaccinate

Your baby gets several rounds of multiple vaccines, as mentioned in Chapter 4. You may want to touch base with folks who keep track of the latest research into the safety of vaccines to know which ones trigger reactions more frequently. Contact the National Vaccine Information Center at 421 East Church Street, Suite 206, Vienna, VA 22180; 800-909-SHOT; or www.909shot.com.

Emphasizing street smarts

Grab a copy of *Street Smarts for Kids: What Parents Must Know to Keep Their Children Safe* by Richard Bentz (Ballantine) and commit his recommendations to memory. The author is a former police officer, so he ought to know the safety score.

Preventing substance abuse and eating disorders

You hope substance abuse isn't in your present or future. The Columbia University CASA program administers www.casacolumbia.org for the National Center for Addiction and Abuse. Information covers the latest studies about substance abuse and what parents can do to keep healthy kids free of alcohol, tobacco, and drugs.

If food and not eating it becomes way too important in your child's life, if you have a perfectionist or two around, or if the pressure about eating seems too much at home, refer to the National Eating Disorders Association, 800-931-2237, www.NationalEatingDisorders.org, to be sure problems aren't brewing in this area.

Finding gender-neutral information

Girls Incorporated, 120 Wall Street, New York, NY 10005, 212-509-2000, www.girlsincorporated.com, publishes training materials about ways to deal with gender bias that can affect your daughter in the classroom and brings confidence-building programs for girls to local institutions.

American Association of University Women, 1111 16th Street, N.W., Washington, DC 20036, 800-326-2289, www.aauw.org, is an organization of 150,000 college graduates that promotes equity for girls and women through publications, grants to improve learning for girls and women, research, internships, and community action programs, such as Girls Can!

Identifying Gifted Resources

Frustrated parents and educators have formed several support groups to share information and give gifted students a chance to shine, and many universities sponsor programs for gifted students. The following national organizations may also be useful and informative:

- ✔ The Association for Gifted (TAG) is a division of the Council for Exceptional Children at 1110 North Glebe Road, Suite 300, Arlington, VA 22201; 703-620-3660; or www.cectag.org. This organization hosts conferences with special parent's programs and produces the *Journal for the Education of the Gifted.* Their Web site connects you to key information for families with gifted people.

- ✔ The National Foundation for Gifted Children (NAGC), 1701 L Street, NW, Suite 550, Washington, DC 20036; 202-785-4268; or www.nagc.org. This national group of parents, teachers, and interested community leaders puts their energies into conferences, information sharing, scholarships, resource links, and *Parenting for High Potential* magazine to address the unique needs of exceptionally talented kids and their education.

- ✔ Supporting Emotional Needs of the Gifted (SENG), P.O. Box 6550, Scottsdale, AZ 85261; 206-498-6744; or www.SENGifted.org, is for adults who come in contact with gifted children and choose to join together to focus on identifying, guiding, living, and working with them through conferences with children's programs, information resources, and communication forums.

- ✔ One publisher that prints a lot of books about and for the gifted is Free Spirit Publishing, Inc., 217 Fifth Avenue North, Suite 200, Minneapolis, MN 55401-1299; 800-735-7323; www.freespirit.com. The company's publications support readers of all ages, which means your gifted child, you, and your child's teachers. Several titles emphasize learning life skills for success and maintaining a positive self-concept.

Finding Special Needs Information

The following organizations provide information and referrals when you question special services for your child:

- ✔ American Speech, Language, and Hearing, 10801 Rockville Pike, Rockville, MD 20852; 800-321-ASHA; www.asha.org/association. This group provides the most up-to-date research and treatments for speech and language differences and referrals to certified speech-language therapists.

✔ National Information Center for Children and Youth with Disabilities (NICHCY), P.O. Box 1492, Washington, DC 20013; 800-695-0285; `www.NICHCY.org`. This national clearinghouse includes information about all special needs, including gifted programs. You can receive free publications, such as parent guides for assessing programs and community schools, and connect with many other research and information sources.

✔ ERIC (Educational Resource Information Center) Clearinghouse on Disabilities and Gifted Education, 1110 North Glebe Road, Arlington, VA 22201; 800-328-0272; `http://erice.org`. Start your search here for information about special needs, including gifted education. ERIC links you to other resources and to the latest education articles. Its National Parent Information Network is a virtual library of approved publications, brochures, and information that encourages parent involvement in education decisions for your child.

✔ The Council for Exceptional Children (CEC), 1110 North Glebe Road, Suite 300, Arlington, VA 22201; 703-620-3660; or `www.cec.sped.org`. CEC is the largest international professional organization dedicated to improving education for kids with special needs. The group has divisions that meet and produce newsletters, journals, and conferences with programs for kids, teachers, and parents.

Your child can be smart and still struggle with a learning disability or problems with attention span (the two most common learning disabilities). These two organizations provide more information to set your mind at ease:

✔ Learning Disabilities Association of America, 4156 Library Road, Pittsburgh, PA 15234, 412-341-1515, `www.ldanatl.org`. This national organization offers information, referrals, local groups, and conferences concerning learning disabilities.

✔ CHADD (Children and Adults with Attention Deficit/Hyperactivity Disorder), 8181 Professional Place, Suite 201, Landover, MD 20785, 800-233-4050, `www.chadd.org`. This parent-run national organization maintains information, referrals, local groups, and conferences concerning attention deficit disorder with and without hyperactivity.

Targeting Specific Parent Groups

Several groups provide support for specific family situations that accompany average parenting trials:

✔ National Foster Parent Association, Inc., P.O. Box 81, Alpha, OH, 800-557-5238, `www.nfpainc.org`. The purpose of this group is to bring together foster parents and the social workers with which they interact, in order to improve the lives of their children.

✔ National Adoption Information Clearinghouse, www.calib/naic.org. Besides links to information and statistics about adoption, the national online directory lets you search for local support groups by state.

✔ About Single Parents, http://singleparents.about.com. This site shares resources and information, polls, chat rooms, and links to anything related to single parenting, including sites for single moms, single dads, and African-American single moms.

✔ Parents Without Partners, Inc., 1650 South Dixie Highway, Suite 510, Boca Raton, FL 33432, 561-391-8833, www.parentswithoutpartners. org. With 400 chapters in the United States and Canada, this group provides education, social, and family activities to single parents and their kids.

✔ Stepfamily Association of America, 650 J Street, Suite 205, Lincoln, NE 68508, 800-735-0329, www.saafamilies.org. Local support groups offer programs, support, and education to separated and rebounded families.

✔ Stepfamily Foundation, 333 West End Avenue, New York, NY 11023, 212-877-3244, www.stepfamily.org. This group offers counseling and a national convention in addition to resources, support, and education for divorced and recoupled families.

✔ Grandparent Information Center, American Association for retired Persons (AARP), 601 East Street NW, Washington, DC 20049, 202-434-2296, www.aarp.org/contacts/programs. Grandparents are just as interested in raising smart kids as are birth parents. If you're on your second round of parenting, this organization can support your efforts by linking you to resources, information, and the free newsletter called *Parenting Grandchildren.*

Finding Educational Toys and Books

You can find simple, inexpensive toy ideas in Chapters 6 and 7. But if you want store-bought stuff, especially items that claim to be targeted for specific learning, consider asking your local small toy store owner or checking with the larger chains.

Each year the national toy store chain Toys "Я" Us publishes "Toy Guide for Differently Abled." If you want to promote development in specific areas, say fine motor or language skills and are unfamiliar with little kids and play choices, this booklet helps you identify toys to do the job. You can find more assistance in selecting toys from the Lekotek Toy Resource Helpline at 1-800-366-PLAY or www.lekotek.org.

Planning Fun and Well-Rounded Activities

Besides local religious (YMCA, YWCA, JCC) and public community centers, these groups promote programs your child may like:

✔ Association of Children's Museums, 1300 L Street, NW, Suite 975, Washington, DC 20005, 202-898-1080, www.childrensmuseums.org. Although this group serves the museum community first, its Web site lets you search for children's museums near you and connect with their site to find out what's happening at those museums.

✔ Boys and Girls Clubs of America, 1230 West Peachtree Street, NW, Atlanta, GA 30309, 404-487-5700, www.bgca.org. These clubs are everywhere, and they provide interesting programs to stimulate interests of smart kids.

✔ Girls Scouts of the USA, 800-GSUSA4U, www.girlscouts.org, maintain more than 230,000 troops in the United States for girls 5–17. Their job is to develop potential through field trips, sports, community service, cultural exchanges, and environmental programs.

✔ Camp Fire USA, 4601 Madison Avenue, Kansas City, MO 64112-1278, 816-756-0258, www.campfire.org. This national youth-development organization serves kids from birth to 21 with child care, after-school programs, and camping and environmental programs designed to build self-reliance and foster intercultural relationships.

Index

FOR DUMMIES®

The easy way to get more done and have more fun

PERSONAL FINANCE

0-7645-5231-7

0-7645-2431-3

0-7645-5331-3

Also available:

Estate Planning For Dummies
(0-7645-5501-4)

401(k)s For Dummies
(0-7645-5468-9)

Frugal Living For Dummies
(0-7645-5403-4)

Microsoft Money "X" For
Dummies
(0-7645-1689-2)

Mutual Funds For Dummies
(0-7645-5329-1)

Personal Bankruptcy For
Dummies
(0-7645-5498-0)

Quicken "X" For Dummies
(0-7645-1666-3)

Stock Investing For Dummies
(0-7645-5411-5)

Taxes For Dummies 2003
(0-7645-5475-1)

BUSINESS & CAREERS

0-7645-5314-3

0-7645-5307-0

0-7645-5471-9

Also available:

Business Plans Kit For
Dummies
(0-7645-5365-8)

Consulting For Dummies
(0-7645-5034-9)

Cool Careers For Dummies
(0-7645-5345-3)

Human Resources Kit For
Dummies
(0-7645-5131-0)

Managing For Dummies
(1-5688-4858-7)

QuickBooks All-in-One Desk
Reference For Dummies
(0-7645-1963-8)

Selling For Dummies
(0-7645-5363-1)

Small Business Kit For
Dummies
(0-7645-5093-4)

Starting an eBay Business For
Dummies
(0-7645-1547-0)

HEALTH, SPORTS & FITNESS

0-7645-5167-1

0-7645-5146-9

0-7645-5154-X

Also available:

Controlling Cholesterol For
Dummies
(0-7645-5440-9)

Dieting For Dummies
(0-7645-5126-4)

High Blood Pressure For
Dummies
(0-7645-5424-7)

Martial Arts For Dummies
(0-7645-5358-5)

Menopause For Dummies
(0-7645-5458-1)

Nutrition For Dummies
(0-7645-5180-9)

Power Yoga For Dummies
(0-7645-5342-9)

Thyroid For Dummies
(0-7645-5385-2)

Weight Training For Dummies
(0-7645-5168-X)

Yoga For Dummies
(0-7645-5117-5)

Available wherever books are sold.
Go to www.dummies.com or call 1-877-762-2974 to order direct.

WILEY

FOR DUMMIES®

A world of resources to help you grow

HOME, GARDEN & HOBBIES

Feng Shui — 0-7645-5295-3

Gardening — 0-7645-5130-2

Guitar — 0-7645-5106-X

FOOD & WINE

Cooking — 0-7645-5250-3

Cookies — 0-7645-5390-9

Wine — 0-7645-5114-0

TRAVEL

Italy — 0-7645-5453-0

Hawaii — 0-7645-5438-7

Las Vegas — 0-7645-5448-4

FOR DUMMIES®

Helping you expand your horizons and realize your potential

INTERNET

The Internet FOR DUMMIES
0-7645-0894-6

The Internet ALL-IN-ONE DESK REFERENCE FOR DUMMIES
0-7645-1659-0

eBay FOR DUMMIES
0-7645-1642-6

Also available:

America Online 7.0 For Dummies
(0-7645-1624-8)

Genealogy Online For Dummies
(0-7645-0807-5)

The Internet All-in-One Desk Reference For Dummies
(0-7645-1659-0)

Internet Explorer 6 For Dummies
(0-7645-1344-3)

The Internet For Dummies Quick Reference
(0-7645-1645-0)

Internet Privacy For Dummies
(0-7645-0846-6)

Researching Online For Dummies
(0-7645-0546-7)

Starting an Online Business For Dummies
(0-7645-1655-8)

DIGITAL MEDIA

Digital Photography FOR DUMMIES
0-7645-1664-7

Photoshop Elements 2 FOR DUMMIES
0-7645-1675-2

Digital Video FOR DUMMIES
0-7645-0806-7

Also available:

CD and DVD Recording For Dummies
(0-7645-1627-2)

Digital Photography All-in-One Desk Reference For Dummies
(0-7645-1800-3)

Digital Photography For Dummies Quick Reference
(0-7645-0750-8)

Home Recording for Musicians For Dummies
(0-7645-1634-5)

MP3 For Dummies
(0-7645-0858-X)

Paint Shop Pro "X" For Dummies
(0-7645-2440-2)

Photo Retouching & Restoration For Dummies
(0-7645-1662-0)

Scanners For Dummies
(0-7645-0783-4)

GRAPHICS

PowerPoint 2002 FOR DUMMIES
0-7645-0817-2

Photoshop 7 FOR DUMMIES
0-7645-1651-5

Macromedia Flash MX FOR DUMMIES
0-7645-0895-4

Also available:

Adobe Acrobat 5 PDF For Dummies
(0-7645-1652-3)

Fireworks 4 For Dummies
(0-7645-0804-0)

Illustrator 10 For Dummies
(0-7645-3636-2)

QuarkXPress 5 For Dummies
(0-7645-0643-9)

Visio 2000 For Dummies
(0-7645-0635-8)

Available wherever books are sold. Go to www.dummies.com or call 1-877-762-2974 to order direct.

FOR DUMMIES®

The advice and explanations you need to succeed

SELF-HELP, SPIRITUALITY & RELIGION

Sex
0-7645-5302-X

Parenting
0-7645-5418-2

Religion
0-7645-5264-3

Also available:

The Bible For Dummies
(0-7645-5296-1)

Buddhism For Dummies
(0-7645-5359-3)

Christian Prayer For Dummies
(0-7645-5500-6)

Dating For Dummies
(0-7645-5072-1)

Judaism For Dummies
(0-7645-5299-6)

Potty Training For Dummies
(0-7645-5417-4)

Pregnancy For Dummies
(0-7645-5074-8)

Rekindling Romance For Dummies
(0-7645-5303-8)

Spirituality For Dummies
(0-7645-5298-8)

Weddings For Dummies
(0-7645-5055-1)

PETS

Puppies
0-7645-5255-4

Dog Training
0-7645-5286-4

Cats
0-7645-5275-9

Also available:

Labrador Retrievers For Dummies
(0-7645-5281-3)

Aquariums For Dummies
(0-7645-5156-6)

Birds For Dummies
(0-7645-5139-6)

Dogs For Dummies
(0-7645-5274-0)

Ferrets For Dummies
(0-7645-5259-7)

German Shepherds For Dummies
(0-7645-5280-5)

Golden Retrievers For Dummies
(0-7645-5267-8)

Horses For Dummies
(0-7645-5138-8)

Jack Russell Terriers For Dummies
(0-7645-5268-6)

Puppies Raising & Training Diary For Dummies
(0-7645-0876-8)

EDUCATION & TEST PREPARATION

Spanish
0-7645-5194-9

Algebra
0-7645-5325-9

The ACT
0-7645-5210-4

Also available:

Chemistry For Dummies
(0-7645-5430-1)

English Grammar For Dummies
(0-7645-5322-4)

French For Dummies
(0-7645-5193-0)

The GMAT For Dummies
(0-7645-5251-1)

Inglés Para Dummies
(0-7645-5427-1)

Italian For Dummies
(0-7645-5196-5)

Research Papers For Dummies
(0-7645-5426-3)

The SAT I For Dummies
(0-7645-5472-7)

U.S. History For Dummies
(0-7645-5249-X)

World History For Dummies
(0-7645-5242-2)

Available wherever books are sold. Go to www.dummies.com or call 1-877-762-2974 to order direct.